A Connecticut Yankee in Penn's Woods

The Life and Times of Thomas Bennet

by
Charles E. Myers

WILKES UNIVERSITY PRESS
WILKES-BARRE, PENNSYLVANIA

A CONNECTICUT YANKEE IN PENN'S WOODS

The Life and Times of Thomas Bennet

by

Charles E. Myers

Publisher's Cataloging in Publication

Myers, Charles E., 1913-

A Connecticut yankee in Penn's Woods: the life and times of Thomas Bennett / by Charles E. Myers.

p. cm.

Includes bibliographical references and index.

ISBN 0-912975-03-2 (pbk.) : $14.95

1. Bennet, Thomas, 1721-1796. 2. Pioneers–Pennsylvania–Wyoming Valley–Biography. 3. Wyoming Valley (Pa.)–History. 4. Susquehanna claim. I. Title.

F157.W9M49 974.8'35'092 Library of Congress #

QBI93-1041 93-60796

Published by Wilkes University, Wilkes-Barre, Pennsylvania

Printed in the United States of America

Designed and composed by Upshur Press, Dallas, Pennsylvania

Cover Art - Joan Schooley

Manufactured by Capital City Press, Montpelier, Vermont

Acknowledgements

I am indebted to Dr. Harold E. Cox, professor of history at Wilkes University, for his help editing this manuscript and preparing it for publication. Most valuable technical assistance in production, design, and editing of the book has been rendered by Mrs. Linda Stallone. Mrs. Barbara Mellon, chief of transcription at Wilkes Barre General Hospital, has done our typing for the past four years. Dr. Christopher Breiseth, Mr. Tom Bigler, Mrs. Marnie Rees, Mr. John Rees, my brother Bob and others have advised me as to content and structure. Mrs. Dorothy Feldman helped to depict phases of the American Revolution. Mrs. Sally Teller Lottick and Mr. F. Charles Petrillo, by their efforts and assistance, have inspired my study of local history.

My wife Virginia, my daughter Mary Anne, and my sons Fred and Charles have patiently listened to me over a period of five years, as the story unfolded.

Mrs. Ruth Bevan of the Wyoming Historical and Geological Society Library, Mrs. Diane Rebar, reference librarian of the Hoyt Library, and librarians of the Osterhout Library in Wilkes Barre have provided significant help. Thanks are also due the libraries at Goshen, Newburgh, and Port Jervis, New York, and Milford and Stroudsburg, Pennsylvania.

Preface

Charles E. Myers, M.D., a fifth generation descendant of Thomas Bennet, tells a vivid story of how the original Connecticut settlers came to the Wyoming Valley, fought, suffered, and stayed. A Connecticut Yankee in Penn's Woods: The Life and Times of Thomas Bennet is more than family history. It is a carefully researched, well written narrative. The book analyzes the clash of cultures among the Connecticut families, who first glimpsed the Wyoming Valley in 1762; the Iroquois nations, who used the valley in summer until ousted by Sullivan's Army in 1779; and the Pennsylvanians, who were determined to affirm their right to the land. Overlapping and conflicting titles from the King of England to the colonies of Connecticut and Pennsylvania laid the basis for the Yankee-Pennamite Wars. The actual warfare between the parties lasted off and on from 1770 to 1784. The final settlement of land titles, securing the ownership for Thomas Bennet's heirs and those of his Connecticut neighbors, did not come until the very end of the eighteenth century.

Dr. Myers demonstrates how local history can illuminate national history. Bennet and such supporters as Col. Zebulon Butler, Lt. Col. Nathan Dennison, and Matthias Hollenback persistently fended off the Indians and their British allies, both before and after the Battle of Wyoming (July 3, 1778). Meanwhile they battled the Pennsylvanians, who scarcely wished them well even in their encounters with the British-Indian enemies. These conflicts reveal much about the internal tensions among Americans during their War for Independence. The Wyoming Massacre of 1778 precipitated General Washington's request for General John Sullivan to mobilize an army to rout the Iroquois nations and their British allies. By pushing the Indians into present-day Canada and upper New York, Sullivan's March initiated the new nation's policy toward Native Americans. Following the War of Independence, the final land settlement secured the area to Pennsylvania, and eventually gave individual land titles to the Connecticut settlers. This resulted from precedent-setting legal and political processes evolving in both Pennsylvania and the new national government to handle private property, a most sensitive right in the new United States.

Dr. Myers includes the big national picture to make sense of what is going on in the Wyoming Valley, just as he uses the Bennets' experiences to make vivid the personal efforts, sacrifices, and triumphs of the Yankees against staggering odds. In addition to the Indian, British, and Pennsylvania antagonisms were the punishment of floods, of harsh winters and scorching summers, of disease and death. Separation of families was a recurring theme. Martha Bennet and her husband Thomas and their children were apart for two years following the Wyoming Massacre of 1778. But the lure of the rich land, the beauty of the Valley, and their sense of community with the other Yankees helped stiffen the resolve of the Bennets always to return. They rebuilt burned out homes, replanted devastated fields, and served in the 24th Regiment and the Continental Army to protect their lands and families and secure their new country.

The Bennet story is not only one of a determined pioneer in Thomas who seems to have been given nine lives to expend in his quest to wrestle a piece of earth for himself and his children. It also includes his wife Martha whose courage and industry were scarcely less than her husband's. When they had lost everything after the Battle of Wyoming, she and her daughter began making clothes to sell as a way of supporting the family. Deprived of a supply of wool, they grew flax to make linen. With their energetic and courageous children, Thomas and Martha helped create in the Wyoming Valley a beachhead for civilization as they knew it. The strength of family is everywhere in evidence in the Bennet story.

One theme recurs throughout Dr. Myers' narrative: the clash of political cultures between the self-governing town meeting democracy of the New England Yankees and the more authoritarian politics of the Pennsylvanians. The implication of this clash for the political culture of our own day in the Wyoming Valley is left implicit, but Dr. Myers' history demonstrates the persistence of this clash throughout Wyoming Valley's formative years.

The tenacious hold on their land is symbolized at the conclusion of this beautifully told story by the fact that when the 1972 flood from Hurricane Agnes washed away a large part of the Forty Fort Cemetery, it came right up to but did not consume the grave of Thomas Bennet. He remains on the land he fought for. His descendant (through his daughter Martha who married Philip Myers) has made a major contribution towards an understanding of how Connecticut Yankees came to the Wyoming Valley, put down their roots, and refused to be ousted, even when Pennsylvania won the right to wrest the area from Connecticut.

Christopher N. Breiseth, President
Wilkes University

Contents

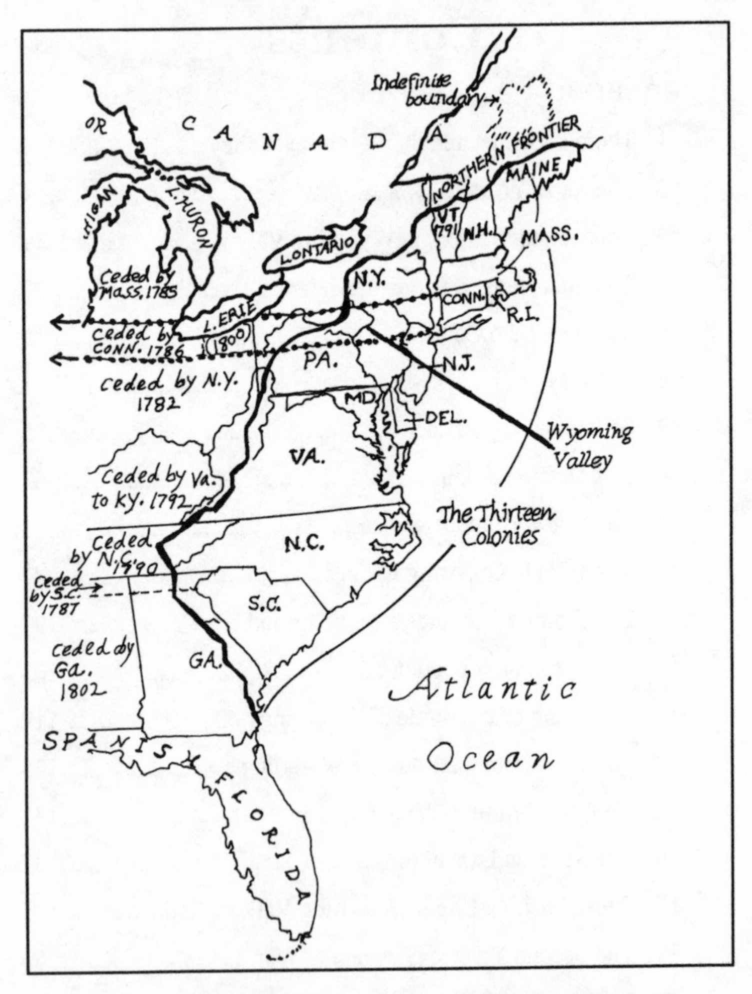

Portion of map from *Miracle at Philadelphia* by Catherine Drinker Bowen. Copyright ©1966 by Catherine Drinker Bowen. By permission of Little, Brown & Co. Author adapted the map to illustrate why conflict over ownership of the Wyoming Valley resulted from the original charters of Connecticut and Pennsylvania.

Shown are the boundaries of the original Connecticut Charter, which extended Westward to the sea. Both Connecticut and Pennsylvania claimed rights to the same territory in the upper portion of what is now Pennsylvania, setting the stage for the forty year conflict for the Wyoming Valley lands.

CHAPTER 1

Thomas Bennet and the Wyoming Valley

The Origins of Thomas Bennet

Thomas Bennet was born in 1721 in either eastern Connecticut or in Rhode Island.[1] The Bennet family is traceable in this country to Edward Bennet, one of the first colonists in Weymouth, Massachusetts, where he was a selectman in 1633. He came from Wilshire, England, and died in Rehoboth, Massachusetts, in 1646. His son, Samuel Bennet, served as a sergeant of militia under the crown and made his home in Greenwich, Rhode Island.

Samuel was voted 100 acres of public land for his military service during King Philip's war (1675-76) and the war with the Narragansets. His grandson, Samuel, born in Coventry, Rhode Island, in 1690, received land as a gift from his father. This Samuel in turn sired Thomas Bennet, the subject of our narrative. Thomas changed the family name from Bennett to Bennet, and all subsequent descendants of Thomas have followed his lead. Back in England, the family is traceable for thirteen generations as a distinguished and honored clan.

The Bennets in this country were part of the movement of westward colonization and migration. They were among many who were disillusioned by the rigidity of the Massachusetts Bay Colony, which became dominated by a group who professed dedication to religious liberty but who within a decade refused this same liberty to others. Also, of course, they were living at a time when the economy and lifestyle was largely agrarian, and tillable land in Massachusetts rapidly became occupied. It was logical for new generations to seek other new lands. Finally, there was an innate restlessness among many of the new arrivals in this great country, a restlessness which spawned the great westward surge of migration which was to last for two centuries.

By May 1639 three small towns (Windsor, Wethersfield and Hartford) organized a government under the name of the colony of Connecticut.[2] It adopted a "Code of Fundamental Orders" which was at the time the first written constitution in this country.

History of the Colony of Connecticut

Something of the history of the Connecticut Colony needs to be reviewed to set the stage for later events in this narrative. Wyoming Valley's earliest historian, Isaac Chapman[3] states that in 1628 the Plymouth Company transferred to Henry Russell and others that part of its territory now forming the state of Massachusetts. In 1630 this same company sold to the Earl of Warwick that part now encompassing the state of Connecticut. The Earl, in turn, by deed 19th March 1631 conveyed to Lords Jay and Seal and others this same territory. Then in 1633 William Holmes, at the head of a small company, took possession of this grant and made the first settlement of the colony on the banks of the Connecticut River just below the mouth of the Windsor River.

A few years later John Winthrop became Governor of this new colony. As the population grew it became necessary to shift the site of colonial government from Plymouth, Massachusetts, to the new site on the Windsor River. A petition for this transfer was approved by the Plymouth proprietaries in December 1644.

Description of the King's Land Grant to Connecticut Colonists

When the new Connecticut colony established its constitution, it sought approval of the crown for self government. A petition to His Majesty Charles II (May 1644) for both a charter of privileges and an approval of the constitution was carried by John Winthrop to the king. On the 23rd of April 1662 such a charter was approved. It included "all that part of our dominions in New England in America, bounded on the east by Narraganset Bay, where the said river falleth into the sea—and on the north by the line of the Massachusetts plantations—on the south by the sea, and in the longitude as the line of the Massachusetts Colony, running from east to west."[4] It should be noted that this agreement antedated the grant to William Penn by nearly twenty years. The terms of this charter from the

Crown were remarkable as they included not only the northern half of Pennsylvania, but part of the present states of New York, New Jersey, Ohio, Indiana, Illinois, Iowa, Nebraska, Wyoming, Idaho, Nevada, Utah, Oregon and California.

The ambiguity of these land grants by the King of England is not unreasonable given the general and widespread ignorance of actual dimensions of this newly discovered continent. In 1681 King Charles II granted William Penn a charter to the Pennsylvania lands to settle a debt to Penn's father. The King's charters to Connecticut and the later Penn grant overlapped in the Wyoming region. The lack of speedy communication, the absence of exact maps, the confusion of *what* was granted and to *whom*, and the colonists' and proprietors' eagerness to expand early land holdings all combined to set the stage for bitter and prolonged disputes over property rights. Of all these disputes on the continent, the most intense and prolonged was to be that between the Connecticut Yankees and the Pennsylvanians in northeastern Pennsylvania.

Origins of the Susquehanna Company

Thomas Bennet grew up in the area of Scituate, Rhode Island. Nothing is known of this period of his life, but it is likely he farmed and worked generally in the fields. He lived not far from Windham, Connecticut, where the Susquehanna Company was formed.[5] A group of citizens in and around Windham, having heard rumors of the beautiful and fertile valley of the Susquehanna at Wyoming, organized a company with intent to develop it as a part of the Connecticut Colony. Thus, the Susquehanna Company was organized July 18, 1753, by about 250 men meeting at Windham, Connecticut. A proposal to organize had been authorized by the General Assembly of Connecticut. The Company sought and won approval by the Connecticut assembly to purchase the Wyoming land from the Indians, with the intent to settle it.

The Journeying Committee

The Susquehanna Company, in October 1753, sent an exploring committee of three men to Wyoming Valley to study the land and its possibilities, and to lay out tentative areas for ultimate settlement.[6] We have no way of knowing what path this trio took from Windham, but they crossed the Hudson at

Fishkill, where a ferry was in operation. They were authorized to sell shares in the company to interested parties en route. From these transactions it is known that they passed through what is now Port Jervis, then went down the Delaware River to what is now Stroudsburg (Fort Penn). From there they struck out through Sciota, Wind Gap, and across the Pocono Mountains following an Indian path to Wyoming. At the valley of Wyoming they found some Indian settlements along with a few of the Moravian missionaries from Gnadenhutten, now Lehighton.

This journeying committee remained at Wyoming for several days and learned from the Indians that the Six Nations claimed the land and exercised jurisdiction over it.[7] On their return trip to Connecticut, they entered the province of New York, and crossed the Hudson at or near Fishkill, thence northward through present Duchess County and over the "Great Road" running from the Hudson to and through New England. To and from the valley they sold shares in the company for two milled Spanish dollars per share, the records of sale establishing the route described above.

This trip of the journeying committee was very disturbing to certain Pennsylvanians in Northampton County, now Monroe, as well as to the Indians dwelling along the Susquehanna. All who heard of it interpreted this visit as a forerunner of a larger body of settlers to come.

At a Susquehanna Company meeting of January 1754, the committee made its extensive report, at which time the total membership was about 400 men. They voted to raise membership cost to four dollars per share, with half shares selling for two dollars each. At this meeting it was resolved to appoint an agent of the company to order, act and transact the purchase of the land from the Indian chiefs.

This action set in motion a vigorous protest from the Pennsylvanians, who had not yet settled the area, and led to a series of top level conferences held in June and July 1754 at Albany, New York, attended by the powerful leaders of the Pennsylvania interests, as well as those from the Susquehanna Company and major Indian chieftains.[8] A deed was executed on July 6th, which was signed by King Hendrik, his brother Abraham, and twenty other chiefs representing all tribes of the six nations. Four hundred pounds, New York currency, was the price agreed upon for all of *southwestern* Pennsylvania. The *unsold* sections included all the lands along the north branch of the Susquehanna and a small portion along the west branch.

The Susquehanna Purchase

While the Pennsylvania agents were holding public conference with the Indians, the representatives of the Susquehanna Company were busily meeting privately and individually with a number of Indian chiefs, mostly in the home of Colonel John Henry Lydius in Albany. By July 11, 1754, fourteen chiefs and sachems of various tribes had signed a deed of transfer of the lands along the Susquehanna River at Wyoming to the Susquehanna Company for 2,000 pounds New York currency. This deed included a specific clause conveying "all and every of the mines, minerals, or ore" in and upon the lands in question. There were 694 grantees cosigning, of which 153 were "half share" proprietors. Subsequent corrections of this list brought the total to 753, with 165 half share owners. The participants in this transaction were in general responsible, sincere leaders, not a scurrilous and reckless gang as the Pennsylvanians later claimed. There was no fraud or trickery and the full amount to be paid was duly received by the Indians.[9]

Sketch derived from map in Harvey, Oscar Jewell. *The History of Wilkes-Barre*–Vol. II, Raeder Press, Wilkes-Barre 1909, facing pg. 790, showing:

1. Bounds of the Susquehanna Company's purchase: x-x-x

2. The western boundary of the town of Westmoreland as of December 1775: o-o-o

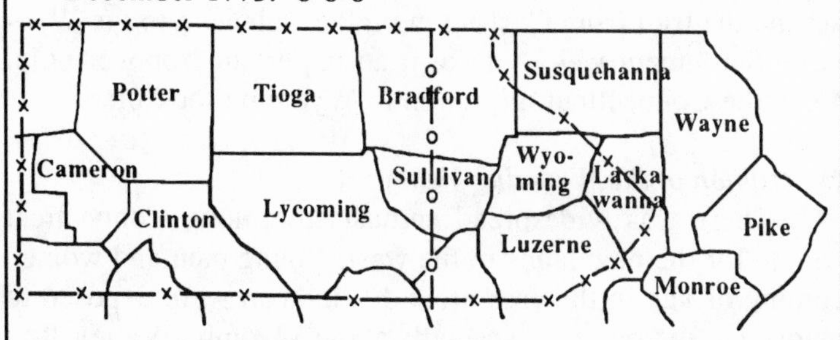

Simplified from the original. Only the upper part of what is now Pennsylvania is shown.

After concluding these negotiations with the Chiefs of the Six Nations, the Susquehanna Company applied to the Connecticut Assembly for its support of a petition to the King requesting authority for the Company to establish a new Colonial government within the limits of their purchase. This authority was approved. The members of the Susquehanna Company had thus pursued an acceptable legal pathway to establish their right to the Wyoming lands. Much has been written about the validity of the Connecticut claim versus that of Pennsylvania. The Connecticut settlers of Wyoming would be faced by dedicated adversaries from the Indians and from Pennsylvanians. Adding to their difficulties, the Iroquois led by King Hendricks refused to sign the deed to Connecticut, and refused to sell the Wyoming lands to *anyone*, preserving them for hunting grounds and for Indian settlement.

In the fall and winter of 1754, a number of inhabitants from Connecticut organized a second land company, initially known as the Delaware Company. Many of its members were also members of the Susquehanna Company. Its agents purchased from the Delaware Indians the lands lying between the Delaware River and a line ten miles east of the Susquehanna.[10] North and south boundaries were the 42nd and the 41st parallels respectively. This company became known as the Connecticut Delaware Company and in the summer of 1755 a few settlers arrived at Coshecton and took possession for the body of the company on the banks of the Delaware River.

In 1748, 12,000 acres of land along the Wallenpaupack Creek had been set aside for the use of the Pennsylvania proprietors. It was first settled by Pennsylvanians between 1750 and 1760 as a part of Northampton County. Its position astride the trail from Coshecton on the Delaware to the Wyoming Settlement was to make it an important stopover point when the Connecticut migration to Wyoming took place. [11]

Description of the Wyoming Valley

There was widespread enthusiasm among Connecticut people for the new lands to the west. Young men and women coming of age in the area around Windham were exposed to many enticing reports, especially about Wyoming Valley. "As early as 1750, a few daring adventurers from New England had crossed the mountains ...from the heights of the mountains along the Susquehanna they gazed upon the most lovely natural landscape which the eye ever beheld. The primeval forests covered the slopes of the mountains, while the plains and river bottom were here and there imperfectly cultivated by the Indians, who as yet held undisputed possession of the country west of the Delaware." [12]

According to Chapman, the valley of Wyoming was a land of great beauty at the time of its first white settlement.[13] Writing his personal observation in 1813, he noted "the broad level plain, the remarkable alluvial fertility and the tremendous growth of huge oak and pine trees. The Susquehanna River courses about 20 miles through this valley, which is formed and bounded by two ranges of mountains nearly parallel to each other. At the time of settlement there were many streams tumbling from those mountains, running across the flat plains to the river. These were plentiful with fish, as was the Susquehanna itself. Wild game, including elk, abounded throughout. In season there was the spectacle of wild flowers and wild grasses occurring especially in the natural meadows."

The Delaware River also held strong attraction for the early settlers. Francis Beck Brandt[14] wrote, "The forty miles of the course of the stream along the base of the mountain from Port Jervis to the Delaware Water Gap is unsurpassed in the variety and beauty of the picture it presents." Brandt goes on to say that "Along the western base of the mountain the river flows majestically onward lighting up field and forest, and adding a charm to a hundred landscapes, diverging from the blue hills at times to give our New Jersey neighbors a portion of the rich valley, and again washing their rocky base; and, receiving the waters of the Bushkill fresh from its little Niagara, and the Broadhead's and Marshall's Creek, the winding stream at length reaches the Water Gap to add the climax to its beautiful creations." Richard Smith had also explored this part of the Delaware and described it in his journal of 1769.[15]

For the colonists in Connecticut and Pennsylvania these new virgin lands promised opportunities of unimaginable proportions. Ownership of land was the symbol of success, of enrichment, and of status among one's peers. It was a time for the young, the strong and the brave of heart. Attempts to settle the new lands would soon begin.

CHAPTER 2

The Early Years

Bennet Marries Martha Jackson

Thomas Bennet grew to manhood in this milieu of dreams of land to the west. He remained unmarried until he was 29 years of age, when he wooed and took as his bride Martha Jackson.[16] Martha came from Litchfield County in Connecticut and had a brother living there.[17] The couple settled in the township of Scituate, Rhode Island, where their first child, Solomon, was born in 1751. The Bennet home in Scituate was not far from Windham, Connecticut, the headquarters of the Susquehanna Company. Like all young men in this region Thomas was aware of the intentions of this Company to settle lands to the west.

The French and Indian War

However, in 1754, hostilities between the French and English resulted in the French and Indian War. This conflict was to last nine years, ending with a treaty in 1763. During that period movements of settlers westward to the new frontiers were halted, awaiting outcome of this so-called Great War. This struggle was of great significance since it would determine whether dominance of the North American Continent would be French or English. The English were victorious, setting the stage for resumption of westward migration.[18]

As this war drew to its close, the Susquehanna Company began once again to pursue its plans for settlement. A largely attended meeting of the Company was held at Hartford, May 19, 1762. At this meeting the following resolution was adopted: "voted, that, for the promotion and encouragement of the speedy beginning a settlement of our Susquehanna purchase, there be liberty for one hundred of the purchasers - by themselves *personally*, and not by substitutes, to enter upon and under the Company to hold and improve, a tract of land within said purchase, ten miles square and easterly of and adjoining the Susquehanna River - to be held and improved by them and their heirs as a *gratuity from this company* over and above their respective shares in the rest of the purchase." [19]

First Settlement at Wyoming in 1762

Shortly after this meeting, some sixteen shareholders journeyed to Wyoming Valley, arriving at Capouse Meadows and thereafter establishing themselves nearby. (Capouse Meadows, named for the Indian King Capouse, is now a part of the city of Scranton.) This was to be the first ten mile tract and the group was to await the arrival of the remaining settlers. However, Chief Teedyuscung approached the sixteen settlers about July 20 and strongly advised them to leave if they wished to escape annihilation by the Indians. Teedyuscung called himself King of the Delawares and was a very prominent Indian leader of his time, albeit too fond of alcoholic spirits. He had established an Indian village in what is now south Wilkes-Barre, and was a converted and baptized Christian. His advice was heeded and the little group of settlers abandoned their encampment to return to the Delaware.[20]

Meanwhile in July, the Susquehanna Company enlarged this group to 200 but designated that the second 100 would take possession of a ten mile tract on the west bank of the river. A directing committee was appointed and by the middle of August a list of ninety-three men was developed to join the sixteen who had encamped at the head of the valley.[21]

Early in September, the two groups met, and shortly thereafter arrived at the eastern bank of the Susquehanna, at the mouth of the Lackawanna River. The composition of these two groups has been debated; but Harvey states that Thomas Bennet was one of those in the group of ninety-three names.[22] This was not his first journey to the new land. His daughter stated that Bennet had visited Wyoming twice before 1763.[23] At any rate, he had left his wife and sons at their Rhode Island home to join this venture. The entire party was made up solely of men, some on horseback, some on foot, traveling over a rough and narrow trail. They carried with them just the bare necessities, and after arriving at the mouth of the Lackawanna they moved down the

Susquehanna to the north bank of what is now called Mill Creek. There they swiftly built some crude huts of logs. This attempt lasted only ten days, the settlers abruptly withdrawing at the pressing request of a delegation from the Six Nations of the Iroquois.

Birth of Young Martha Bennet

By late September 1762, Thomas Bennet had returned to his home in Scituate, Rhode Island, no doubt shaken and disappointed at this turn of events. As it turned out, his wife was pregnant and gave birth in January 1763 to a daughter, Martha, destined to become a prominent person in the history of the settlement of Wyoming. Shortly after the birth of this daughter, Bennet rented his Scituate property and moved his little family to the Minisink area on the Delaware.

At the time of his move from Rhode Island, there was an established wagon path to the mouth of the Fishkill on the Hudson River. The town of Fishkill was a very early settlement in Dutchess County and the path traveled from it down hill to the nearby Fishkill landing.[24] Bennet and his family entered the town, walking and riding horseback over the heavily forested lofty ridge of hills. From the summit of the mountain the view of the Hudson River was beauty unsurpassed, and the road heading down to the landing was winding and steep.

The ferry across the Hudson River to Newburgh had been operating since the summer of 1743.[25] Alexander Colden had obtained letters patent enabling him to establish the ferry. This ferry became of increasing importance to the movement of New England men to the Susquehanna. In 1769, Richard Smith sailed up the Hudson to inspect the great tract of New York land known as the Smith patent, which he had just acquired. "We took a turn on shore at Denton's Mill, 60 miles upstream from New York and walked about two miles down the River to Newburgh, a small scattered village, and to the ferry. We found excellent cyder at both.—This town has some trade and may be a place of consequence as the *fine* country of Goshen is said to lay back about 12 or more miles. The New England men cross here and hereabout almost daily for Susquehanna; their route is from here to Minisink, accounted only 40 miles distant." [26]

Bennet Family Moves to the Delaware Settlement

The Bennet family crossed over the Hudson from Fishkill to Newburgh; they then had another steep climb up to the high plateau at Newburgh. Their destination was Goshen. Goshen had been a settlement for about seventy-five years and was situated in the midst of a fertile, gently rolling plain. Passing through Goshen, the family arrived at Minisink and moved into a large stone house along the Delaware, a house shared by several others and used as a fort from time to time.[27] The Minisink area covered about sixty square miles, a strip along the Delaware River, three to four miles wide and from twenty to thirty miles long, extending from Bushkill on the south to Port Jervis on the north.[28] Describing this area at the time, Smith states "We lodged last night at Peter Kirkendahls (now Port Jervis)-there is a tolerable farm and the first we have seen for some time past. Here hills on the river open to right and left and let in some good flats. The lands along the Minisink are not so rich as I expected; very little meadow is visible, the ground rather unfit for the plow and somewhat sandy like ours about Burlington and accordingly they raise more rye than wheat. Not many houses are to be seen and those quite mean, the flats in many places narrow, flanked still by the Range of Hills."[29]

Rittenburg and Clark[30] described the Minisink as rolling and hilly, the slopes generally free from rocks, and soil susceptible to cultivation. The southern part of this area, around Bushkill, was much more fertile, supporting the growth of wheat and rye. For the most part the area is preserved in its natural state today. Many buildings and small towns were removed in the 1970s as a result of an abortive plan to construct here a huge lake for recreational purposes. One can still see the beauty of the gently flowing Delaware and the fields and forests as of yore.

Bennet, now residing along the Delaware, attempted to create a suitable habitat for his family. Shortly after he moved there, groups of his friends and acquaintances–those who had been driven out of Wyoming by the Iroquois in 1762 – filtered back to the Susquehanna area. Bennet was sorely tempted to go along, but his family persuaded him to stay on the Delaware.

At about this time the English government issued an order to the Connecticut legislature to cease settlement along the Susquehanna and Delaware rivers, until the issue of rights could be laid before the king. However, official word of this order did not arrive until after the colonists had begun settlement at Mill Creek and after the Bennet family had moved to the Delaware. In any event, the case for Connecticut was appealed to the crown in London by a Colonel Dyer, who, with others, had secured from the sachems of the Mohawk and the chiefs of other nations a new deed confirming the earlier contested one of July 11, 1754.[31] A legal opinion in England on this issue was to the effect that the Charter of Connecticut would have to stand because it anteceded by several years that given to Penn, unless the Penns could establish the right of prior occupancy, which they could not.

The Mill Creek Massacre of 1763

Thomas Bennet felt some insecurity during these legal arguments. His enthusiasm was considerably more dampened by the fact that the Mill Creek settlement on the Susquehanna was destroyed by a ferocious massacre on October 15, 1763.[32] Some of the survivors of this Indian attack fled over the mountains to the Delaware settlements. This group from Mill Creek had gained great initial success, had planted several hundred acres of corn and other grain and had cut a large amount of hay. They had built a sawmill on Mill Creek and had completed a large block house.

Refugees from this massacre arrived on the Delaware in a confused and hysterical state, but after a few days most of them proceeded back to their friends and families in Connecticut. At that time there was a bitter boundary struggle among the settlers of New York, New Jersey and Pennsylvania, concerning the ownership of these lands along the Delaware. [33] Armed battles of small scale occurred sporadically among the white settlers. To these were added the very frequent raids of unfriendly Indians, with resultant murders, scalpings, destruction of grain and livestock, and burning of isolated homes.

Bennet Moves from the Delaware to Goshen

For the Bennets, life along the Minisink proved to be increasingly unpleasant. Thomas debated what to do to improve his circumstance. The Wyoming massacre of 1763 so thoroughly alarmed him that he temporarily abandoned the idea of moving to the Susquehanna. Early in 1764, after having lived along the Delaware for one year, he reconnoitered some farm land in nearby Goshen. Shortly thereafter he moved his family from the Minisink settlement to a comfortable farm at Goshen which he leased for a period of six years.[34] Goshen was astride the path from Connecticut to the Delaware and to Wyoming, and Bennet was constantly exposed to any movement of settlers and others to and from these areas.

For two years after the Mill Creek massacre of 1763 there was no further organized attempt to settle Wyoming by the Susquehanna Company, and the beautiful valley was abandoned, uninhabited except for scattered groups of Indians. In this interval the Pennsylvania proprietors were very active, being now alerted to the intentions of the Susquehanna Company. All this was thrown into disarray when, in October 1768, Sir William Johnson convened the Great Council of the Indians at Fort Stanwix (Rome, New York).[35] A deed was signed by a sachem of each of the Six Nations granting to Thomas and Richard Penn lands which included those already claimed by the Susquehanna and Delaware companies.

At this startling news, the Connecticut people convened at Hartford, December 28, 1768, and resolved that "Forty persons upwards of the age of 21 years, proprietors in sale purchases, and approved by the committee to be nominated, proceed to enter upon and take possession of said land for and in behalf of said company by the first day of February 1769."[36]

Before proceeding with the journey of the "first forty" settlers, let us update the activities of the Pennsylvanians in order to understand the hostilities about to develop.

Activities of the Pennamites

Beginning in 1763, the Pennsylvania Proprietors had kept up an aggressive campaign to deny the lands of Wyoming to the Connecticut settlers. Some idea of the intensity of their concern can be gleaned from a letter of May 1763 written by Governor Hamilton (Pennsylvania) to Colonel Bard.[37] "I have lately received intelligence with fresh complaints from the Indians of Wyoming, that the Connecticut people still persist in prosecuting their scheme of settling the lands about Wyoming; and with the advice of the Council (of Pennsylvania) I have thought it proper to issue a proclamation and I desire that you will immediately take a journey to Wyoming with such assistance as you shall judge proper and use your best effort to persuade or drive away all the white people you shall find settled or about to settle, there, or any lands not yet purchased from the Indians ...and if they shall go away peacefully, you will then, after their departure, see all their buildings and improvements destroyed ...if you find these persuasive measures shall not succeed...I would have you, either by stratagem or force, to get three or four of the ring leaders...apprehended and carried to the gaol."

So it was that an expedition of Pennsylvania militia under Captain Asher Clayton in October 1763 arrived at the charred remains of the massacre at Mill Creek, which had taken place a few days previously. Instead of "driving out" the settlers, they found mutilated and dead bodies which they buried. Before departing, they further destroyed whatever crops and cabin remnants they found.

In the summer of 1765, Captain Amos Ogden, Captain John Dick and John Anderson came to Wyoming Valley to establish a trading post under joint authorization by the Commissioners for Indian Affairs of Pennsylvania and Sir William Johnson for the Indians.[38] Near what is now the intersection of Ross and South River Street, Wilkes-Barre, they erected a rather substantial log building for use as a store and warehouse. An active trade with Indians up and down the river flourished for a few years.

Pennsylvania proprietors fully believed that the original charter to Penn from the king gave title to the Wyoming lands to the Penns. To strengthen their position, through Sir William Johnson, they persuaded the Indians at Fort Stanwix in 1768 to deed these same lands to Pennsylvania. This was accomplished after much pressure; several Indians protested that they had already sold these lands to the "New England white people, had received their pay for the same, and could not sell the same lands again."[39]

Manor of Sunbury

Governor John Penn then authorized a survey of the Susquehanna lands to lay out two manors: one on the west bank to be the Manor of Sunbury, and one on the east bank to be the Manor of Stokes. Sunbury included what is now Plymouth, Kingston, Forty-Fort and Wyoming. Stokes is now Wilkes-Barre and all of its suburbs.

Manor of Stokes

Soon after the manor survey was completed Governor Penn executed a lease for seven years to Captain Amos Ogden and his associates for the use of 100 acres in the Manor of Stokes on condition they would maintain the trading post and would defend themselves and those who might go on the lands under them "against all enemies whatsoever.'[40] Ogden and his two cohorts then selected 100 acres in the north corner of the manor, to include the land at the mouth of Mill Creek. They moved to the site originally occupied by the Connecticut group at the time of the massacre of 1763. There, they built a new block house and soon moved to it all the goods stored in the house at the bend of the river.

Governor Penn now also issued a proclamation offering various Wyoming lands to any willing settlers under the same terms, and, although several lessors signed up, few actually fulfilled the requirement of occupying with promise to defend themselves. By January of 1769 Ogden was well seated at the Mill Creek log house and some new settlers had arrived from Pennsylvania and New Jersey, occupying sites near the Mill Creek headquarters.

The stage was now set for the prolonged series of confrontations between the Pennsylvanians and the Connecticut settlers. This strife was destined to persist for twenty years, with periods of quiet alternating with fierce civil war pitting white against white. This struggle and its grief would be enhanced by episodes of ferocious Indian raids, including massacres, in all of which Thomas Bennet and his family would be involved.

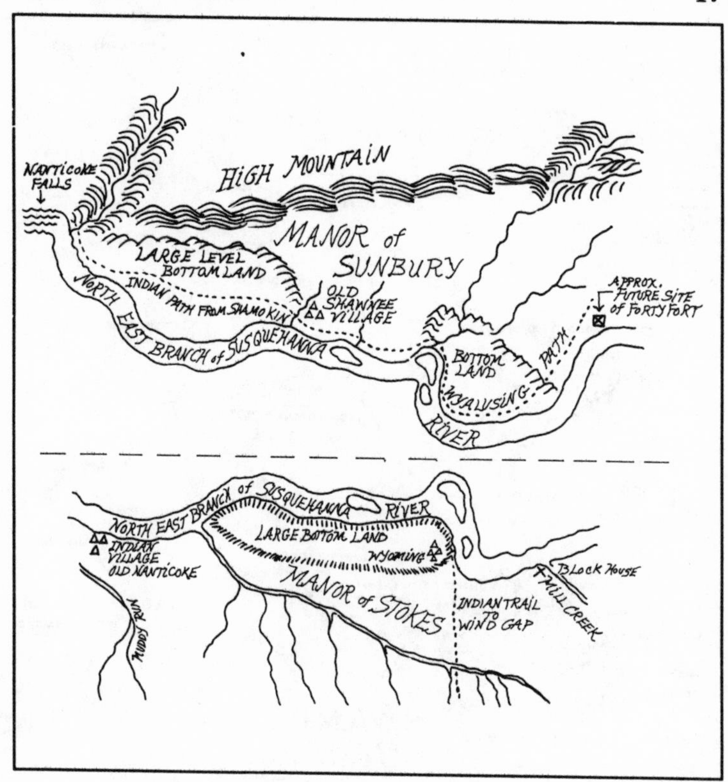

VACANT LAND

The Manor of Sunbury was to be a tract of 20,000 acres on the west side of the river. The Manor of Stokes was to be 9,800 acres, the latter to be entirely within Wyoming Valley. As can be seen, the course of the Susquehanna River is somewhat different and the maps are not precisely accurate, but they show the early relationships of terrain and water shed.

Maps adapted by the author from: Harvey-*The History of Wilkes-Barre*, Vol. I, pp. 454, 455, Raeder Press, Wilkes-Barre, 1909, from the original Pennsylvania Survey ordered by Governor Penn.

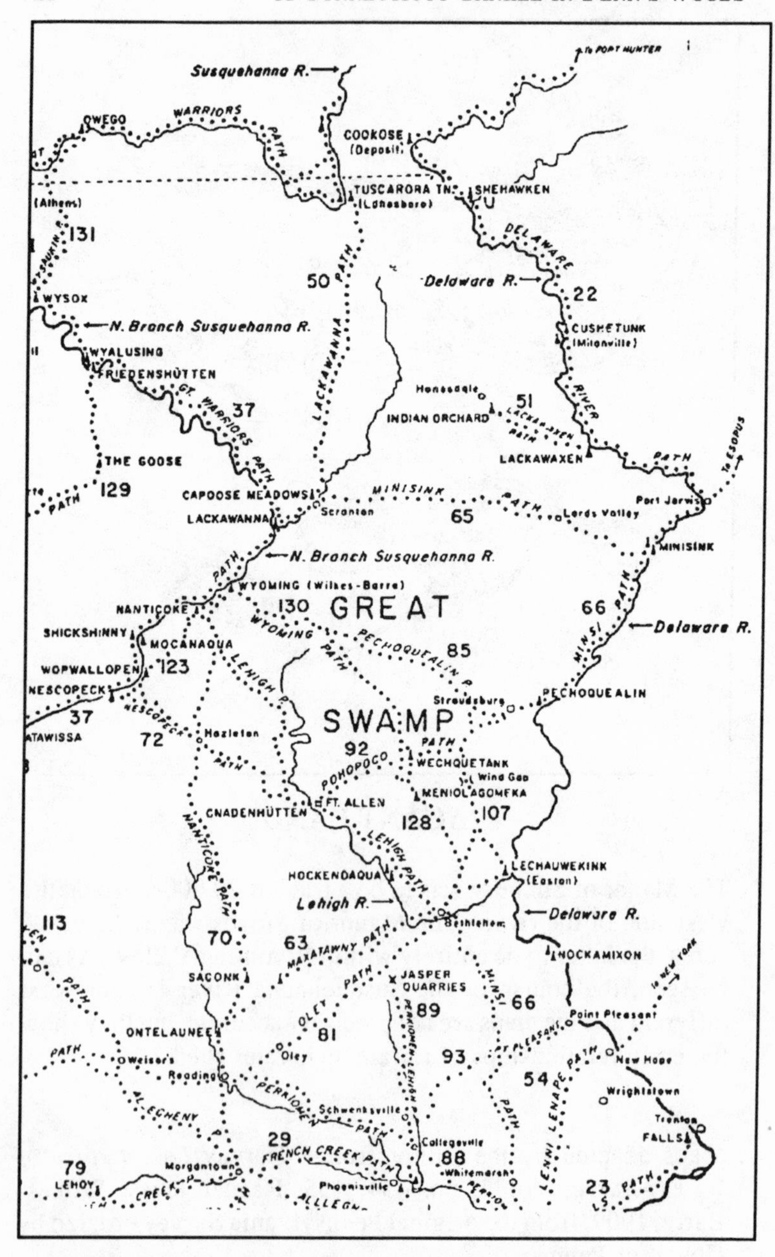

Following three maps from *Indian Paths of Pennsylvania* by Paul A. Wallace, 1965. Reproduced with permission of the Pennsylvania Historical and Museum Commission, Harrisburg.

CHAPTER 3

Connecticut Settlers in Wyoming Valley

Description of Indian Trails to Wyoming

In all of the migration to the west toward the frontier, there were many formidable natural obstacles to overcome, and the state of man's equipment to get there was quite primitive. Overland was the primary method to travel east to west since the flow of major rivers was north to south. A major waterway flowing from east to west would have facilitated transport of the immigrants as it did along the James, Potomac and Savannah Rivers far to the south.

Indian pathways had long been developed, and it was some of these that became established roadways for the movement of the white settlers to the western frontiers. Paul A. Wallace emphasizes that such paths were dry, level and direct wherever the terrain permitted.[41] "They followed river terraces above flood level or…they followed well drained ridges. Rivers

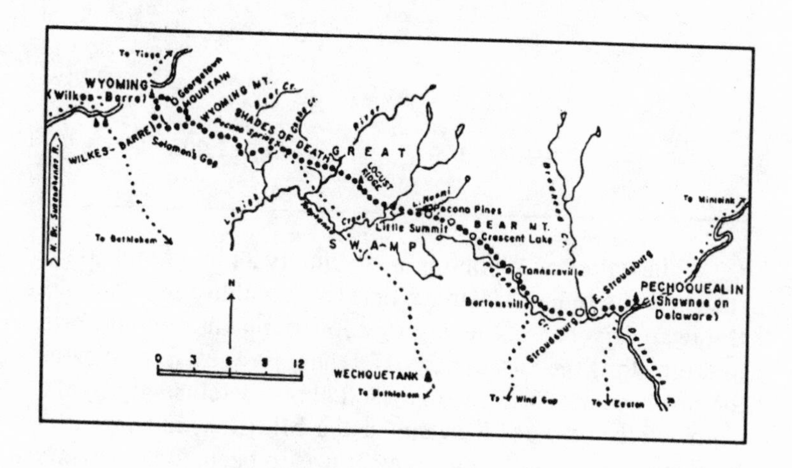

and creeks had to be forded. ...The Indians seized every advantage offered by the terrain. Most paths managed to keep so direct a course ... they were actually less winding, and therefore shorter, than most of the river roads built by the white man." Wallace gives the Indians credit for being naturally skilled terrain engineers.

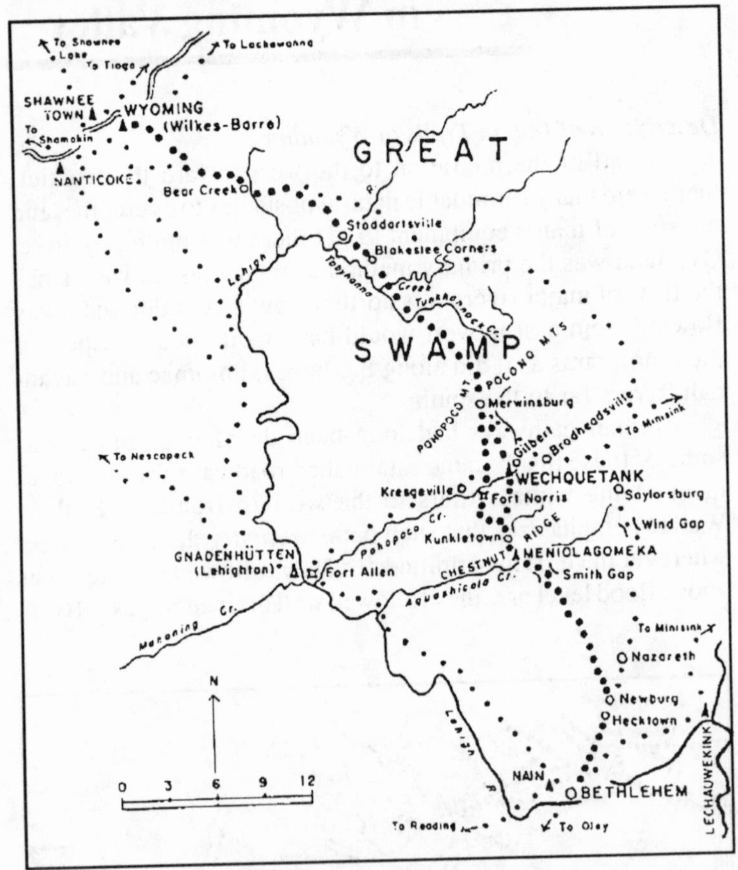

The valley of Wyoming was actually an important crossroads for the Indians. Wallace lists five notable paths from the Delaware River area, converging upon four paths running north to south along the Susquehanna. Of these five east to west paths the northernmost was the one used almost exclusively by the Connecticut settlers. It began in the Minisink, not far from Minisink Island, and close to what was to become Dingman's Ferry along the Delaware. The path rose abruptly along the

Raymondskill through a gap in the mountains. Entry to the path from the Delaware was "overlooked" by Indian Point and Pow Wow Hill, both situated on the high plateau above the Raymondskill. There is a marker on current Route 209 which is close to the old opening of the path. In fact, one can very closely follow this path over beautiful high ground to Lord's Valley and Blooming Grove. About twenty miles from the Delaware is an active spring, called "Bubbling Spring," where there is a little clearing in a quiet area said to have been a stopping point and camp site for early Connecticut immigrants.

Passing through the present communities of Lord's Valley and Blooming Grove, the path crossed current Interstate 84, over high ground to Paupack Church. Its progress thence to Hamlin is at present interceded by the large artificial Wallenpaupack Lake. From Hamlin it proceeded to Mt. Cobb, from which height the early settlers could see the head of Wyoming Valley. Descent from that elevation then coursed through present Dunmore to the western terminus of this old pathway at Capouse Meadows, now Scranton. Holister[42] describes Capouse Meadows as a meadow surrounded by all of the wilderness of mountain and valley. Here Capouse was King of a Muncy tribe — "Where the council fires lit up the valley long before the arrival of the whites." It was the Indian custom to burn over the surrounding hunting grounds annually, so that there was little or no sapling growth to interfere with the chase around the meadow; besides this, all lower limbs of adjacent trees were hacked off with the hatchet.

The first Yankee settlers called this area Capouse Meadows, after its great chieftain, and described it as a flat beautiful meadow land literally scooped out of the Moosic Range. In 1769, when the First Forty settlers arrived here, game of all kind abounded. Perch, pike, and chub swarmed the Lackawanna River in fabulous numbers while "every fair water brook that bubbled from the mountain was alive with trout."

Holister, continuing, states that the trail from the Delaware to Capouse in general kept to the higher ground where the woods were less dense, because the warriors preferred climbing over considerable elevation to the labor of cutting a trail through more level or lower ground. Besides, overlooking points permitted them to discover the approach or presence of the enemy.

Certain features of the Minisink trail are worth considering. There were frequent copious fresh water springs. Holister notes the presence of a large bubbling spring close to the summit of Moosic Mountain, beside the trail, lying between the valley and Mt. Cobb. Swamps and marshes were generally avoided and at appropriate intervals, camp sites could be identified. The entire trip from the Delaware to Capouse Meadows could be made in three days, more easily in four, the time consumed depending upon the season and upon the strength and endurance of the traveler.

The Susquehanna Company Sends Settlers to Wyoming

When the Susquehanna Company authorized the enlistment of forty adventurers who would take possession of the Wyoming lands, there was little difficulty developing this list and by January 1769 it was completed. These forty were to have their choice of lands among the five planned townships. A directing committee was appointed to provide support and maintenance for this expedition. These settlers were required to be on site no later than the first day of May 1769.

Harvey describes this action as follows: "For the encouragement of the 'First Forty' settlers, as also of the 200 who should join them in the spring, the Company voted to lay out five 'gratuity' towns, or townships, of land within the Purchase. Each town was to be five miles square, and three of the towns were to be located on one side of the river and two on the other side — 'adjoining and opposite' to each other, only the river parting; at such place on said river as they (the settlers) may think proper. Each of said towns to be five miles on the river, and extend in width back five miles, and to be and belong to the said "Forty" and to the said 200 persons, over and above their respective shares and proportions in the remainder of the general purchase."[43]

The Forty were, first, to have their choice of one of these towns and then the remaining four towns were to belong to the 200 other settlers. However, the Forty and the 200 proprietors had to be there on the date mentioned, and were required to continue thereon, "holding and improving the same by themselves, heirs, or assigns — for the space of five years after their entry as aforesaid."

According to Brewster,[44] a part of the group of Forty set out from Windham, Connecticut, late in January 1769, in the middle of winter. On horseback they crossed the Shetucket River just below what is now Willimantic, then wound over the snow capped mountains into Lebanon, where they found additional comrades awaiting them. All joined for a celebration at the Alden Tavern, then the enlarged party proceeded to Hartford, where a few more of the Forty joined them. They then rode through Litchfield County to Duchess County, New York, and across the Hudson River on the ferry from Fishkill Landing to Newburg.

Climbing the bank to Newburg they rode on to Goshen, New York, where they picked up seven more members, including Thomas Bennet. The party proceeded across this part of New York and arrived at the Delaware at a site destined to become Port Jervis. There the path ran twelve miles down the eastern side of the Delaware, through the Minisink area, to Dingman's Ferry.

According to William Fitten, in 1743 Andrew Dingman obtained his first land patent at this site.[45] Dingman was a pioneer of Dutch extraction from Kinderhook, New York, who had developed considerable experience and talent trading in land with the Indians. He examined this land along the Delaware and finally was able to acquire rights on both sides of the river. The area was long known as "Dingman's Choice," and as the time went on a small village developed. Shortly after he obtained this land he began to ferry travelers and locals across the river — for many years this was the only such convenience along the northern Delaware River.

Today, the town of Dingman's Ferry has been demolished. The actual ferry has been replaced by a privately owned steel bridge (toll $.50 per car). The river at this point flows quietly and deeply through a green forest. A haunting stillness prevails in this area and envelops one standing along the bank.

Pennamites Arrest Settlers

The group of forty settlers ferried across the Delaware at this point, then followed the "upper path" to Wyoming. On about February 6, 1769, they looked down on the valley lands from Moosic Mountain. Descending to Capouse Meadows, they followed the Lackawanna River down to its mouth. In the process they decided that they would choose the flat meadow lands on the west side of the Susquehanna. But they found the Susquehanna River too swollen for a crossing at that time, and camped at the mouth of the Lackawanna River, where they hastily built two or three log cabins at the site of present Pittston. They had just begun to settle in when, on March 13, a posse of the Pennsylvanians under Sheriff Jennings and Justice Gordon arrived from Easton. They found the Connecticut settlers secured within their log houses and were unable to persuade them to surrender. Forcible entry was required and finally thirty-one of them were captured and arrested.[46] Thomas Bennet, in his deposition given at a later time (1771), stated that he too was taken prisoner by Jennings but that he managed to escape his captors while still in the valley.[47] Although it was winter and extremely unpleasant weather, he fled north along the river to Capouse Meadows and thence over the upper trail to the Minisink. Arriving at Goshen he rejoined his family at the farm which his sons and wife had been maintaining in his absence. His stay there was destined to last just a few months, his visions fixed upon the ultimate settlement of Wyoming.

Additional Settlers Sent

Back in Connecticut, the Susquehanna Company met at Hartford April 12, 1769, and voted to generate an additional list of 300 more settlers, over and above the "First Forty" plus the 200 additional men approved in December 1768. This would bring the total to be recruited to 540 settlers. Organization and maintenance of this migration was placed under the direction committee appointed in December. This committee comprised Isaac Tripp, Benjamin Fallett, John Jenkins, William Buck, and Benjamin Shoemaker.

The committee had little difficulty developing its list, made up of proprietors or appointed alternates. This time the company directed that the 540 were to be organized as a common whole, a compact unit, properly fortified, without regard to any town or township which might later be laid out. The men would be divided into task forces—tillage, labor, fortification, scouting, husbandry, and a small force to maintain peace and order during the early phases of settling.

They also voted to provide a minister or teacher of religious matters and to issue to him one whole share of property rights, as well as to order his sustenance and maintenance as a responsibility of the committee. Additional provisions were ordered, and the sale of more shares was approved in order to support the new venture.

Major John Durkee of Norwich County was appointed to lead the new group of settlers, and in late April about 110 men gathered at Norwich, to set out for Wyoming. Major Durkee proved to be an excellent choice, at age forty years a man of "considerable experience as a soldier in time of war and as a man of affairs in time of peace."[48] He also possessed a sense of fairness, was of calm and deliberate demeanor, and knew how to exert discipline and to render punishment to those offending the common decency and laws of his group.

This new group journeyed across Connecticut, crossed the Hudson at Fishkill, crossed through Goshen, New York, Sussex County, New Jersey, and crossed the Delaware at Dingman's Ferry. Along the way they picked up individuals from the "First Forty" who had tarried at Minisink after their release from the Easton jail; some, such as Thomas Bennet, joined this group as it passed through their districts.

From the Delaware they coursed over the "Minisink path" to Capouse Meadows on the Lackawanna. By 1769, this path was well established by the Connecticut settlers, and through repeated use, overnight sites for encampments had been developed at convenient intervals. Fresh water and grasses were sought, especially for the irreplaceable horses.

Provisions for such a journey depended upon the time of year. Wild game could be found along the way, and fish were plentiful. In season, wild berries and nuts could be harvested. Barrels of salt pork, along with dry corn, were frequently strapped to some of the horses. Tents or shelters for overnight encampment were occasionally used, but many nights were spent under the sky with minimal protection. When it rained, everyone got wet and stayed that way until dried by the sun and air. Rarely was a party under Indian attack, but it was customary to have scouts and sentinels posted for safety.

Arriving at Capouse Meadows at dusk, on May 11, 1769, the settlers' observation of valley detail was impossible, but in the bright early light of morning, a beautiful spectacle of spring time greeted them on all sides. Close by were the early grasses and wildflowers. Scattered clumps of wild honeysuckle were intermingled with the blossoms of wild cherry and plum. The clear waters of the Lackawanna tumbled into the Susquehanna. Down the valley floor was the reflection of the river. Ample groves of pine were intermingled with the delicate first leaves of hardwoods. Closer to the river they could see the fertile and treeless flatlands on the west side, verdant with early spring grasses. The fresh odor of springtime came up from the valley floor, and once again, these settlers were enchanted by the beauty of what they considered to be rightfully their lands.

This was the fifth entry into the valley by Thomas Bennet —a fifth attempt to settle. By now he was forty-nine years of age, strong, vigorous, and tall. Not by nature quarrelsome, he was endowed with natural survival abilities and unquestionably was a man of purpose. He had left his wife and children– Solomon, age eleven; Martha, age six; and Andrew, age five –at his farm site in Goshen. According to his daughter, Martha, he was a determined man, with heart set upon moving his family to the Wyoming settlement. Prior experiences cautioned him and in the migration of spring, 1769, he decided to go on with the party of settlers with the intent of coming back for his family just as soon as the situation appeared stable and there were adequate living quarters available.[49]

Riding down along the Susquehanna that May morning, he once again experienced a warm feeling of belonging to this new and beautiful valley. Approaching the Mill Creek settlement of Ogden, Stuart, and others, he followed Major Durkee's lead to bypass this establishment. However, the party was observed by Stuart and some brief shouting interchange occurred. Major Durkee was eager to avoid any confrontation or struggle and made no formal contact. But Stuart recognized Bennet and several others and later that day he wrote an urgent message to Governor Penn at Philadelphia, reading in part ..."This afternoon at about 3 o'clock 146 New England men and others, chiefly on horseback, passed by our houses and are now encamped on the east side of the river. Among them are Benjamin Shoemaker and John McDavitt with several of their neighbors. I spoke to Mr. McDavitt, who informed me that at least as many more are on their way and will be here tomorrow, and I have other intelligence that they will in a few days be 500 strong. If this is true, we can only act defensively until we are reinforced, as presently we are about twenty-four men. On my way up the river from Shamokin I was hailed by a man at the mouth of Fishing Creek, named James McClure, who told me that he and four others were an advanced party of 100 going to join the New England men, and that they chiefly would be from Lancaster County.

From the view I had of those gentry, in their procession by our houses, they appear to be...of the very lowest class, but are almost all armed and fit for mischief....I have enclosed a list of the names of as many of them as I could possibly collect in so short a time."[50] The list totaled thirty-one names, and included Thomas Bennet plus five others of the "First Forty."

Bennet proceeded with the Durkee party to the site of the old storehouse of Ogden, then still evident southwest of what is now the intersection of Ross Street with South River in Wilkes-Barre. The site overlooked the bend of the river on the west, and on the south it was bordered by a deep ravine. Harvey states,[51] "The location was a favorable one because, in the first place, it was in a measure protected against the near approach of would be assailants...on one hand by the river, and on the other by the ravine; in the second place, clear and unobstructed views of the upper and lower reaches of the river could be had from that point, and the approach of boats up and down the river could be seen for some distance; in the third place, the ground there had been almost entirely cleared of trees, having been utilized in building the house and fences required by Teedyuscung of the old Indian village in South Wilkes-Barre ...and in building Ogden's storehouses."

Creation of Fort Durkee

The majestic sweep of the Susquehanna is no longer seen in its primeval glory and beauty. The flood dike and its massive pile of earth, rocks and metal pilings now prevent one from standing on this site, with the original open view described by the early settlers. One can still get a sense of this, however, standing on the dike. Down river is seen the next bend as the river courses toward Plymouth. In springtime the river bank is lined with aspens and willows, showing light yellow-green, backed in the middle distance to the west by the low hillside of what is now Larksville and Larkmount Manor. In the far distance is the western mountain range bordering the valley, providing a bluish-lavender background for the scene. The river reflects the sky and mountains, and shows various moods, changing many times during the span of one day.

On this site, Major Durkee and his party set to work to erect a fort to be known thereafter as Fort Durkee. Within little more than one week they had built twenty log houses plus the fort itself. All of these houses could be entered only through the central port of the fort and all had firing slits rather than windows on the side facing outwards. The Fort Durkee settlement functioned like a military outpost in a foreign land. Sentinels were posted round the clock, passwords were required, and no one could leave the fort without permission of Major Durkee. Although ultimate personal possession of Wyoming land was understood and anticipated, there was at this early point a common effort to establish the settlement.

In July, 1769, Major Durkee adopted the name Wilkes-Barre. The name was chosen to honor John Wilkes and Isaac Barré, members of the English Parliament, who supported the colonialist rights in America in opposition to King George III. By July they had two or three hundred acres of the flat land under cultivation, marked off by a split rail fence. An ample reserve of hay was available and the corn was maturing nicely. There was much reason for self confidence and for some pride in accomplishment. Fish and wild game of all types were plentiful and aside from one threat from the Pennamites there was no serious confrontation with them or with the Indians.

The Connecticut settlers who had been jailed in Easton the previous March had been liberated on bail after a brief confinement. Trial had been set for early June, and when this date arrived Major Durkee and two others set out to attend the trial. The trip proved unnecessary and a genuine waste of time and energy, for when they arrived in Easton they were informed that the case against the Yankees was continued to the September court, with bail of the defendants renewed. Many of those men returned to Wyoming but a few returned to their respective homes in Connecticut. While Major Durkee was away on this trip, a Colonel Turbot Francis arrived from Fort Augusta (Sunbury) with a large party of armed Pennamites. He demanded immediate possession of the houses and fort, and threatened to kill the settlers and set everything aflame, should the settlers refuse. After much haggling, Francis realized that force would be required to accomplish his goal, but judging the Yankees too strongly fortified he withdrew to his base at Fort Augusta, awaiting further orders from the governor.[52]

Connecticut Settlers Driven Out

During the summer and early fall of 1769, Captain Ogden and his group dwelt in and around Mill Creek, extending their cultivation of the area and generally improving their little settlement. The two communities carried out daily activities, carrying defensive weapons as they went about their work. Occasional physical confrontations and rare violence between parties are noted, but in general they seem to have avoided one another.

In September there was a serious skirmish in which physical wounds were inflicted. This hastened the preparations of Sheriff Jennings (at Easton) for his expedition to Wyoming Valley, which he was to make in compliance with instructions from Governor Penn. Accordingly, about twenty men set out from Fort Augusta, armed with an iron four-pounder and ample stores of ammunition. This party came up the river in several bateaux and arrived at Mill Creek on November 8. A few days later Sheriff Jennings set out from Easton with about 200 men. These two forces were charged with the conquest and dissolution of the Yankee settlement at Fort Durkee.

Ogden, learning of the approach of Jennings, gathered his forty men and on November 11 made a surprise raid on a small working party of Yankees some distance from Fort Durkee. By chance one of the party was the fort commander, Major John Durkee, whom Ogden arrested and promptly dispatched in irons to the Philadelphia City Jail.[53]

On the very next day Sheriff Jennings reached Wyoming, and on November 14 he led the combined forces to Fort Durkee; later, after some parley and discussion, the Connecticut settlers surrendered. The articles of surrender permitted fourteen of them to remain to tend the livestock and to harvest, pending legal pursuit of the rival claims. But a few days later, Ogden, independently and contrary to the agreement, launched a campaign of burning and destruction, driving away cattle and horses and generally making the little settlement untenable.

Bennet Flees to Goshen

The original arrest warrant developed by Sheriff Jennings at the time of the capitulation listed the settlers of Fort Durkee.[54] One of those named was Thomas Bennet; however, no arrests were made. Since Bennet was not named as one of the fourteen settlers to be left at the fort, he once again traveled the upper path back to the Delaware and thence to his farm in Goshen, New York.

Recapture of Fort Durkee

Some of the Fort Durkee settlers in 1769 were actually Pennsylvania farmers from the area around Lancaster and Hanover, in Lancaster County. These men had applied earlier to the Susquehanna Company to let them join the further defense of the Company's claim at Wyoming. The Company granted to roughly fifty Hanoverians a plot of land six miles square, the exact site to be determined at a later date; for their part, they were to defend and to develop the settlement but to follow the rules and regulations already decreed by the Susquehanna Company for the Connecticut settlers.

In mid-January 1770, Captain Zebulon Butler and Ebenezer Backer were dispatched by the Susquehanna Company to proceed to Hanover Township in Lancaster County. Upon their arrival there they found about forty men organized under Lazarus Stewart ready to march to Wyoming to defend the Connecticut settlement. When this party neared Wyoming it was joined by eight or ten men who had been among those who surrendered the fort the previous November. They arrived at Fort Durkee quietly on Sunday, February 11, 1770. Harvey states "At that time Fort Durkee was garrisoned by a band of Pennamites—Ogden was in New Jersey and Sheriff Jennings and his posse had returned to Philadelphia. Captains Butler and Stewart had little difficulty evicting the Pennamites, and then took up quarters there."[55]

Just when Bennet returned to the fort is not documented, but he was there by early March 1770. A warrant was issued by Justice Lewis Gordon for his arrest, along with that of thirty-six other men who were said to be at the fort at that time. By mutual agreement, Captain Zebulon Butler was commander overall, with the Lancasterians under the command of Lazarus Stewart. Major Durkee was at that time waiting near Sciota for a number of New Englanders who were to march with him to Wyoming as reinforcements, bringing along a supply train of much needed ammunition and provisions.

Captain Ogden had by now returned from New Jersey to his Mill Creek block house, and was in command of a small group of Pennamites remaining at the site. In late April, Major Durkee and his reinforcements arrived, and he at once assumed command of Fort Durkee; it was he who confronted Ogden and finally persuaded him and his group to capitulate and to depart the area.

Brief Peace and Prosperity

In the months that followed, there was at first a good deal of destruction of Pennamite property by the Yankees, and many of the former Pennsylvania settlers were forced to leave the area completely. Gradually, however, an atmosphere of peace and prosperity settled over Wyoming. "Hope, joy, and confidence began to prevail."[56] The summer months saw the completion of the surveys and laying out of the several townships, as ordered and approved by the Susquehanna Company. The township plot of Wilkes-Barre was laid out as a parallelogram, and the four other settling towns were surveyed: Nanticoke, later Hanover, Pittstown (Pittston), The Forty, later Kingstown and now Kingston, and Plymouth.

A list of the proprietors of the five townships was prepared at Wilkes-Barre on June 17, 1770, showing 238 names, including that of Thomas Bennet.[57] These men were busily improving lands. Bennet and a party began working on the flat plains across the river, where they constructed a few log houses. Such work was done by day, the party under orders to return to the main fort each evening.

Drawing of Lots

On July 7, 1770, the allotment of Kingston lands was made to the "First Forty" settlers. Slips of paper, each with the name of a proprietor present, were placed in a hat, while in another hat were deposited slips with all the lot numbers of the township being allotted. From each hat a slip would be drawn and subsequently matched.[58] During the summer of 1770, following the drawing of west side lots by the First Forty, there began the construction of log houses and cultivation of rich

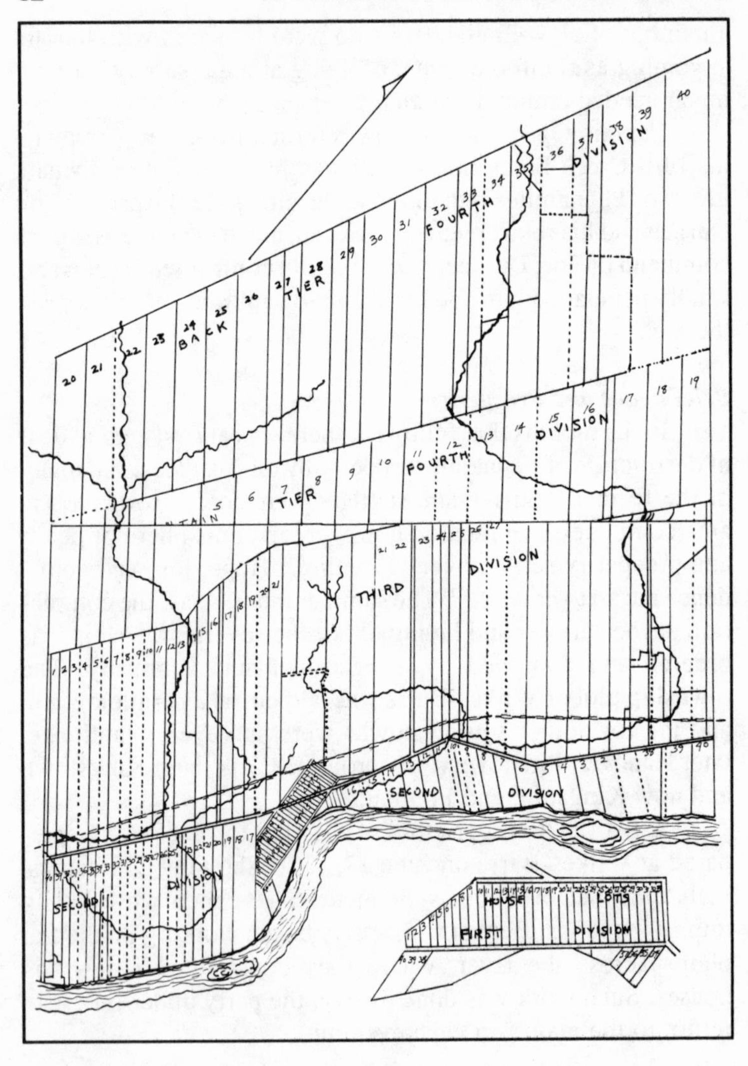

Map from Wm. Brewster, *History of Certified Township of Kingston, Pa.* 1930. Lots, divided among first forty settlers, with most prized house lots along the river.

fields in what is now Forty Fort, with some activity in Kingstown as well. The first records of a town meeting in Forty Fort or Kingstown referred to one held shortly before July 3, 1770. At that meeting it was voted to lay out the third division of lots known as back lots. Thomas Bennet drew lot No. 8 and also became owner of first division home lot No. 19, and of second division meadow lot No. 13. Later, when the fourth division mountain lot was drawn, Bennet was given his "settling right" of No. 24.[59]

Some concept of the scope of this land is of importance if one is to understand the determination of the early settler to hold and to defend his rights. At Forty Fort, the first division, or town lot, was divided into forty pieces, each of the First Forty settlers receiving one such lot by drawing. The lots faced the beautiful Susquehanna River, were above the general flood plain and were considered by these settlers to be ideal for home plots. A part of this section was set aside as the town plot; the old church, the meeting house, part of the cemetery, and the site of the present town hall of Forty Fort all lie on this town plot.

The second division, or meadow lots, consisted of the fertile bottom lands lying in the upper and lower Kingstown flats. Over the years these flatlands were repeatedly flooded, developing a rich alluvial soil. Parts of these lands had been cleared and cultivated by the Indians long before the white man came to the valley. Lot No. 1 of the second division lay in lower Wyoming, and Lot No. 40 abutted the Plymouth Township line.

The third division became known as the "Great Back Lots." These lots became the site of the great farm estates which once lined Wyoming Avenue, extending from the "Great Road" back to the mountains in the west. Most of present Kingston Township lies in the third division. The mountain tier or fourth division remained undivided until 1787, when it was parcelled into forty sections, each original settler being awarded one fortieth of the division.[60]

Beginning in June and July 1770, each of the first forty settlers became a holder of several hundred acres, some in timber, some in meadow and field, and some bordering the river. Bennet held an enduring and steadfast interest in development of this land, in the construction of the fort and associated cabins, and the cultivation of rich meadow land.

As formal town meetings began in the summer of 1770, it seems certain that about this time the settlers began construction of the public house, later to become the fort. Minutes of the meeting of July 3, 1770, describe a vote for adjournment to the "center of the town at the house building on the bank of the river, near the Great Springs, on the first Tuesday in July, next, at 2:00 O'clock in the afternoon."[61]

The clearing of the land and its cultivation, the construction of cabins and the fort, the development of roads and highways, all combined in 1770 with the maintenance of regular town meetings. These efforts would thenceforth flourish when the Yankees were in control.

Bennet Goes for his Family

The summer of 1770 was one of great progress for the settlers in all the townships, and a sense of stability and security led some of them to bring family and close friends to the valley. One of these was Thomas Bennet. About September 12, 1770 Bennet departed from the settlement to bring his family in from Goshen, New York.[62] Before leaving the valley he had selected a site on his house lot some distance upstream from the fort, on the bank of the Susquehanna. He had built a cabin, had cleared some land and put in some seed. "He had examined the ground; he understood all the hazards of the enterprise; his courage was equal to the danger, and the question was settled. As to property, he had but little before, for he had sold his farm in Rhode Island on personal security, and both the purchaser and the security had failed, and the whole was lost."[63]

Pennamites Recapture Fort Durkee

While Bennet was on his trip, and unbeknownst to him, Fort Durkee had fallen to the Pennamites under Ogden. The Connecticut settlers were driven off, their properties destroyed. Ogden had also sent a detachment of men across the river to the cabins of the First Forty, demanding that the occupants surrender. Bennet's cabin and fields were devastated and largely destroyed by this armed detachment, as he would later discover when he returned.

Meanwhile, in Goshen, Thomas Bennet loaded everything possible on pack horses, leaving behind only what was immovable. The family now commenced its journey to "the promised land." From Goshen they advanced to Port Jervis, thence to the ferry at Dingman's and on over the Minisink path. Near Shohola (Pike County) they met and were hospitably entertained overnight by a Quaker named Wires, who had a house and family there.

They took leave of Shohola the next morning, and Wires accompanied them as far as a spot known then as "the little meadow," where the little caravan stopped for some refreshments. Mrs. Bennet was boiling some chocolate over a fire made by the side of a log. She was unusually depressed and Peck in *The Story of Wyoming* quotes her saying, "I don't know what I am about to meet: I think something pretty heavy."

While they were still paused for refreshments, several men came down the path, one bleeding from a head wound. The Bennets were shocked at the news they bore: the fort had been taken by the Pennamites, who were busily ousting all the New England settlers. But Bennet, a man of cool courage, had made up his mind to try his fortunes upon the fertile soil of Wyoming; and he was not to be turned aside from that purpose by anything but stern invincible necessity. Bent upon going on, Bennet had to decide what to do with his family. They held a conference, Mr. Wires in attendance, and Mr. and Mrs. Bennet decided to go on, leaving their three children in the care of the Wires family.

Before following their course back to the Valley, it is appropriate to review the bitter and destructive attitudes which had developed between the Pennamites and the Yankees at the Wyoming settlements. In the Northampton County Court held in Easton in mid-September 1770 a presentation was set forth describing how on the 2nd of May 1770 the men on the warrant list had broken and entered the house of Amos Ogden, Esquire, carrying away goods worth 100 pounds; this list, which included the name of Thomas Bennet, was the object set forth by the judge for a warrant for the arrest and confinement of all by whatever means necessary.

As a consequence, Nathan Ogden, brother Amos, Captain Dick and several others raised a posse of 140 armed men from the Easton area and from New Jersey. This force began its march at Fort Allen (Lehighton) and approached Wyoming over the southern or Nescopeck path. They arrived at Solomon's Gap, overlooking the valley, at dusk on September 21. Early the next morning, Ogden, with telescope, observed several work parties leaving the protection of the fort. Ogden dispatched several assault groups to capture as many of the work parties as possible. They were to use stealth, cunning, and surprise, and to bring their prisoners back to the mountain camp. The tactic was eminently successful, and most of the men were captured without firing a shot and without violence.[64]

Among those captured was Major Durkee, the fort commander, an action which led to much confusion and despair to those Yankees remaining in the fort. That evening, at a meeting of the principal men in the fort, it was decided to hold out while they sent a few messengers for help to Coshetunk on the Delaware. But these messengers were captured by Ogden, who learned from them of the confusion and consternation existing in the fort. As a result Ogden decided to attack at once, and before dawn on September 23 his forces silently approached the fort. Ogden then sent Captain Craig with an assault detachment into the fort. Craig is reported to have surprised a sentinel on duty, to have knocked him unconscious, and then to have rushed into the fort itself. A short struggle ensued. Harvey states that although several were wounded, there were no deaths. All the men were taken as prisoners to the Easton jail, the women and children remaining at the fort.

At Easton, Major Durkee, Captain Zebulon Butler, and Major Simeon Draper were transferred to the Philadelphia jail where they were all subsequently indicted. The Easton prisoners were released after three weeks of miserable deprivation in jail. In an affidavit given by Captain William Gallup he refers to the events as follows: "Sometime in the month of June 1770 he, with a number of Connecticut settlers, returned to the Susquehanna, where he remained unmolested until sometime in September when he and the Connecticut settlers, in the dead of the night, whilst in their houses asleep, was broken in upon by the Pennsylvania party and abused to a great degree by beating with swords, staves and other enormities, and took from him his horse and saddle, and destroyed a large quantity of grain and then carried under a strong guard and committed to prison at East-Town, where he was kept on coarse bread and water only...about 20 days and then released without any tryal by law."[65]

As Miner[66] wisely remarks, one might wonder why such a powerful and proximate force of the Pennsylvania colony could not have completely controlled the sequence of events at Wyoming. Governor Penn and his government were not popular and much Pennsylvania sentiment favored the Yankees. "There had been longstanding contention between the people of the province and the proprietaries, in respect to taxation chiefly, connected with numerous other points, exciting feelings of mistrust and enmity." On the other hand, the Connecticut Assembly had not claimed the little settlement as its own. It was the sustained enthusiasm of the Susquehanna Company that kept the Yankees returning again and again to take and to hold the property at Wyoming.

CHAPTER 4

First Yankee-Pennamite War

Thomas and Martha Bennet return to Wyoming

Following evacuation of the Yankee settlers, Nathan Ogden assigned roughly twenty men to hold the fort, then accompanied the remainder of his force and his prisoners to Easton, subsequently returning to his home nearby. There was a general feeling that matters had finally settled and that once and for all the Yankee intrusions had been put to an end.

Shortly after this action, Thomas and Martha Bennet arrived at last at Capouse Meadows after a trying trip on horseback from Shohola. It was the dead of winter and their journey had been unusually arduous. They had intended to seek temporary quarters with a Mr. Chapman, whom they had known previously as a neighbor in Goshen. Chapman had built a cabin near Mill Creek. The Bennets, however, found the area greatly disturbed "as though by a war," and were unable to locate Chapman. They took possession once again of the small log house Bennet had previously built on the flats just above Forty Fort. He had stored and concealed considerable grain when he departed in September, and he was relieved to find this undisturbed, available for use during the winter months. Within the month the children were brought in from Shohola, and Bennet and the family were comfortably situated in the cabin.

This story is derived chiefly from Peck,[67] and differs from that told by Harvey,[68] who states that the Bennets came directly to Fort Durkee which was at the time occupied by the Pennamites. The tale as narrated by Bennet's daughter is fully told in Peck's book. She would have been about six years of age when these events took place, but the story is told by her in advanced years. Bennet's affidavit supports Harvey and placed him in a cabin in the fort by mid December; he was definitely at the fort on the night of December 18, 1770. It is worth noting that Bennet, a

Yankee, was able to obtain such shelter at Fort Durkee at a time when it was occupied by the Pennamites.

Lazarus Stewart Reclaims Fort Durkee

Meanwhile Lazarus Stewart, the intrepid and daring Lancastrian leader of "the Paxtang Boys" had organized a band in preparation for a return to Wyoming, but remained in hiding until that preparation could be completed. He had been arrested and had escaped his captors in a series of wild maneuvers; a warrant for his arrest and confinement was known to be active. Stewart had actually attracted new support from Captains Craig and Brady, as well as from John Dick, all of whom once had been part of Ogden's posse. By the eighteenth of December (1770) Stewart, with about thirty men, reached and entered the fort through its north gate at eleven at night. All of the Pennamites were ousted on the spot, just as mercilessly and precipitously as had been the Yankee settlers in the previous exchange.

As previously noted, Bennet was at that time occupying a cabin within the fort. In Bennet's affidavit given later, he stated that initially he concealed Colonel Clayton, the Pennamite garrison commander, and one other soldier in his cabin briefly to prevent their being injured.

Concerning this most recent exchange, a sense of the crisis experienced is derived from the deposition of Mr. Van Campen, one of the Pennamites in the fort: "About three O'clock in the morning (of Tuesday, December 18, 1770) the people of the fort being abed, the fort was entered by a body of men from Hanover, Lancaster County, armed with guns and clubs, and commanded by Lazarus Stewart; that they immediately proceeded to break open the doors of the houses of the fort; that they broke open the deponent's door, took him prisoner, beat him and abused him unmercifully, and put him in a prison under guard; that they then proceeded through the fort, in the same manner treating all and ordering them to depart immediately, and would scarcely give them time to collect a small part of their effects. That there were in the fort eighteen men (Pennamites), six of whom made their escape and twelve who were made prisoners, and a considerable number of women and children who were driven out of the fort by the said Lazarus Stewart and company in a cruel and inhuman manner."[69]

That Bennet and his family were part of the melee is certain. Recognized by Stewart as a Yankee, he was spared the fate of all the others and was permitted to stay as a resident of the fort.

More Settlers Sent from Connecticut

Early in January 1771 while Captain Stewart was still in possession of Fort Durkee, the Susquehanna Company met at Windham, Connecticut and adopted six orders:

1. That the 240 settlers previously authorized were to proceed forthwith to Susquehanna to assist those now in possession of the lands.

2. That a committee, headed by Colonel Dyer, should approach the Governor of Pennsylvania for a settlement of the controversy in a legal and constitutional way.

3. That this committee draw up a binding agreement between the settlers and the company, to be signed by all.

4. That Captain Zebulon Butler, Captain Lazarus Stewart, Major John Durkee, and John Smith, Esquire, be the governing committee "on the spot," so to speak. Both Butler and Durkee were still in the Philadelphia jail at the time. The proprietors of the five townships were each authorized to name one representative to join these gentlemen to form one overall governing committee.

5. That Captain Stewart and his cohorts be authorized to settle Hanover Township as a reward for their services.

6. That Lackawanna Township, not so good and valuable as had been expected, be granted to the thirty-five proprietors already there.

The above is extracted from the minutes of the Susquehanna Company's meeting of January 9, 1771.

Fort Wyoming Built by Pennamites

Events were now to explode abruptly. In the court of Northampton County a new writ was issued to take Thomas Bennet, Lazarus Stewart, and eleven others specifically named for inciting to riot in connection with retaking Fort Durkee, and by January 11 a warrant for their arrest was authorized.[70] Again, a posse was organized, and on January 18, 1771, a fully armed force of 100 men arrived in Wyoming Valley. Captain Ogden and his men immediately began the construction of a strong wooden fort about "125 rods" north of Fort Durkee close to a "fine bubbling spring" and at that point along the river bank from which activities of Fort Durkee could be closely observed; this new post also provided overview of the pathways to the "upper road" to the Delaware used by the Yankees and to the "Pennamite path" to the Lower Road leading from Wyoming to Easton. This new structure was to become Fort Wyoming and would soon completely replace Fort Durkee.

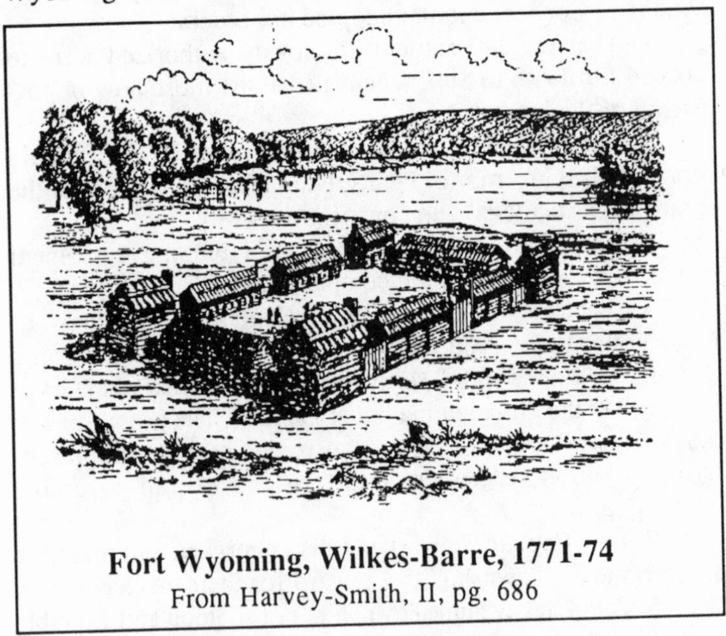

Fort Wyoming, Wilkes-Barre, 1771-74
From Harvey-Smith, II, pg. 686

Simultaneously with the work of construction, attempts were made over a period of twenty-four to forty-eight hours to enter Fort Durkee peaceably to carry out the arrest warrants in the hands of the sheriff accompanying Captain Ogden, but Lazarus Stewart stonewalled any such effort, completely rejecting any and all conciliatory efforts. He knew full well he would be arrested and placed in jail. On Monday, January 21, an armed confrontation took place in which Nathan Ogden, brother of Captain Amos, was shot and killed. Affidavits and reports vary to some extent, but there seems to be agreement that Lazarus Stewart fired the first shot, the one that killed Ogden, after a heated exchange of shouting. Gunfire from both sides followed and three or four Pennamites were wounded.

Fort Durkee Destroyed

That night, under cover of darkness, Captain Stewart and his Lancastrians stealthfully escaped into the woods and disappeared. Left behind were ten to twelve Yankees who elected to surrender the following morning. All were taken to the Philadelphia jail, there to join Major Durkee and Captain Butler who were still incarcerated. Bennet's affidavit states that he heard a gun go off, but did not know who fired. He heard his wife say that Nathan Ogden was shot. He further stated that the only time he appeared in arms was "to keep sentry in his turn."[71] This conflict again left the Pennamites in control of the valley and its settlements; it witnessed the last use of Fort Durkee and the creation of Fort Wyoming.

CHAPTER 5
Yankees Take Control

Bennett Family Moves in with the Mannings

When Bennet was carried away as a prisoner, he sadly bid farewell to his wife and three children. No time was allowed for him to arrange for their care and support. During the few months preceding these events, Mrs. Bennet had become an intimate friend of a Mrs. Manning, whose husband was a Quaker, a noncombatant at the time, accepted by both sides. The Mannings lived in a cabin on the flats south of Fort Durkee. When Bennet was taken prisoner, Mrs. Manning invited his family to come to live with them. Worried about the constant conflict and threat of war in and around Fort Durkee, Manning had built a new shelter on Scovell's Island near what is now Pittston, at the head of the valley. This cabin used a huge fallen tree as the center beam of the roof and had a large room on each side. A few days after Bennet was taken prisoner, Manning, his family, Mrs. Bennet and her children moved up the river in heavily laden canoes, taking with them all the meager household goods and provisions they could muster. Arriving at Scovell's Island, they made a temporary home there, expecting to remain until the situation became more favorable.[72]

Thomas Bennet in Philadelphia Jail

Meanwhile, Thomas Bennet, always a man of freedom and of the open spaces, was crushed by his jail experience. The Philadelphia jail, in common with jails of the period, was a cold, unheated, grim affair, where provisions were scant and insufficient. The jails in this country were noisome, loathsome places and the life led by the majority of their inmates was little more than beastly. The "Pennsylvania Packet" (Philadelphia) of January 4, 1770, states: "Who would expect to hear of objects amongst us whose sufferings and miseries are beyond the power of words to describe? But such in reality is the miserable condition of the unhappy criminals in our gaol every winter; not so much for want of food, as from cold and nakedness, for private families daily send them more or less (food), and in hard winter the religious societies make public collections." In the issue of March 16, 1772, there was the following: "We hear that three of the prisoners confined in the gaol of this city died during the last week, and the coroners inquest have found that they perished through want of necessaries - the very refuse of your kitchens, beds, and wearing apparel could be received by them with joy and thankfulness."[73]

Some of the inmates had the practical and emotional support of relatives living nearby, but the Connecticut settlers in the Philadelphia jail were isolated from their families, a fact which added to the injury of their confinement.

Release from Prison

In April 1771 the Susquehanna Company met at Windham and among other actions they voted to send fifty pounds to Major Durkee, Thomas Bennet, Simeon Draper, Silas Gore and Asa Ludington for the purpose of ameliorating their sufferings while in the Philadelphia jail. Of this, thirty-four pounds was for Major Durkee, and four pounds each to the other men. In the text of this motion is the following statement: "whereas, Major John Durkee and several others of the proprietors of the Susquehanna purchase are confined in the common gaol in the Province of Pennsylvania, and are there destitute of friends and money...which renders their situation extremely distressing and affecting to all who have any just ideas of their sufferings ... votes that the sum be immediately raised and sent."

Bennet was released from prison in April 1771. He was physically depleted and worn out by his experience, and was terribly discouraged. He found his way back to Wyoming and there joined his family at Manning's cabin at Scovell Island, where he began his rehabilitation.[74]

Pennamites Control Wyoming

While he had been in jail the Pennsylvanians occupied Fort Wyoming with a garrison of about thirty men. From January to July 1771, the Pennamites were securely established in Wyoming Valley. They built a sawmill near the mouth of

Mill Creek as well as a small block house to protect it. Gradually a number of small dwelling houses were built scattered about the valley. Single men generally occupied Fort Wyoming, while married couples occupied the new small houses.

During this period the provincial deputy surveyor of Pennsylvania, Charles Stewart, layed out the manors of Stokes and Sunbury. Stokes included Wilkes-Barre and all of the lands on the east bank of the Susquehanna lying within the Valley of Wyoming. The Manor of Sunbury included Forty Fort, Wyoming, Kingston and Plymouth Townships. Stewart's action added to the great confusion of land titles which would plague the area for several decades. Each owner-settler felt entirely justified in his own claim.

A number of Jerseymen and Pennsylvanians moved into the valley; among them were Captain Amos Ogden and Charles Stewart, Esquire. Several large plots were transferred to men of prominence in Easton and in Philadelphia, men who would never become residents of the area. Fort Wyoming was gradually enlarged and strengthened, while Fort Durkee was abandoned and dismantled.

David Ogden Attempts to Murder Bennet

Bennet had returned from prison to Scovell's Island in April 1771. David Ogden, brother of Captain Amos and of the killed Nathan, learned of Mr. Bennet's return. David was still in a mood of bitter revenge for the death of his brother, and organized a small posse with intent to capture or murder Thomas Bennet. Through a love affair between a young Pennamite and one of their daughters, the Mannings were warned in advance of the approach and intent of David Ogden. Against his objections, Mr. Bennet was pushed out a rear door of the cabin and was hidden in the nearby forest. When Ogden arrived, the Mannings and the Bennets denied his presence or any knowledge of his whereabouts.

After the passage of several hours, the Bennet boys gave their father the all clear signal, believing that Ogden had disappeared. However, Ogden and his party were lurking nearby at a concealed spot. A short time after Bennet reentered the cabin, Ogden returned; he found little Martha seated on her father's lap, closely embracing him. The sight softened the heart of Ogden and he and his party departed, leaving Bennet unharmed. "Ogden afterwards said he intended to have shot Bennet, and should have done it but for the fear of killing the child."[75]

During the spring of 1771 Bennet slowly recovered his strength, and began once again to help in the daily labor of clearing, building, sowing and hunting. Nothing is known of his relationship to Fort Wyoming, which at that time was occupied by the Pennamites. Bennet remained at the Manning cabin on Scovell's Island, waiting for the situation at Fort Wyoming to change. He did not have long to wait.

Captain Zebulon Butler, a jailmate of Bennet in Philadelphia, was also released from confinement in early April 1771. Shortly thereafter he was placed in command of a small Connecticut force of about sixty men, and was directed by the Susquehanna Company to proceed to Wyoming and to be on the Wyoming lands no later than July 10. His men were nearly all proprietors who had previously been to the valley; they were required to furnish their own weapons and ammunition, horses, and emergency rations. This force went through Goshen, New York, and about July 3 they were joined by Lazarus Stewart and a small force of armed men in Northern Sussex County, New Jersey.[76] Their approach to the Delaware River became known to the proprietors of Pennsylvania. Intense efforts were made to organize a posse of armed men to stop the "invaders." There was little support among Pennsylvanians for armed confrontation because this was a busy season for the agrarian economy upon which their livelihoods depended.

Colonel Butler Reclaims Fort Wyoming

Unopposed, Captain Butler arrived at Wyoming on July 8, 1771, and took over the Mill Creek block house and the old mill. On July 9 Butler met with Colonel Asher Clayton, commander of Fort Wyoming, and after a brief discussion the two parted without reaching terms.[77] In the fort at that time were eighty-two men, women and children huddled with a store of provisions and other personal effects. The Pennamite garrison had plenty of fresh water from the spring, but badly needed food and ammunition. Butler wisely elected not to make a direct armed attack upon the fort; instead, he chose to isolate it from all outside support. He threw up three small fortifications or redoubts, one on the west side of the river opposite the fort, one south of it, and a third on the high eminence above the site of the present courthouse. A fourth redoubt was near the intersection of present Northampton and Main Streets.[78] From these he could command all pathways to the fort, and successfully ambush relief parties, seizing horses and provisions.

Between August 11 and August 15 the fort was subjected to constant musket fire. Provisions had been entirely consumed and Colonel Clayton decided to surrender. Under the favorable terms of capitulation, the occupants of the fort were allowed to leave unharmed and families were given two weeks to clear out of the area. This action marked the end of combat between the Yankees and the Pennamites for the next four years, and ushered in a period of expansion, peace and prosperity for the frontier settlement.

CHAPTER 6
Forty Fort

The Mannings expelled

On the day of the capitulation, (August 15, 1771) one of the Yankee officers rode up to the Manning cabin and expelled the Mannings as suspected Pennamite sympathizers. Manning and his family left the area for settlement along the west branch of the Susquehanna, never to return. Bennet and his family were invited to move into Fort Wyoming, and thereupon they took their meager belongings down river with the purpose of residing within the fort. Bennet did not like the situation and refused to live there on any basis other than temporary. He fitted up an old horse shed in Forty Fort and created for his family a residence described as "comfortable."[79] Here he resided for over two years, and it was here that another daughter, Polly, was born.

Settlement Expands

There now entered into the valley a large number of Connecticut settlers, and the community expanded in many ways. Thomas Bennet built a double log house on his land. "We removed to our new house, raised good crops of grain, and had a fine stock of horses and cattle. We sold grain and bought articles of convenience from the Middletown boats. The father and brothers hunted beaver, bears, deer, raccoons, wild turkeys, etc. and we were in comfortable circumstances. One night a ferocious animal entered the yard, and so wounded one of the young cattle that it was found necessary to kill it. The father and brother seized their guns when they heard the disturbance, but the savage beast bounded out just in time to save themselves ... it was a panther."[80]

Construction of Forty Fort

Settlers on the west side of the river now worked steadily towards completion of the fort (Forty Fort). However, able-bodied men on the west side continued to serve on the guard duty roster of Fort Wyoming in Wilkes-Barre. Guards were posted at the main fort around the clock, and during this period the headquarters of the entire settlement of five townships remained at Fort Wyoming. Each township had its own town meetings and elected officials; regular town meetings were held at the main fort.

In a general meeting of the Wyoming settlers held at Fort Wyoming on December 18, 1772, it was noted "that for the future there shall be but one guard kept from this time until the first Monday in March next, and that there shall be but eight men to guard (as rotation) the 24 hours this winter season...and for those of our bretheren who live over the river and the upper end of Plymouth as far as Evelands, to come over and guard the block house, and to be brought over and carried back over again (on the ferry) on *free* cost, provided they come between sunset (in) and daylight (out); *whenever Kingstown shall build a guardhouse*, to guard in by themselves, somewhere in the center of the inhabitancy..."[81]

Construction of Forty Fort was arduous and difficult, requiring many man hours of labor. Sheldon Reynolds describes the fort as enclosing an acre or better of ground.[82] Its outline was rectangular, with gates north and south and with sentinel towers at the four corners. With great forethought, the settlers built close to the river bank where there was a gushing spring. In time, they excavated a tunnel from the fort to the spring and covered the path to conceal access at the time of siege. The tunnel also provided an all-weather approach to the spring.

As was the custom at this time, they made the walls of the fort of sturdy logs, settling each heavy log upright in a five foot trench. The logs extended twelve feet above the surface of the ground, and were sharpened at the tops. Another tier of logs was secured against the first, overlying the crevices and thus forming a formidable and durable barrier to attack. Barracks or cabins were built along these walls, the roofs of which formed a continuous platform around the perimeter. In the center was the parade ground. The settlers also excavated an underground room in which they stored provisions and other reserves for use in case of siege. The roof and entrance of this room were concealed as ordinary flooring and trapdoor.[83]

The work required extensive excavation by hand; the timbers had to be cut with axe and fitted one by one. All who were able gave time and labor to this endeavor. The work had to be shared since each man also had many other tasks to perform. Bennet and the other men were busy providing for their families, hunting game, catching fish, clearing and cultivating the land. Women worked long days doing the many things necessary to maintain the home.

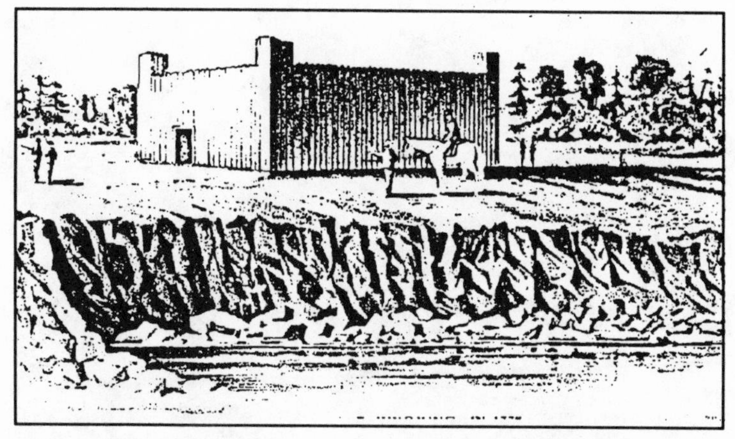

Forty Fort, Wyoming, in 1778 reproduced from Brewster. Original drawing by Edmund L. Dana first appeared in Pearce's *Annals of Luzerne County*, 1860.

CHAPTER 7
Settlement Established

Local government organized

There now entered into the valley a large number of new Connecticut settlers. The period from August 1771 to the outbreak of the American Revolution in 1776 was one of free activity in this new frontier settlement. Up to 1774, it was essentially on its own insofar as government was concerned, existing only as a project of the Susquehanna Company but not recognized as a colony by the government of Connecticut. The group of settlers now established at Wyoming proceeded to organize a government for themselves. Chapman[84]states "they laid out townships, formed settlements, erected fortifications, levied and collected taxes, passed laws for the direction of civil suit, and for the punishment of crimes and misdemeanors, established a militia and provided for the common defense and general welfare of the colony."

Supreme power was vested in the "whole body of the people." This power was exercised by the "meeting of the Proprietors"—an open meeting assembled whenever business made it necessary. Issues were resolved by majority vote of the proprietors, each meeting having its own elected president pro tem. Minutes were maintained by a clerk specifically elected for each meeting. An Executive Committee consisted of one person from each township, called the "Committee of Settlers." It was authorized to decide all matters of minor importance, civil and criminal, and to call a town meeting of the proprietors when it deemed necessary. There were three levels of judicial power. The supreme court was the meeting of the proprietors, where appeals were heard and where the merits of each case were subject to revision; here decisions already made could be corrected. The Committee of Settlers was the Executive Court with power to enter judgments and issue writs of execution.

Townships Designated

Each township had its own constable and its own common court made up of three landowners. Decisions and awards by the common township court had to be returned to the Committee of Settlers. Early meetings of courts at any level were held in the homes of the settlers. Many years later, the first court of the newly organized Luzerne County was held on May 27, 1787, at the house of Colonel Zebulon Butler.[85]

From 1771 to 1773 this system of governing was used, but it was modified at the full meeting of the proprietors July 8, 1773. It was then decided to appoint a "Board of Directors" instead of the Committee of Settlers. A sheriff and other officers were provided for. The new agreement had to be signed and agreed to by all the proprietors. Failure to do so meant expulsion and land forfeiture.

Thus the settlement was carefully organized as a town. All proprietors were involved, and initially meetings were held at various homes. The *land* and its ownership was *the* economic factor at the bottom of the social structure. Land owners governed by equal participation in town meetings; it was they who were taxed to support schools, early teachers of religion and the churches. Strength was lent to the enterprise by the unity of the congregationalists, who dominated daily life and who insisted upon adherence to puritan standards.[86]

First School System

As in other Connecticut settlements, three equal shares were reserved for support of the church, for the first settled minister, and for a school in each of the townships. Shareholders were required to settle the land and to improve it within a specific time. The admission of subsequent inhabitants to the town was within the discretion of the original proprietors. It was no haphazard milieu in which the Bennets raised their family of two sons and two daughters. It is likely that these children attended school and church services, as soon as such service became available. The first record of any public action taken by the settlers of Kingstown regarding schools was that of the proprietors at the meeting held December 21, 1773, when three committeemen were appointed to divide the town into three divisions for the keeping of schools. This school system was developed sixty-two years before the state instituted its own school system.[87] Kingstown also began to arrange for a religious leader, reaching an agreement shortly thereafter with Reverend Wadhams who had begun preaching in Plymouth.

Laying Out of Roads

During this period a system of roads was laid out. Plans for the "Great Road," now known as Wyoming Avenue, were drawn by a committee of the "First Forty" as early as May 1770.[88] This road, 100 feet wide, extended for about nine miles, beginning at the Plymouth-Kingston border, and running north as far as the ferry to Pittston. It stands intact as a highway with few equals in the towns of the United States today.

Grist and Saw Mills

One of the early needs was the construction and availability of a grist mill. Whole grain and corn were of course available, but before the first grist mill, householders had to grind their own grain by hand in a crude hollowed out stump with a pounding log rounded and fashioned for this purpose, suspended from a bent sapling. The hominy or cornmeal thus prepared was the most important food staple for these early settlers, especially during the long winter months. The first sawmill and the first grist mill were built at Mill Creek, and one of the first roads from the west side settlement ran from Wyoming Avenue, on a line extending Union Street to the banks of the Susquehanna opposite Mill Creek. There was a ferry across the river at this point, constructed in about 1772, making the mill available to those living on the west side, but as the population expanded during 1772-1773, the mill and its supply of grain were unable to meet the food needs.

The Winter of 1772-73

Miner, describing the near starvation of the winter of 1772-1773, states the following: "The month of February 1773, had so nearly exhausted the provisions of the Wilkes-Barre settlement that five persons were selected to go to the Delaware, near Stroudsburg, for supplies. Mr. John Carey, then a lad of sixteen, volunteered as one of the party. The distance was fifty miles through the wilderness; numerous streams, including the deep and rapid Lehigh, were to be crossed. Had these been frozen over so as to be passable, their toils would have been sensibly mitigated; but the ice had formed on each side, many feet from shore, leaving in the center a deep, rushing flood. Stripping naked, tying their clothes and sacks on their heads and shoulders, cutting a way through the ice from the shore to the stream...they waded through, dressed themselves, and found warmth in marching rapidly, arriving at the good old Scotchman's and sending in to make known their errand. (The Scotchman was John McDowell, who had a farm in Cherry Valley near what is now Saylor's Lake. It was one of the few substantial houses west of the Blue Mountain at that time.) Mr. McDowell came out rubbing his hands in great glee, bade them welcome, but...told them he had a house thronged with company, on the occasion of his daughter's wedding. Among the guests were (Pennsylvania) magistrates and others, whose enmity was to be dreaded if they knew a party of Yankees were within reach; but he gave directions that they should warm themselves noiselessly at an outhouse, then take shelter in the barn, where comfortable blankets were spread on the hay mow, a most royal supper sent them, with spirits and wine; their sacks were filled with flour, and their pockets with provisions. The four men took each a hundred pounds, young Carey seventy-five and welcome was their return to their half-famished friends at Wilkes-Barre.

Never was an opening spring, or the coming of the shad, looked for with more anxiety or hailed with more cordial delight. (The shad run occurred annually in early April and lasted until late May. Several thousands of fish were caught each day in seines constructed for the purpose.) The fishing season, of course, dissipated all fears, and the dim eye was soon exchanged for the glance of joy."[89]

This experience gave urgency to the construction of a second mill on the west side. A commission was appointed to search for a likely spot. In 1773 a site on Toby's Creek was designated in the western portion of what is now Luzerne; a new mill was built. An access road, now Bennet Street, was laid out from Wyoming Avenue following the higher ground westward along the border of the back lot of Thomas Bennet to the current intersection of Kelly Street, where the road turned left and coursed downhill to Toby's Creek and thus to the new mill. The bridge over the creek to the mill was a short distance upstream from the present stone bridge. Much of the land on the southwest border of Toby's Creek was wetland, prohibiting construction of the access road on the south side of the creek. A new bridge, opened in December 1989 at the site of the original one, gave direct egress from Kelly Street.

Critical Road Construction

Another early road was built from what is now the intersection of Wyoming Avenue and Northhampton Street (Kingston) eastward to the river, where Parshall Terry operated a ferry to Wilkes-Barre in 1773. This road became Northampton Street and took a straight course to the river's edge.[90]

Wyoming Avenue, Union Street, Northampton Street and Bennet Street were the earliest roads laid out on the west side, and provided access to points critical to the settlers on the west side of the river. Accurate surveys were required and remain a matter of record. Township borders were essential, the one between Plymouth and Kingston causing prolonged disagreement and altercation. Specific proprietors' committees were appointed, and Bennet is known to have been added to the Plymouth-Kingston Committee appointed to resolve that border dispute.

The area of the Wyoming settlement was in every way frontier; access roads were little more than bridle paths. However, it could be reached by riverboats in some seasons. Early traders, both Indians and whites, came down the Susquehanna from upstream, with bateaux carrying merchandise from as far as Schoharie in New York State. There was seasonal river access from the down river settlements, but river routes proved inadequate for growing communities. It was apparent to the settlers that improved overland routes of communication and transport would be required, leading eastward to the Delaware River. By the spring of 1772, "A tolerable road had been constructed from Wilkes-Barre to Pittston,"[91] and in the fall of 1772 the Wyoming settlers generally turned out a revolving labor force to build the road from Pittston to the Delaware. This closely followed the old "upper path" running along the Lackawanna River to Capouse Meadows, then directly to Shohola, and southeast to Dingman's Ferry. Though possible for a wagon to travel over the road by fall 1772, it was a very rough and primitive road, barely passable.[92]

Additionally, it seemed desirable to establish a direct route to Easton, which by then had developed into an important trade and supply base. At a town meeting on December 7, 1772, it was decided to levy a road building tax upon each settling right to finance the construction of the road to Easton following the "lower" path (approximately Route 115).[93] This route crossed the "Great Swamp" and the "Shades of Death."

The Great Swamp was a wet area of great timber growth about twelve miles across, lying twelve miles southeast of Wilkes-Barre. In the midst of this area was a region of dense forest with trees of enormous heights. Because of the sense of gloom on the footpath through this region, it was termed the "Shades of Death." What is now called "Shades Creek" marks the general area.

It was decided to pay three shillings per day to those men laboring on the road between the Delaware and the western border of the Great Swamp, while those improving the road from Wilkes-Barre to the eastern edge of the Great Swamp would receive one shilling per day. In order to assure collection of the tax and thus payment to the workmen, a committee of tax collectors was appointed, one man from each township.

Until 1779 this road was seasonally difficult because of the swamp, dense growth, and steep grades, but it remained the most direct route from the Wyoming settlements to the established community where supplies could be purchased or traded. In 1779 it was surveyed, realigned, and substantially improved by army engineers under the direction of General John Sullivan.

The influx of new settlers and their families placed a burden on the administrative system for local government. Miner[94] states, "At no time until 1772 were there more than 130 men on the ground at once, some being on the way out, and others returning home. As there was no mode of enforcing discipline, the association being voluntary, each man acted as prompted by his own sense of interest and propriety." There was a growing sense of need for the structured government all had experienced in Connecticut. Disagreements over offenses and punishments occurred with increasing frequency as the population expanded. Thomas Bennet, himself, was ordered to forfeit all of his land holdings to the colony because he failed to report for guard duty—an order which was rescinded the following month. This sense of need culminated in a memorial completed October 3, 1772, addressed to the General Assembly of Connecticut, signed by 241 men, one of whom was Bennet.

"The memorial of us the subscribers inhabitants of Wyoming on Susquehanna and within the colony of Connecticut humbly sheweth that we being *destitute of the advantages of civil authority* which weighs us under many disadvantages by reason of our settlers being very numerous and consequently some unruly persons among us who commit disorders to the great disturbance of the inhabitants...which to prevent we pray your honours to take into your wise consideration our unhappy and distressed condition and either incorporate us into a county and appoint us proper authority; or annex us to some one of the counties or in some other way grant us relief as your honours in your wisdom shall think proper....(We would humbly suggest that something of this kind would not only tend to suppress vice and immoralities among us but promote virtue and be a means to spread the gospel through these western parts)...dated in Wilkes-Barre...October 3, 1772."[95] No action having been taken by the General Assembly, another petition of like tone was made April 3, 1773. In this petition, however, the plea is made "for our defense, security, and protection against the *vile encroachments of our neighbors, the Pennsylvanians,* which keep us good order and regularity among ourselves." The document lists 350 men as petitioners.[96]

An issue in these memorials and indeed at every town meeting of Wilkes-Barre during this period was the fervent need for a sound government. The General Assembly of Connecticut, in its first response, designated three commissioners to meet with Governor Penn to *negotiate* a settlement of the ownership of the Wyoming lands. This, they felt, ought to be accomplished before the assembly took any further action to incorporate the new lands formally with the State of Connecticut. While no new armed confrontations occurred between the Yankees and the Pennamites until 1775, there was a constant undertone of disagreement and contest between the two colonial governments.

Although the commissioners met with Governor Penn in a conciliatory manner with the stated purpose of gaining compromise, Penn flatly denied claim or right of the Connecticut colony to the contested lands. The commissioners reported this disappointment to the General Assembly of Connecticut. Shortly thereafter the Susquehanna Company once again appealed to the Assembly on behalf of the Wyoming settlements, "As a settlement at Wyoming was not sufficiently powerful to protect itself in a state of war against the province of Pennsylvania on the one hand, and the combined British and savage enemies on the other."[97]

Town of Westmoreland Created by Connecticut

The General Court of Connecticut, considering the problem, passed an act in January 1774, establishing the new town of Westmoreland. "The country extending from the river Delaware westward 15 miles beyond Wyoming, and in extent north and south the whole width of the charter (Connecticut Charter) bounds" describes the huge area of which this new town consisted. For administrative purposes it was attached to the County of Litchfield in Connecticut. The act prohibited all persons from settling in this area except by permission of the Colony of Connecticut.[98]

A general meeting of the Wyoming settlers was called by Zebulon Butler and Nathan Denison, both newly appointed justices of the peace. At this meeting all civil officers were elected by the proprietor-settlers, and thenceforth the laws of Connecticut were carried out in full force. There was a logical sequence of events for the Wyoming settlers. The original proprietors-settlers, those coming before 1772, generally knew one another and several were close friends back in Connecticut. A new colony, they brought with them an organized body, which enabled them to develop self government during those years when they were awaiting recognition by Connecticut. When one considers the many tasks facing these frontiersmen, it is remarkable that they could and did spend so much energy and time forging the civil government, and the code of laws by which they were to live. The entire movement was developed and fostered through the very democratic pathway of the town meeting, in which each proprietor-settler had a vote. As in many other colonies on this continent, the spirit of independence and of representative government was already glowing and would one day burst into flame.

CHAPTER 8
Self Defense

Westmoreland organizes

The creation of the town of Westmoreland in January 1774 provoked marked acceleration of the controversy between the colonies of Connecticut and Pennsylvania.

Following an interchange of letters between Governor Turnbull of Connecticut and Governor Penn, the latter issued a public proclamation which was published in the Pennsylvania Packet of March 7, 1774. Essentially, this proclamation forbade the inhabitants residing in the area of Westmoreland to give any obedience whatsoever to the details of the Connecticut Act which created it. "And I do, in His Majesty's name, charge and command all persons whatsoever within the said counties to yield due submission and obedience to the laws of this government."[99] To all of which the residents of Wyoming paid no heed. Or, as Chapman states it: "but this proclamation appears to have been regarded with as little attention by the inhabitants of Wyoming as would have been a royal edict issued by the King of Spain."[100]

At the first town meeting of Westmoreland held in Wilkes-Barre on April 11, 1774, the list of officers and committee members involved 100 of the active proprietors; Thomas Bennet was appointed to the Committee of Surveyors of Highways; also named were the selectmen, the town treasurer, the constables and collector of taxes.

The Twenty-Fourth Regiment

At the meeting held on June 27, 1774, it was noted "By this town of Westmoreland that they will now form themselves into companies in ye military way for ye defense of this country," one company for each district of Westmoreland. This action on the part of the town meeting was a response to the proclamation of the Connecticut Assembly, which directed that Westmoreland would develop a new regiment of the Connecticut line, "to be called by the name of the The Twenty-Fourth Regiment." Colonel Zebulon Butler was placed in command, with Lieutenant Colonel Nathan Denison his second. Connecticut law relating to the militia was quite specific. All males within the colony from sixteen to fifty years of age were required to bear arms and to attend musters and training drills. No one over forty-five years of age could be compelled to serve in the militia. Excused by law were physicians and surgeons, attorneys-at-law, justices of the peace, members of the assembly (the upper house), schoolmasters, gristmill operators, etc.

Every soldier was required to "always be provided with, and have in continual readiness, a well fixed firelock—the barrel not less than 3 1/2 feet long—or other good firearms to the satisfaction of the commissioned officers to which he doth belong; a good sword or cutlass; a worm; a primer and priming wire fit for his gun; a cartridge box; one pound of good powder; four pounds of bullits fit for his gun, and twelve flints - or penalty of three shillings for want of such arms."[101]

Each company had the right and privilege to nominate its own officers (above the rank of sergeant), the nominees then being commissioned by the Connecticut Assembly. Training days were designated well in advance and failure to attend brought a fine or penalty of three shillings.

A Soldier's Equipment

The establishment of the Twenty-Fourth Regiment reached into every household. Next to his axe, a male of this period cherished his gun. He was thoroughly accustomed to the use of his firearm, chiefly for the procurement of food but also for defense. But the enactment of the Assembly set standards which all could not meet at once.

The commonest firearm of the period was the musket and it was the standard for infantrymen of all countries. It was a muzzle-loading flintlock, highly inaccurate at over fifty yards.[102] There were however, several of the new rifles becoming available, shoulder guns with accuracy up to 400 yards. The Pennsylvania German gunsmiths of the period had developed a light rifle (1 1/2 turns in the barrel). It could be loaded without the use of a mallet by wrapping an undersized lead bullet in a greased piece of cloth or leather and shoving patch and ball together into the barrel. The gun was fired by a flintlock. It was a remarkable advance over the musket and became known as the Pennsylvania (and later, the Kentucky) rifle.[103]

Making Gun Powder at Home

Gunpowder was also to be provided by the newly enlisted soldier. This requirement was not easily fulfilled and many households had to make their own supply of it. Although gunpowder had been known for centuries, it was Roger Bacon, an English monk, who had stripped it of its magic and mystery by showing that this reported gift of the devil to mankind was a mixture of very earthy materials.[104]

The most critical ingredient of gunpowder was salt peter. Since Bacon's time this was obtained from decaying animal refuse, such as one might find in a dirty stable. It appeared as a whitish scum, resembling mold, collecting on the surface of old manure. By washing this material with water, then boiling off the water, one could get a hand full of more or less pure crystals of salt peter. Bacon emphasized that he refined these crystals by reboiling until they were white, clean, and odorless. A preparation of salt peter was the critical step, and required the greatest attention. Salt impurities in the crystal residue contributed to persisting moisture in the salt peter and thus to loss of its explosive potential when it was mixed with charcoal and sulfur. Gunpowder was difficult to keep dry under any circumstances, and storing it for any length of time was even more difficult. The need for producing it locally was recognized by all, and when the Continental Congress issued a call to arms in late 1775, it published and distributed a little manual detailing the method for making gunpowder at home.[105]

The Twenty-Fourth Connecticut Regiment from Westmoreland consisted of nine companies; the Second Company was developed in Kingston, to which Bennet belonged. The Seventh, Eighth and Ninth Companies were from Exeter, Lackaway, and the region around Tunkhannock. There was no standard uniform, although officers generally wore identifying badges. Even so, there was another standard costume for the frontiersmen of the period, and it accommodated quite well the requirements of the infantrymen.

Clothing in the summer was made of linen, and in the winter it was of linsey-woolsey. A man's shirt was long and hung halfway down his thighs. It was open down the front and confined by a belt tied in the back. Hanging from the belt was a tomahawk or hatchet on the right, a long knife on the left, and a bullet bag in front. The shirt was lapped far over in front to make a roomy pocket for bread, jerked meat, rifle tow, and tobacco. At his right side hung a large pouch from a shoulder strap. In it were carried extra lead and a mold for bullets, plus flint and steel. Tied to the same shoulder strap, above the pouch, was the powder flask.

Thus equipped the soldier was trained intensively in the care and use of his gun. Since his very life might depend upon this discipline, he made every effort to develop skill. Care in loading was essential since a frequent and ever present danger with the muzzle loading gun was accidental discharge when loading. Another problem was frequent fracturing of the ramrod, which at times would accidentally be left in the muzzle and fired out by the excited soldier. Since gunpowder was black and dirty, the gun barrel easily became fouled. Cleaning was a dirty but necessary job, performed frequently. The gun was able to discharge a single bullet, and the exercise of reloading had to be repeated over and over so that in the stress of combat a soldier could fire the second or third volley within a matter of minutes. Fortunately, many of the Wyoming men were already somewhat familiar with all these matters; but the officers had much to do to prepare them for actual combat.

Harvey Smith states,[106] "It is more than probable that, owing to the unsettled and precarious affairs throughout the country, efforts were made during the summer and autumn of 1775 by the officers of the 24th Regiment to perfect themselves and their men in military service and discipline."

The 24th Regiment was commanded by Colonel Zebulon Butler, a distinguished leader respected by all. Colonel Butler had had a military career which began in 1756 during the French and Indian War, as a commissioned ensign in an infantry company of the Connecticut line. Between 1756 and 1775 he acquired several periods of combat experience at the company and regimental levels and was a mature, forty-four year-old senior officer when he assumed command of the Westmoreland Regiment.[107]

Second in command was Lieutenant Colonel Nathan Denison, age thirty-five, with demonstrated leadership capabilities but with little previous military experience. Several commissioned officers of company grade had seen service in the French and Indian War. Thus a cadre of officers was immediately available to begin training in military discipline.[108]

Colonel William Plunkett and the Battle of Rampart Rocks

During the spring and summer of 1775, a group of Connecticut settlers from Wyoming attempted to make a settlement on the west branch of the Susquehanna River. A group of violent men from Sunbury, acting on behalf of the Pennsylvania proprietors, seized the Yankees and sent several of them to the Philadelphia jail. Valuable property and livestock were taken as booty, and the new settlement was completely dispersed.

This armed force from Sunbury was organized and commanded by a Colonel William Plunkett. Plunkett had had combat experience in the French and Indian War, and had held a series of commissions in the Pennsylvania Batallions. He had been a practicing physician in Carlisle (1751 to 1756), having graduated in medicine from the University of Dublin. By 1775 he owned extensive lands along the west bank of the Susquehanna and resided in Sunbury. He was a prominent man in the inner circle governing Pennsylvania and was known as an ardent and long time opponent of the Yankee settlers at Wyoming. He was greatly encouraged by the success of his troops in eliminating the Yankees from the west branch and resolved to do the same to those living at Wyoming on the north branch of the Susquehanna.

Over a period of a few weeks, Plunkett enlisted some 600 or 700 well armed and well equipped men for his ambitious foray. The Continental Congress had admonished against any further interstate confrontation and so Plunkett named his combat unit "Posse Comitatus"—a civil rather than a military thrust—to be accompanied by the sheriff of Northumberland County.

The Wyoming settlers kept themselves informed of the preparations going on at Sunbury. An excerpt from a letter written to Zebulon Butler at the time reveals the spirit of these informants as well as the nature and intent of the planned attack, despite its civil action masquerade. We quote, in part: "keep this letter secret and do not discover the author...you may surely depend upon their (the Pennamites) coming up to Wyoming, for they will not be stopped by Congress, but are now mustering their men at Sunbury....you may depend on their plundering you of all your effects, for they are determined to rob and plunder the country; and you will find them as inhuman as the Devil. For God's sake put yourself in readiness, and fight for your lives and fortunes." (Written in Sunbury about December 10, 1775.)[109]

This and other communications created much concern among the Wyoming settlers. There was some intelligence suggesting that Pennamites from the north and from the east were appearing to join in a common strike against the Yankees. Rumor had it that Colonel Stroud, despite his long history of Yankee support, had switched interests to the Pennamites, and that the Governor of Pennsylvania was himself a Tory with no real support of the peaceful proclamations of the Continental Congress.

In mid-December, when Plunkett was preparing his forces and stores, young Benjamin Shoemaker, Jr., and a companion were seized while on their way up the river from Middletown (below Harrisburg). These young men were laboriously poling a few bateaux laden with merchandise and stock for the general stores they were keeping in Wyoming. Plunkett adopted the stores and bateaux for his own use and held young Benjamin Shoemaker captive, planning to place him in the lead boat when he finally launched his expedition

News of this seizure reached Wyoming and served to crystallize available information into the channel of most probable thrust—that of an attack from below, up the river from Sunbury. Colonel Zebulon Butler was given blanket authority over the military defense of the settlement, and he placed all able-bodied men of the town on alert, in readiness to leave their homes at any time. "Every man able to bear arms was directed to hold himself in readiness to march at a moment's warning, his arms in order, with all the ammunition needed for a week's muster, and provisions for at least three days."[110]

The total force Westmoreland could bring into the field totaled about 285 but several of this number were from the Lackawaxen settlement or from the Delaware, forty miles away. Furthermore, there were probably twenty to thirty persons of Pennamite loyalty living right in the valley, so that an effective combat force could not have exceeded 250 men, some of whom had no guns.[111]

Colonel Butler did not officially call up the 24th Regiment, seeking instead to swell his force to as many able-bodied men as the town could provide. But the large part of his armed unit was made up from the regiment, all of whom were well armed and prepared in the basics of military science. Butler realized, more than anyone, the overwhelming numerical odds against him—250 Yankees against 700 of Plunkett's Pennamites. He dared not risk a confrontation on the open flat land of the valley, where he could easily be outflanked. With this in mind, he and others reconnoitered the south end of the valley, where the river passes through a narrow canyon for three or four miles, and where a difficult span of rapid water poured out of the valley (Nanticoke Falls).

He recognized the defensive potential of the area where Harvey's Creek flowed into the Susquehanna and chose this spot for joining the battle. On December 23 (Saturday) he marched his forces to this area and camped for the night on a piece of flatland on the north bank of Harvey's Creek. Among members from the Second Company of the 24th Regiment were Thomas Bennet, now age fifty-four, and his son Solomon, barely sixteen.[112]

Colonel Butler's plan of defense was at once placed in action. His main force constructed a log and earth barricade based upon a large shelf of rock overlooking the river. He placed a small force at a spot higher up the elevation, with instructions to prevent outflanking of the barricade. He sent Ensign Alden downriver about one quarter of a mile to act as an advanced post, occupying a small level spot where the river created a bit of back water into the west bank. Captain Lazarus Stewart was dispatched, with another small force, to an area of concealment on the opposite bank of the river—with intent to ambuscade any attempted landing force there.

The weather had been unusually mild and the river was open for the most part. Thin shelves of ice projected out from each shore for a few feet here and there, but the main channel would take bateaux with little difficulty. A number of these boats were used by Colonel Plunkett, but several of his men walked the distance on shore. His progress was slow and tedious; he departed from Sunbury on December 15 and it was December 24 (Sunday morning) when Ensign Alden reported the approach of Plunkett's troops. Alden and his men then withdrew to join Colonel Butler's main body on the ramparts.

Colonel Plunkett ordered his men to follow Alden and thirty minutes later the battle began with a sharp volley of musket fire from the breastworks. There were some Pennamite casualties, and confusion and apprehension spread among them. Seeing the impregnable position of the Yankees, Colonel Plunkett and his troops withdrew without firing a shot. He then directed his men to carry two of his heavy boats by land up the river to a point above the falls, concealing this portage from hostile fire. Several of his men accompanied him, with the intent of crossing over to the east side of the river in detachments which would then advance directly to Wilkes-Barre. Colonel Plunkett waited until nightfall and then, with the captive Benjamin Shoemaker in the lead boat, he led two boatloads of men (plus a small cannon) across the river. Nearing the opposite shore, the boats were detained by the thin shelf of ice extending from the bank; the boats "were, without warning, fired upon by Captain Stewart and his men who were concealed in the thick woods on the bank. Two or three men in the first boat were wounded, and one subsequently died. All the occupants of this boat would have been killed had not Benjamin Shoemaker called to the Yankees to desist from firing."[113] Colonel Plunkett, riding in the second boat, flung himself down flat and ordered withdrawal. Two boats hurriedly backed astern into the rapids and were hurled rapidly downstream to the quiet water below.

Early the next morning, Plunkett sent a detachment up the mountain in an attempt to turn the right flank of the ramparts. This move had also been anticipated by Colonel Butler and there was a unit of Yankees up there awaiting the Pennamites. The battle lasted most of the day, with periods of activity and exchange of fire, casualties being inflicted on both sides. Towards the end of the day, Monday, December 25, Plunkett withdrew his forces and began his retreat down the river.[114]

During this confrontation Martha Bennet rode down the west side of the river on horseback, leading a second horse loaded with much needed provisions. According to Peck,[115]

Thomas and Solomon Bennet were involved in this expedition for nearly two weeks. There having been no supply train, help from many households sufficed to provide "quartermaster" support to the troops.

This battle was of great importance to the Wyoming people. It determined that the Yankee culture would be the one to endure on this frontier until after the revolution. It was also a classic in defensive tactics. The intelligence gained and received by the commanding officer was correctly interpreted. Colonel Butler chose a spot for the battle, and took the time to prepare his defense. His deportment of troops was precisely what was needed. Loss of life and total casualties were held to a minimum, and his numerically inferior unit defeated a much larger force. This brilliant tactic and its resulting victory demonstrated the consummate skill and leadership of Colonel Zebulon Butler.

CHAPTER 9
The War for Independence

Resentment in the Colonies

During the years leading up to the Declaration of Independence, people in several colonies were exposed to pressures imposed upon them by their mother country, Britain, pressures which were largely economic.[116] As a result of decades of war with France, the treasury of the crown was sorely depleted, all domestic sources of revenue having been taxed to the ultimate. It was logical for George III to focus his attention on the American colonies for new taxes and new monies for the treasury.

A series of acts was designed to do just that, each provoking intense reaction among the colonists. The sentiments of the colonies were eagerly expressed to the King and to Parliament. Indeed, in a letter dated December 18, 1754, Benjamin Franklin clearly set forth the basic complaints which ultimately led to the War for Independence—excluding the people of the colonies from all share in the choice of representation, and taxing them by act of Parliament when they had no representation.[117] Variations of these themes were played out by the several actors over a period of several years. All along the way, Britain could have salvaged her colonies, for basic loyalty to the crown was widespread, but George III was obsessed with the sovereign right to tax "in the face of evidence that the attempt would be fatal to the voluntary allegiance of the colonies."[118]

Tuchman[119] states, "The British attitude was a sense of superiority so dense as to be impenetrable. A feeling of this kind leads to ignorance of the world and of others because it suppresses curiosity. They (the British) were not interested in Americans because they considered them rabble or at least children whom it was inconceivable to treat...as equals. Uniquely George III combined a tendency for strong prejudices with an ill-framed mind," and in the last analysis as reigning monarch he had ultimate power, all of which enabled him to lose America. The people of Britain shared in the creation of this dilemma. Trevelyan[120] stated, "Londoners were unwilling to read anything about Americans if it appeared a little lengthy.... They avoided consideration of anything other than what immediately concerned them, so that they could pursue their usual amusements without being disturbed."

The ministries of Granville, Rockingham, Chatham-Grafton, and North passed through a decade of mounting conflict with the colonies without ever sending a representative, much less a minister, across the Atlantic to make acquaintance and to find out what was actually endangering the relationship and how it could be improved. The ministries reflected the Crown's obsession with their dignity, sovereignty, and honor and made these their goals rather than reconciliation with the colonies.

Agitation and resentment in the colonies was not a steadily increasing foment. The very unpopular Stamp Act stirred the people everywhere to be "more attentive to their liberties, more inquisitive about them, and more determined to defend them."[121] But the crown, under pressure, repealed the Stamp Act and reaction in the colonies was one of widespread relief. Trevelyan quotes John Adams in November 1766, six months after its repeal: "The people under the sun [were] as little inclined to tumult, riots, seditions, as they were ever known to be since the first foundation of the government. The repeal of this Stamp Act has composed every wave of popular disorder into a smooth and peaceful calm."[122] But George III proceeded within the year to enact a series of revenue bills calculated to light the fires of resentment once again.

Although the initial focus of resentment by the colonies was largely economic, the publication of Thomas Paine's article "Common Sense" persuaded large numbers of the populace that the colonies were destined to "prepare in time an asylum for mankind." Paine had been a wanderer, a defeated European, but he had grasped the "continental dimensions of the American struggle, and flung it in the face of all humanity as a challenge."[123] Benjamin Rush and Benjamin Franklin encouraged Paine to write his pamphlet, finding his words both unorthodox and interesting. First published in January 1776, it set forth in logical fashion the history of the independence movement. Through a series of arguments Paine outlined the weakness of monarchy and of hereditary succession, portrayed reconciliation as a "fallacious dream" and concluded that "nothing but independence (i.e. a continental form of government) can keep the peace of the continent and preserve it inviolable from Civil War."

Paine's pamphlet was widely read, even more widely discussed. It rapidly sold over 120,000 copies within three months, and by all measurements then and now, was a powerful instrument persuading many undecided colonists to swing to the support of the independence movement. "People of those times were very much like ourselves; which is to say they were often confused, usually divided in sentiments and now and then rather badly discouraged about the possible outcome of the struggle."[124] Independence was fervently supported by roughly one third of the colonists, and equally opposed by another third.[125] The remainder were undecided and it was upon this fraction that Paine's writings had the most effect.

In the passage of 200 years we have glorified independence; we have grown to look upon the events of 1776 as one harmonious, nearly unanimous movement. Not so. Some of the colonies, particularly those in New England, strongly supported independence. Others, more distant from Boston and still following proprietary governments under the crown, were lukewarm, even opposing the movement.[126]

The First Continental Congress

This division of sentiment was seen in the meeting of the First Continental Congress in September 1774. A resolution of May 10, 1774, had recommended that "where no government [of a colony] sufficient to the exigencies of their affairs have been hitherto established, [an assembly should] adopt such government as shall, in the opinion of the representatives of the people, but enduce to the happiness and safety of their constituents in particular, and Americans in general."[127] This resolution provided room for broad application, and was adopted by both conservatives and liberals.

However, John Adams asked the chair, Hancock, for a committee to write a preamble. Adams was appointed chairman of this committee and was empowered by his colleagues,

Rutledge of South Carolina and Lee of Virginia, to construct the preamble. In part, it stated "whereas it appears absolutely irreconcilable to reason and good conscience, for the people of these colonies now to take oaths and affirmatives necessary for the support of any government under the crown of Great Britain, and it is necessary that the exercise of every kind of authority under the said crown should be totally suppressed, and all the powers of government exerted, under the authority of the people of the colonies, for the preservation of internal peace, virtue, and good order, as well as for the defense of their lives, liberties and properties, against the hostile invasions and cruel depredations of their enemies; etc."[128]

Wilson of Pennsylvania was shocked by the wording and spoke eloquently and vigorously in opposition. He stated in part, "if that preamble passes, there will be an immediate dissolution of every kind of authority; the people will be instantly in a state of nature. Why then precipitate this measure? Before we are prepared to build the new house, why should we pull down the old one, and expose ourselves to all the inclemencies of the season?"[129]

When the preamble came up for a vote, it passed six to four. But the division of the colonies was spelled out in this vote. The four New England colonies, plus Virginia and South Carolina, voted aye. North Carolina, New York, New Jersey, and Delaware voted nay. Georgia was absent and both Pennsylvania and Maryland abstained. Protests were loud and widely rendered. Governors, judges and other officials held their commissions from the King, and legislators were required to swear allegiance to him.

John Adams found the Virginia delegation most to his liking. It was plain that at that time Virginia and Massachusetts would have to lead the liberty party, while Pennsylvania and New York worked their hardest for accommodation with Britain and for business as usual. Adams stated that of the forty-odd delegates to this Congress the liberty men could be counted on one's fingers: Richard Henry Lee, Patrick Henry, Colonel Washington (all of Virginia); Gadsen of South Carolina, Roger Sherman of Connecticut, Governor Hopkins of Rhode Island. There was obviously a large conservative majority against the liberty men.[130]

Colonies Divided on Independence

Page Smith quotes David Ramsay—"The revolution (and independence) had its enemies, as well as its friends, in every period of the war. Country, religion, local policy, as well as private views, operated in disposing inhabitants to take different sides. The New England people, being settled by one sort of people, were nearly of one sentiment."[131] New York State and New York City had large numbers of loyalists, while in Pennsylvania there were many dissenting faiths. Quakers, German-Lutherans, Moravians, and Presbyterians stood as a solid block against the liberty movement. Furthermore, Governor John Penn was torn between the two factions and owed allegiance to the crown for his power and authority. The highly intelligent and conservative political leader in Pennsylvania was clearly John Dickinson, who wanted liberty, but held out to the last for some kind of reconciliation.

The south was, in general, also divided. The rich planters were in debt and saw independence and the revolution as a way out of their situation. The Southern frontier, however, became the only region in Colonial America that could properly be called a Tory stronghold.[132]

On May 15, 1776, the Convention of Virginia instructed its delegates to propose to Congress an official declaration of independence. The motion was to declare that "these unified colonies are, and of a right ought to be, free and independent states, that they are absolved from all allegience to the British crown, and that all political connection between them and the state of Great Britain is, and ought to be, totally dissolved."[133]

On Saturday, June 8th, Congress took up debate on this "Virginia Resolution." Delegates from the middle colonies (Maryland, Delaware, Pennsylvania, The Jersey's and New York) argued against accepting these measures "at this time." It was held that the people of these colonies were *not yet ripe* for bidding adieu to Britain, and that no capital step should be taken until the voice of the people drove the respective delegates to affirmative votes. On the other hand, John Adams led the arguments in support of the declaration, pointing out that the people were actually waiting for the delegates to lead the way. He and others pointed out that there was little or no argument against the policy of separation; that the chief stumbling block was one of timing; that it could be vain to wait for several months for perfect unanimity, "since it was impossible that all men should ever become of one sentiment on any question."[134]

Because of these debates, it was apparent that the middle colonies plus South Carolina, were not yet ready to support a declaration of independence; but the mood of the people was rapidly moving to that position. Rather than risk a negative vote of the Congress, the leadership considered it prudent to postpone the final decision to early July. Meanwhile, in order to minimize any delay, a committee was appointed to prepare the actual Declaration of Independence. John Adams of Massachusetts, Dr. Franklin of Pennsylvania, Roger Sherman of Connecticut, Robert R. Livingston of New York, and Thomas Jefferson of Virginia comprised the committee. Jefferson was selected to draw up the declaration, which was completed and presented to the House on Friday, June 28th.

Meanwhile, on June 14, 1775, the Connecticut Assembly voted that its delegates to the Continental Congress propose to that body "to declare the united American colonies free and independent states." Four days later Governor Turnbull issued his Proclamation of Reformation, a document referred to as Connecticut's Declaration of Independence.[135]

On Monday, July 1st, the Continental Congress resumed consideration of the original Virginia Resolution, which had remained on the table. By day's end, approval was carried, Pennsylvania and North Carolina voting against it. By the next day, both states joined in approval "for the sake of unanimity." New York, which had originally abstained, finally joined the others a few days later.

On the same day, Congress began to consider Jefferson's Declaration of Independence. To gain the full support of the delegates, it was necessary to modify the original statement. The clause deploring the enslavement of Africans was dropped completely, along with those passages conveying censure on the *people* of England. On the evening of July 4th The Declaration of Independence was approved by the House and signed by every member present except Mr. Dickinson.[136]

The Pennsylvania delegation of eight men was known to have a majority to vote negative on independence, but on the day of the vote three of these delegates were absent, including John Dickinson. The caucus vote was three affirmative and two negative. The vote, three to two, in caucus, resulted that Pennsylvania's single vote was yea for the Declaration of Independence.[137]

The Pennsylvania delegates were sympathetic to the sentiments of the people they represented. The large number of Quakers in and around Philadelphia, the German majority in Lancaster, York, Berks and Northampton Counties, the Moravians and the Mennonites, the Amish, and the German Baptists were all against the bearing of arms. This sentiment led them to favor reconciliation with the crown, and subsequently influenced many of these well-to-do persons not to support the revolution financially.

Yankee Sentiments at Wyoming

These matters related strongly to the course of events in the Wyoming colony, which was Yankee in sentiment and policy. The Wyoming settlement, in fact, was a mirror image of the parent in Connecticut and shared the ardent stance for independence taken on June 14, 1775, at Hartford. At a meeting of the proprietors and settlers of the town of Westmoreland on August 1, 1775, it was declared that, "this town does now vote that they will strictly observe and follow the rules and regulations of the honorable Continental Congress now sitting at Philadelphia." They further declared themselves willing to make any accommodation with the Pennsylvania party "that shall conduce to the best goal of the whole, not infringing on the property of any person, and come in common cause of liberty in the defense of America."[138]

Existing, as it did, as a pocket of independence and patriotism in northeast Pennsylvania, the Connecticut settlement of Wyoming posed as a sore thumb in the province of Pennsylvania. It is likely that this profound difference in political philosophy influenced the coming Pennsylvania response to the repeated requests for help by the isolated frontier settlement of Wyoming.

Throughout the thirteen colonies Committees of Safety were established at the suggestion of Congress.[139] It was Congress' intent that dissenters (i.e. Loyalists and Tories) would be identified by these committees and arrested. Westmoreland's Committee, centered in Wilkes-Barre, was organized early in 1776, probably comprising Nathan Denison, John Jamison and

William Stewart.[140] The establishment of this committee had become pressingly necessary, as, with the breaking out of the war, and the prohibition on the part of Connecticut of any further emigration to Wyoming, there had come in new families from Minisink, Westchester, New York, Kinderhook, and the Mohawk, none connected with Pennsylvania nor Connecticut, between whom and the old settlers there was neither sympathy in feeling, nor community of interest.

At first, attempts were made to win over Loyalists by social and economic pressures; failing these, Committees of Safety used harsher methods, such as whipping, coats of tar and feathers, fines, confiscation of property, banishment, and even death. "Loyalists, in turn, met bitterness with bitterness and savagery with savagery, especially in the border warfare along the great frontier.[141] The actual numbers of Tories worrying the colonists of Westmoreland must remain uncertain. The total population of the town in the summer of 1776 was about 2900 of whom 625 lived in Wilkes-Barre and another 625 dwelt in Kingston and Forty-Fort.[142]

It is not possible, now, to judge whether the many arrests and evictions were justified. Zeal and patriotism created the milieu for abuses. On the other hand, some of the loyalists did inform and assist the enemies of the colonists. Miner[143] states "some of them it is known immediately opened communications with the enemy....we are not prepared to say therefore, that the people were to blame in taking the most energetic measures to remove...the more avowedly disaffected."

Westmoreland Companies of the Connecticut Line

The Connecticut colonists, as early as 1772, had instituted the concept of local militia, with a company in each of the five townships. These were formally organized as the 24th Regiment of Connecticut in 1774. A form of military training existed in these companies, so that self-defense was an integral part of their daily thinking.

After a series of communications from the Westmoreland Assembly to the Continental Congress,[144] wherein were pleas for some kind of defense, Congress, on August 23, 1776, ordered "that two companies on the Continental line establishment be raised in the town of Westmoreland, and stationed in proper places for the defense of the inhabitants of the said town and parts adjacent till further orders...that they be liable to serve in any part of the United States when ordered by Congress."[145] Enlistment was for the duration. The two companies comprised one hundred sixty eight men; added to this number were the thirty or more men enlisted for the Continental Army during the previous summer. Sheldon Reynolds[146] has stated that Wyoming sent about eight times its fair quota of men into the service.

The 24th Regiment

Robert Durkee and Samuel Ransom were each elected captain of one of the two companies, with Colonel Zebulon Butler in command of the 24th Regiment. Colonel Butler was directed to obtain and to send 200 pounds of powder and a proportionate quantity of lead for the use of these two new companies. But adequate arms were constantly in short supply and from time to time many soldiers were actually without.

The settlers were constantly apprehensive for their own safety and at the town meeting held August 24, 1776, voted that "It now becomes necessary for ye inhabitants of this town to erect suitable forts as a defense against our common enemy."[147] The field officers of the 24th Regiment were authorized and instructed to survey the defense capabilities of the several townships, and particularly to examine existing fortifications and to make recommendations for improvement. In each township, the people belonging to any fort were to carry out this work without either fee or reward from the township. The scope of this effort was considerable in view of the available persons in the township, particularly since these same people had to continue their daily tasks of maintaining an agrarian economy, attending the town and committee meetings, serving guard duty, and many other duties.

Building the Forts of Wyoming

Among the forts, that at Forty Fort was the most strongly constructed, containing a good source of water. It was strategically located at a bend of the Susquehanna River, on high ground, and had a good view of the river both up and downstream. The Inspecting Committee directed it to be strengthened and improved, but the basic construction was already completed. Just above the Exeter-Kingston borderline, the

Wintermute family had built a log house which they stockaded in spring of 1776. This fort was constructed without the sanction of any authority; and the Wintermutes were thought to be Tories and in communication with the enemy. These suspicions proved to be justified as events transpired.

At the Westmoreland town meeting of August 1776, it was decided to build a stockade around the home of John Jenkins, subsequently known as Jenkins Fort. It was situated in West Pittston a bit north of Wintermute and was considered a countercheck to that structure.

Across the river was Pittston Fort, begun as authorized in 1772. Situated on high ground overlooking the river, it permitted broad views of the river and its traffic, as well as of movement on the west side. It was not completed until 1779, and at the time of the massacre (1778) it was made up of three block houses surrounded by a stockade; it was considered adequate for temporary defense only.

Wilkes-Barre Fort was authorized in August 1776 to be built on a site at Public Square, modeled essentially to resemble the construction at Forty Fort. It was finished in 1778 a few months before the massacre, but it seems never to have been planned as a definitive site for siege defense.

In Plymouth a block house was constructed in 1772. Complying with the August 1776 resolution, a heavy stockade was built around the block house. Located on high ground on Garrison Hill it occupied a strategic site guarding the south entrance to the settlements. It was intended primarily as a place of refuge for the inhabitants on the Shawnee flats, south and east of the fort.

In addition to the forts, there were several block houses. In Hanover Township there were two such structures, one built by Lazarus Stewart, and, not far away, a second one built by Rosewell Franklin. Rosencrans' block house was in Plains Township, while there was yet another built on the west side of the river opposite the foot of Northampton Street, Wilkes-Barre. These structures served as local rallying points during raids by Indians, but were not involved in any overall plan of community defense. From this appraisal of defense capabilities and the description of the work to be done, it can be seen that much hard labor faced those settlers able to shoulder the load.[148]

Between August 1776, when the defense resolution was passed, and December 1776 the two companies of Westmoreland infantrymen were trained as a battalion, under Captain Ransom. The troops were either billeted in Wilkes-Barre or lived nearby at home, reporting every day for training.

Washington's Army Dispirited

During this same period, the War for Independence had not progressed well for the Americans. During the summer and fall of 1776, General Washington managed to keep his little army intact through a series of retreats; actually his opponent, General Howe, could likely have surrounded and destroyed it had he been just a bit less cautious and followed up his victories at White Plains and at Fort Washington with vigorous pursuit and entrapment of the retreating patriots. On the other hand, General Washington proved himself to be a clever tactician, continuing his retreat through New Jersey with the lightning thrusts at Trenton and Princeton. "In fact, it could be persuasively argued that the Jersey campaign was a turning point in the war. Washington's main army had been saved and patriot morale had been in large measure restored."[149]

Harvey quotes Marshall: "At no time during this retreat did the American Army exceed 4,000 men and on reaching the Delaware was reduced to less than 3,000, of whom not quite one third were militia of New Jersey. The Commander-in-Chief found himself at the head of this small band of soldiers, dispirited by their losses and fatigues, retreating, almost naked and barefooted, in the cold of November and December, before a numerous, aggressive and victorious army."[150]

General Washington's private feelings at the time were reflected in a letter to Lord Washington dated December 17, 1776, in which he concluded: "A large part of the Jerseys have given every proof of disaffection that they can do and this part of Pennsylvania are equally inimical. In short, your imagination can scarcely extend to a situation more distressing than mine. Our only independence now is upon the speedy enlistment of a new army. If this fails, I think the game will be pretty well up."[151] Washington's army was sharply reduced in strength and material and he was grievously troubled and disillusioned by the lack of support given by the local populace.

Thomas Paine

On December 19, 1776, Thomas Paine published the first of his "Crisis Papers." Paine had been a member of the Continental Army and took part in its retreat from New York to the Delaware. This paper, familiar to all subsequent generations, began with the statement "These are the times that try men's souls. The summer soldier and the sunshine patriot will, in this crisis, shrink from the service of their country, but he that stands it *now* deserves the love and thanks of man and woman.... The harder the conflict, the more glorious the triumph." He concludes his message—"I shall not now attempt to give all the particulars of our retreat to the Delaware; suffice it for the present to say that both officers and men, though greatly harassed and fatigued, frequently without rest, covering, or provisions, inevitable consequences of a long retreat, bore it with a manly and a martial spirit."[152]

Continental Duty

The two Westmoreland Companies were ordered to Continental duty during this period. They departed Wilkes-Barre on January 1, 1777, in the midst of a very cold spell of winter, and marched over the lower road to Wind Gap and Easton. The trip was exhausting and arduous but the troops approached their task with a flame of patriotism. Realizing the acute need for them to join the main army, they were sustained by the conviction that they would be returned to Wyoming just as soon as the "emergency" subsided. They reached the main army at Morristown on January 9, 1777.

Everyone "back home" supported this movement of the two companies, but initial enthusiasm gradually faded, then drifted toward anxiety and panic as the months passed. Security at home depended upon an effective body of men capable of defending against the enemy. The home front was sorely depleted of such manpower, and was largely made up of women, children, old men, and the sick or disabled.

Miner[153] describes the picture for Wyoming as 1777 drew to a close: "The colony was now in its sixth year of age. Nearly all their able bodied men were away in service. The remaining population in dread of the savages were building six forts or stockades requiring great labor and without fee or reward. All the aged men...exempt by law from duty, were formed into companies to garrison the forts....Of the militia the whole were in constant requisition to go on to scout, and guard against surprise. The smallpox pestilence was in every district." This bleak picture at home was balanced by an awareness of the acute needs of the Continental Army for fresh manpower.

CHAPTER 10
Contrasts in Opposing Armies

Burgoyne's Grand Strategy

As the months of 1777 passed by, the needs of the Continental Army for manpower became more and more urgent. There was no possibility that the independent Westmoreland Companies could be released and transferred back to Wyoming for defense of the frontier.

It seemed to the British that the Americans were literally "hanging on the ropes" and that with proper strategy the war could be brought to a close. In January 1777 General John Burgoyne returned to London for a visit, and while there constructed a grand plan which, if successful, would bring the termination of the war, with Britain victorious.

The plan consisted of a three pronged attack. A body of troops would descend from Canada to Lake Champlain, would take Ticonderoga, establish a large supply base at Crown Point, and proceed to Albany. Simultaneously, General Howe would come up from New York and New Jersey and meet Burgoyne at Albany. A third force, under St. Leger, would come from Niagara across the fertile and rich Mohawk Valley, finally closing at Albany with the other two generals.[154]

Although the overall strategy was well conceived and had the approval of everyone in London, the plan failed due to flaws in its execution. In June 1777, Burgoyne moved south with a force of about 7,000 infantrymen plus 400 Indians, and some artillerymen. The entire train was huge and cumbersome, and the logistics of supply by water and through dense forests became a chief deterrent to ultimate victory. Expecting the support of the local populace as they moved south, they found determined sabotage and opposition instead. Constantly in need of provisions and of horses, Burgoyne's army was heavily occupied foraging the countryside as it proceeded. One such attempt met disaster and defeat at Bennington, where a patriot force under the brilliant and determined leadership of General John Stark crushed and destroyed a British force which had been detached to search for badly needed horses.

The cautious General Howe never did commit himself to a march north to Albany; he became fully occupied with the army of Washington, pursuing it to Philadelphia. Although Washington lost at the Brandywine and did not emerge a victor at Germantown, these maneuvers in retreat kept Howe fully occupied. As Howe perceived it, taking Philadelphia was much more important than advancing north to a meeting with Burgoyne.

The Siege of Fort Stanwix

The third prong from Niagara encountered unexpected delay and unconquerable resistance at Fort Stanwix, now Rome, New York, along the Mohawk River. A determined, well-armed combat unit of 700 men occupied the fort. Several artillery pieces and adequate reserves of ammunition supported this unit. General St. Leger with a force of about 1,800 men, comprising Tories, Indians and Butler's Rangers, attempted to reduce the fort. But St. Leger did not count on the fighting spirit of General Peter Ganswort who commanded the stronghold.

Unreliability of Indians

One of the problems favoring the defeat of St. Leger was the unreliability of the Indians making up a majority of his force. As on other occasions, the force of Indians and Rangers, lacking artillery and heavy weapons, could not reduce a fortified position containing a well led and determined garrison of defenders. Their great combat successes were always in ambuscade, or in attacks upon isolated homes and communities where the odds could be greatly in their favor.

It was during this action at Fort Stanwix that General Herkimer's relief force was successfully ambushed at nearby Oriskany. But because of their poor discipline the Indians failed to destroy the rear of the force, permitting the escape of large numbers of Herkimer's troops. Concerning this ambush at Oriskany, Lieutenant Colonel Barry St. Leger wrote to General Burgoyne on August 27, 1777: "The impetuosity of the Indians is not to be described; on the sight of the enemy (forgetting the judicious disposition formed by Sir John Johnson and agreed to by themselves which was to suffer the attack and begin with the troops in front, while they should be on both flanks and rear), they rushed in, hatchet in hand, and thereby gave the enemy's rear an opportunity to escape."[155]

British Lose at Saratoga

In October 1977, General Burgoyne was defeated at Saratoga. Although both General Benedict Arnold and General Schuyler were, in the minds of many, the commanders whose brilliant and courageous actions led to an American victory, General Horatio Gates took the actual credit. St. Leger's force never did reach Albany and Burgoyne's army was eliminated from further combat.

Westmoreland Companies

News of the victory at Saratoga spread throughout the colonies and boosted spirits everywhere. The two Westmoreland Companies serving with George Washington shared in this enthusiasm, but were fully occupied as combat troops at the battles of the Brandywine and of Germantown. It was obvious that they could not be released to return to the defense of their homes in Wyoming. Miner speaks of "treachery, a trick to entrap them into service under so fair a pretense, and then to force them away, leaving their homes wholly exposed and unprotected, implied a degree of cruelty they could not even comprehend."[156] But in reality General Washington could spare no one; indeed it was his tenacity in holding his little army together during 1777-1778 which was probably his major contribution to the success of the war. The companies were to remain on active duty, spending the difficult winter of 1777 at Valley Forge, along with the rest of Washington's army.

In early December 1777, after the battle at Germantown, what remained of Washington's army gathered at the east bank of the Schuylkill, while some of their engineers and watermen built a makeshift bridge by placing a number of wagons end to end, connecting these with wooden rails. One snowy, cold night, the men crossed the river to the west side, and made camp near what is now Gulph Mills. Here they pitched tents and spent several days. It was during this encampment that Congress ordered a day of thanksgiving, intending, no doubt, for there to be feasting and reverence. According to one soldier "our country, ever mindful of its suffering army, opened her sympathizing heart so wide upon this occasion as to give something to make the world stare. ... It gave each and every man half a gill of rice, and a tablespoonful of vinegar."[157]

The Winter at Valley Forge

The army was now not only starved but nearly naked, lacking shirts, trousers, shoes, blankets. In this condition they marched to Valley Forge, in the words of General de Kalb one of the poorest districts of Pennsylvania, the soil thin and uncultivated, almost uninhabited, without forage and without provisions. They arrived at Valley Forge a week before Christmas in the dusk of evening, thirsty and fatigued, only to find that there was no fresh water available unless one walked a good distance from the camp. There was no shelter and a cruel race began to get huts built before these half naked, starved soldiers might freeze to death.[158]

The encampment was established on a bleak hill, with huts built in clusters housing detachments separated from one another. It could have been a difficult site to defend and there is no explanation why it was chosen for the winter camp, except that it was central to the area of responsibility. Daytime was spent in construction details, with some detachments being sent out to forage for provisions, and some being charged with harrassing the enemy. But neither of these efforts was supported by the starved, ill clad, sick soldiery. At night, a blanket would be shared by several men, attempting to sleep with its protection by turn; and always there would be the huddles of men sitting up all night around the several campfires. Wood was the only source of heat and gathering it became an increasing chore, the supply of dry kindling and good burning wood growing more and more distant from camp.

Illness was rife everywhere, resistance to infection weakening under the burden of malnutrition. Most of the soldiers developed intense generalized itching of the skin, which was accompanied by scabs and scratch wounds. One could conclude that the encampment was infested with body lice. It is possible that typhus was rampant, and certainly pneumonia and gastrointestinal fevers were prevalent. In many instances, a soldier could not have eaten even if the food was available.

Deaths were frequent, as many as 2,500 soldiers being lost during this dreadful winter.[159]

What forces combined to create and to perpetuate this evil milieu for our courageous men? In the first place, no large scale farming had yet developed in this hilly, heavily wooded, essentially uninhabited land, so that foraging was to become fruitless. Contrast this with the rich and extensive farmland north and south of Philadelphia, along the Delaware, extending to Wilmington - farmland easily accessible to parties of the British dispatched from Philadelphia.

Then, too, the populace of Philadelphia and of its suburbs was heavily Loyalist and Quaker, the latter unwilling to support any armed revolt by sharing their wealth with the Patriots. In fact, there was widespread disaffection for the independence movement leading to the failure to supply Valley Forge with provisions of any kind.

Finally, those in charge of the Commissary must be thought of as inefficient and inept. George Washington in his letter to the President of Congress, December 23, 1777, complains that "the present commissaries are by no means equal to the execution (of the office)."[160] He goes on to say that the army had no assistance from the Quartermaster General with regards to provisions, soap, vinegar, clothing, shoes, or blankets, nothing since July, and Brandywine. He figured that there were 2,898 men "now in camp" unfit for duty "because they are bare foot and otherwise naked." As of December 23rd he calculated that he had about 8,000 men fit for duty!

Nevertheless, it was during this winter of little hope that Washington's army grew into a better fighting force than ever. Several foreign military officers came to live and work with the troops, exposing them to skilled and sensible military training. These experts were no doubt attracted to the idea of a new kind of liberty and government, the "asylum for mankind" portrayed by Thomas Paine. In this group was Baron Friedrich von Steuben, a former staff officer under Frederic the Great, who became very popular with the troops at Valley Forge. Others included Louis Duportail and Johann de Kalb from the French service; Thaddeus Kosciusko and Count Casimir Pulaski from Poland; and finally the Marquis de Lafayette. This impressive group helped immeasurably to build morale, to support General Washington, and to keep alive the struggle for independence.

One cannot leave this period without devoting a few words to the British troops and officers simultaneously occupying Philadelphia. During the winter of 1777-1778, the city became a scene of war prosperity, offering the occupying force an extremely snug and hospitable retreat. Theaters were crowded and the coffers of the Loyalist and Quaker merchants swelled. All of this was in such sharp contrast to the state of affairs at Valley Forge as to defy the imagination.[161]

General Howe could very likely have successfully attacked and eliminated Washington's forces at Valley Forge; the British soldiers were well equipped, highly trained, well nourished, and outnumbered the Americans at a ratio of over two to one. But Howe never made a move against the Americans. He attempted to recruit Loyalists, expecting to swell his own forces, but this was not successful. Disappointed in the conduct of the war, the British King and his government relieved Howe and gave the command to his subordinate Sir Henry Clinton, who arrived in Philadelphia May 8, 1778.

But before Howe departed, the city gave him a farewell ball the elegance of which becomes apparent. The celebration included a regatta, a mock tournament, a gala dinner and dancing until 4 a.m. One of the British officers describes the end of this event as follows: "towards the end of supper, the Herald of the Blended Rose, in his habit of ceremony, attended by his trumpets, entered the saloon and proclaimed the King's health, the Queen, and Royal Family, the Army and Navy...the knights and their ladies in general: each of these toasts was followed by a flourish of music."[162]

Almost coinciding with the arrival of Clinton, news of the treaty of alliance with France reached Philadelphia on May 6. This treaty had as its ultimate end the "absolute and unlimited independence of the United States." By it, France was bound to defend American territory in North America, and the United States to come to the defense of the French West Indies. Coupled with an agreement of amity and commerce, the treaty had a profound negative effect upon British and Loyalist morale in America, at the same time raising the spirits of the American armies and of the Congress. A new determination and confidence spread throughout the several states. Washington's army remained at Valley Forge until June 1778, while the Continental Congress continued to hold sessions at York, Pennsylvania. In the middle of June the British forces completely withdrew from Philadelphia.

Westmoreland Companies Transferred to Wyoming

In April and May a few detachments were sent out of Valley Forge to perform special duty. One of these was made up of the two Westmoreland Companies, assigned to guard a collection of British and Hessian prisoners of war confined to barracks in Lancaster, Pennsylvania.[163] Through deaths, discharges due to disabilities, desertions, and fulfillments of enlistment time, the two companies' combined strength had dropped to eighty-six men. Congress then ordered the formation of one company from this group, appointing Lieutenant Spaulding as the commanding officer. By late June 1778 this "new" company of poorly equipped infantrymen was finally ordered to march to Wyoming to take part in the defense of the settlements there.

CHAPTER 11

The Frontier Becomes a Battleground

Indian Forces Along the Frontier

The settlers at Wyoming were a part of the American frontier and in due time this frontier would be intimately exposed to the war. The frontier stretched from Maine to Georgia in a great arc, and represented a large part of the American territory as well as of its population. But it was, throughout the war, exposed to constant depredations on the part of the Indians, and those who lived on the frontier were in constant fear of some new violence. It was inevitable that the weak outer flank of the new country of America would soon receive the attention of the British and of the Indians.

Early in the conflict, both sides tried to entice and to hire Indians in the prosecution of the war. Contrary to popular belief, it was the Americans who had actually taken the first step. Even before the battle of Lexington, the Massachusetts Provincial Congress enlisted the Stockbridge Indians, and early on, through its Indian commissioners, the Continental Congress made repeated overtures to involve Indians on the side of the Patriots.[164]

As time went on, however, it became clear that the Indians would become involved on the side of the British. "The British had the supplies, the articles for trade, the fur-trading posts; the British seemed to be there as their defenders; it was the Americans who were advancing into their hunting grounds. It was inevitable that the Indians would be caught up in the war."[165]

The entire civilized world was soon shocked by news of the barbarity of Britain's savage allies and England probably gained very little by using them in the conflict. Besides, the Indian was not a dependable soldier and frequently escaped control. He disliked taking casualties, shied away when confronted by the odds against him in battle, and was not effective in taking a well fortified position. But British regulars and their combat units were filled out by adding Indians and Loyalists, neither of which proved to be very reliable soldiers.

For a few years after 1772, the Wyoming settlement contained scattered families of Indians who were generally on friendly terms. The little frontier town was remarkably free from Indian raids or attacks. But with the outbreak of the revolution there was a gradual shift toward hostility,and by the winter of 1777 most Indians had migrated north toward Niagara and the Indian settlements of the New York frontier. Even during that winter, however, the region lying between Niagara and Wyoming was not burdened by conflict with the Indians.

The Wyoming settlers began to send out scouting parties as patrols, ranging as far north as Wyalusing. Sometimes these parties took prisoners (both Indians and suspected Tories) and at other times a Yankee patrol would be taken by the foe. Actions on both sides were at times fierce. Cruikshank[166] quotes General Robideau (British): "the confiscation of the effects of the disaffected (Tories) is very irregular, the brutality offered to the wives and children of some of them... in taking from them even their wearing apparel, is shocking."

Butler's Rangers

In the fall of 1777, British preparations for prosecuting the war along the Pennsylvania frontier were beginning to take form. John Butler had been authorized to form a corps of rangers to serve with the Indians. There were to be eight companies, two of which were to comprise men who spoke "the language of the Indians and (were) acquainted with their customs and manner of making war."[167] All members of the corps wore green uniforms, trimmed in scarlet, with flat caps of green carrying small brass plates at the front bearing the monogram G.R. (George Rex).

Training of this force was in general distinct and separate from that of regular troops. There was little need for the forms of parade or drills. Trained in the skills of dispersing rapidly and of forming ambush, members were required to be sturdy, alert, and capable of priming and loading their weapons as swiftly as possible. A large number of displaced Loyalists were enrolled; a roster printed in 1780 listed thirty-six names recognized as former inhabitants of Westmoreland. Tory refugees who kept drifting into Niagara gave fresh tales of hardship and ruthless persecution. They reported that many more of their friends were merely waiting for a favorable opportunity to enlist in the Loyalist cause.[168]

Concerning Butler's Rangers, Cruickshank states in his preface that "many thousand descendants of these brave men who formed Butler's Rangers are now living in Ontario and other British provinces. I hold that they have no reason to be ashamed of ancestors who were eminently distinguished by the none too common virtues of inalterable loyalty, unfailing courage, and unconquerable endurance, who sacrificed everything for the cause which they embraced...these were hard, fierce and revengeful men but...they lived in stormy times, in a hard, fierce, revengeful world."

The organizer and commander of the Rangers, John Butler, was born in New London, Connecticut, in 1725, where he was educated. His father was a career officer with the British crown, and during this service made himself useful to Sir William Johnston, the head of Indian affairs, thus gaining favor and ultimately a large 60,000 acre estate of land in New York State. John Butler grew up in a staunchly Loyalist family—even though his native part of Connecticut became intensely devoted to the Patriot cause. By December 1777, his son and other members of his family (and friends) were "in irons and badly treated."[169] John Butler could speak several Indian dialects fluently and was an ideal leader for his Corps of Rangers.

Joseph Brant–Indian Ally

Butler's main Indian ally was Joseph Brant, distinguished among the Iroquois for fearless leadership and statesmanship. Brant's date and place of birth are uncertain but he is said to have had the blood of Indian chieftains. He was educated by the Reverend Joseph Wheelock, first president of Dartmouth. An intelligent Indian, he performed early as interpreter, and became a fearless warrior and leader. He was constantly grieved and disturbed by the genocide of his race. During his youth and early manhood, his name spread panic and terror among settlers because of his ferocious and savage leadership. He conducted lightning raids all along the New York and Pennsylvania frontiers. Brant died in 1807 in Canada, where he had a comfortable home and thirty or forty Negro slaves working his land.[170]

Unadilla became the base for the Rangers and Indians; it was conveniently located as a supply and support center for the planned raids along the New York and Pennsylvania frontier, and its population was largely Loyalist. The few Patriots living in the area were soon dispersed until, in 1778, "not a patriot remained."[171] Butler and Brant devised a plan in which the latter would have the main purpose not to kill frontiersmen but to obtain food—food for his own men and for those of Butler, who expected soon to follow him into the Susquehanna Valley, his destination being Wyoming. Brant also aimed to collect men who as Tories would serve under Butler and he was "not to fight or make any alarm if possible...to avoid it." Brant was quite successful in this venture; he raided the upper Delaware and got about seventy head of cattle as well as some horses, while he recruited sixty or seventy inhabitants to join his forces. In May and June he raided and destroyed Cobleskill and Springfield, carrying much booty back to Unadilla.

Plans to Attack Wyoming

In all of this Butler represented the cause of England, not the cause of the Indians, and there in Wyoming Valley lay one of the most populous and defenseless settlements that existed remote from the seaboard. To attack and destroy it was to invite detachments for its defense at the expense of the American Army which Howe, Cornwallis and Clinton sought to overthrow.

On the other hand, Brant's fierce hostility and that of the Mohawks under him was directed not against Pennsylvania but against the New York frontier where lands, rightfully theirs, were theirs no more.

In June of 1778, a conference of Rangers and Indians was held at Tioga Point at which it was agreed that Brant would continue his forays for provisions and other supplies, while Butler and his forces would speedily descend upon Wyoming.

Meanwhile, at Wyoming the spring had gently changed to summer. Everywhere the crops of corn, wheat and other grains were thriving. The spring shad run had been prolific and fish had been salted, smoked, and dried, held in barrels for future consumption or for barter. The cattle were thriving on the fields of pasturage and on the ample fresh water. Women, children and the aged were busy from first daylight to sundown.

But beneath this appearance of abundance and comfort lay anxiety bordering on panic. This restlessness had begun in the fall of 1777 when many of the able-bodied young men departed with the two independent companies of Westmoreland. Rumors had spread that the Indians were going to join the English in a new series of attacks on the frontier settlements.

Settlers Prepare for Attack

In late fall young Martha Bennet spotted a party of Indians canoeing upstream and saw them land and disembark a short distance above the Bennet farm. Martha ran to inform her mother, and the two women went to visit the Indian party, which had encamped on the flat land overlooking the river. Chief of this party proved to be Queen Esther, the shrewd and intelligent Seneca who had organized and managed "Esthertown" (near Ulster, New York).[172] Martha described Queen Esther as an old and gray woman. Mrs. Bennet asked Queen Esther if the Indians were going to attack the Wyoming settlers, whereupon the Queen shook her head "no" with tears coming to her eyes. After about three weeks, the small band of Indians left this campsite, continuing up the river.[173]

"Queen Esther's influence with the natives was unbounded. When she appeared among them she was treated with the utmost deference. Her costume was rich and showy with a profusion of pure white beads. " Queen Esther, prior to the 1778 massacre, was portrayed as a woman of tolerance and compassion, kind to the white prisoners. Stone rejected completely the belief that Queen Esther was present at the massacre, but several settlers claimed to have seen her, among them being Martha Bennet, who knew her from prior close contact.

During the winter of 1777 and 1778, settlers at Wyoming had made numerous appeals to Congress for help. Harvey,[174] speaking of members of Congress, states "they saw, felt and acknowledged the exposed and defenseless situation of these frontier settlements...but the whole force under control of Congress was being concentrated for an important and decisive campaign." Finally on March 16, 1778, Congress resolved that one full company of foot soldiers be raised in the town of Westmoreland for defense of the settlement. Soon thereafter, Dethick Hewitt was appointed Captain and commissioned to raise this company from those men still remaining in

Westmoreland. Captain Hewitt raised about forty men within a period of six weeks, but they were poorly equipped and essentially untrained.

Support for Wyoming

By late May and early June, intelligence reports began to confirm the intent of the English to attack Wyoming. About the first of June, Lieutenant Colonel Zebulon Butler arrived in Wilkes-Barre on leave from his regiment, then stationed at West Point. Seeing the situation at the settlement he at once set out for York, Pennsylvania, where the Continental Congress was then in session. It is likely that he made contact with Colonel Timothy Pickering, a member of the Board of War. Colonel Pickering dispatched a letter to General Washington on June 19, 1778, on behalf of the Board, making these points:

1. He enclosed letters from General Wolcott (a Connecticut delegate to Congress) and Lieutenant Colonel Dorrance for Washington's perusal.

2. He stated that Durkee's and Ransom's companies "are now so very much reduced" and would not be missed (by Washington) as an effective fighting force. He requested that they be detached and ordered to the defense of the Wyoming frontier.

3. He further suggested that these two companies be combined into one, and that Lieutenant Colonel Zebulon Butler be permitted to remain at Wyoming to direct operations there.[175]

Colonel Butler returned to Wilkes-Barre from York by way of Lancaster and informed Captains Durkee and Ransom first hand of the desperate situation at Wyoming. Immediately thereafter they both resigned and, along with Lieutenant Wells, departed for their Wyoming Valley homes.

Captain Spaulding and his company began the march from Lancaster on about June 26, taking the Reading road up to Bethlehem and Wind Gap, and from there over the "Lower Road" to Wilkes-Barre—a distance of at least 125 miles, over rough terrain.[176]

Settlers Move Into the Forts

In the middle of June 1778, a few weeks before the battle of Wyoming, the Bennets had seven horses disappear, and the two sons and their sister, Martha, ventured afield in search of them. Martha intended to pick some cherries along the way. The boys discovered unmistakable evidence that the horses had been stolen by a party of Indians, and hastily the Bennets returned to their home. Not long after this the Bennet family moved into the Forty Fort, along with many of the settlers.[177]

Forty Fort was the largest and strongest of the six forts constructed in the valley and it became the site where most of the settlers collected in June and July 1778. Although frightened and worried the settlers had some sense of security as they assembled within the fort. It is recalled that the fort was a stockade with double thickness logs, with sentinel towers on the four corners and with a walkway constructed four or five feet below the tips of the upright logs. There was no artillery piece—a four-pounder existed at Wilkes-Barre but there was no ammunition. Defense depended entirely upon the accuracy and volume of small arms fire. The fort was, however, surrounded on three sides by a large open field of fire, and on the fourth side by the river. A determined group of men trained and experienced in the use of small arms, supplied with ample ammunition and artillery might have been able to stand some days of siege, especially if the attacking force had only small arms to fire.

CHAPTER 12
The Battle of Wyoming

The British Descend the River to Wyoming

Action on the part of the British forces was not long in coming. Major John Butler with his assault command of Rangers and Indians departed Tioga Point on Saturday, June 27th and descended the river swiftly and silently. Harvey, after reviewing all available information, placed this command as numbering about 700—"250 Rangers, 350 Seneca warriors, and probably 100 miscellaneous Indians."[178] They came down the river by means of a huge flotilla of canoes and small boats. There were no cannons or field pieces; rifles, muskets, tomahawks and arrows were the only assault weapons.

On June 30th, Butler and his command put ashore at Bowman's Creek, about 29 miles up river from Forty Fort. Here he divided his forces into two groups: troops from the small boats were ordered to continue on foot down river along the western shore, whereas the Indians and some white soldiers floated downward in their canoes. They all reassembled on shore about twenty miles above the Fort at "Three Islands." Here Butler again divided his command into two forces. Butler led the bulk of his Rangers, plus some Indians, over land to the top of Mount Lookout, a spot overlooking much of the valley. Mount Lookout was the highest point of the mountains lying on the western side of the Susquehanna; it was a lookout point favored by Indians, commanding a view from which all but the most concealed activity could be detected on the valley floor below. The other force, consisting of several Indians plus four or five "Rangers," marched quietly down the right bank of the river.[179] By this maneuver, Butler cleverly avoided passing his main force through the river's narrow entrance to the valley, where he might have been ambushed, while also gaining the tactical advantage of superior observation of his enemy.

Meanwhile, the Wyoming settlers were aware of the advancing foe. As early as June 26th, Captain Dethick Hewitt led a small scouting party up the river, returning on the evening of June 30th with the news that a large party of the enemy was slowly advancing toward the valley. It is likely that Hewitt observed the full flotilla before Butler divided his forces. Then early on June 30, before the return of Captain Hewitt, a party of twelve men and boys went from Jenkins Fort up river to Sutton's Creek (a distance of ten miles). This group was ambushed but five survivors escaped, returning to Jenkins Fort with the alarm of impending attack. It is likely that they had met the Indians of Butler's force coming down the right bank of the river. This detachment of Indians wrought havoc amongst the scattered settlers in upper Exeter township, burning and killing as they approached the valley, then joining Major Butler on Mount Lookout early in the morning of July 1st. Butler at that point bivouacked in nearby Orange, consolidating his forces once again, and laying plans for the next few days.

Early that same morning, about 400 men, armed and equipped, had set out from Forty Fort under the command of Zebulon Butler and Nathan Denison. This was a reconnaissance in force, intending to meet and to destroy the enemy. They proceeded as far as Sutton's Creek but met no opposition. They were under constant surveillance by Major Butler's outpost on Mount Lookout. Returning to Forty Fort that evening, the group disbanded, several of the men proceeding then to their respective homes and families.

Surrender of Fort Wintermute

On this same busy day, also early in the morning, two of the Wintermutes left their fort in Exeter township and quietly found their way to Mount Lookout to meet with Major Butler. The Wintermutes had long been suspected of being Tories with clandestine contact with the enemy.

It is still possible today to appreciate the wise and strategic placement of Wintermute's Fort. The plateau of Abraham's Plains rises rather abruptly at the upper end of what is now Exeter, and it was at the top of this incline that their fort was located. It looked down upon the gravelly plain, which was bordered on the west by an extensive marsh or wetland lying along the foot of Mount Lookout, and on the east by the river.

The Wintermutes escorted Major Butler and his aides back to their fort the evening of July 1st. There was no struggle, the small detachment perceiving the futility of resistance. It was there that Major Butler established headquarters with his troops bivouacked nearby.

Both Sides Prepare for Battle

Each of the valley forts had its own small garrison. When the settlers became aware of the approaching enemy they generally withdrew to the protection of these forts.

By July 1st, between three and four hundred men were gathered at Forty Fort, more or less prepared for combat. Miner[180]says, "So that there were 230 enrolled men, and seventy old people, boys, civil magistrates and other volunteers." Harvey describes the force in great detail and states that there were between 300 and 400 men–probably 375–assembled in the fort, and as many or more women and children.[181]

A total of 700 people were milling around within this enclosure, which by all estimates was a little over one acre in size. Thomas Bennet and his family were fortunate to occupy one of the cabins built along the inside wall of the fort, but most of this number had to be in the open space of the parade. Providing for the disposal of human waste, for sleeping space, for food and water, must have been a tremendous task. The logistics made a prolonged defense of the fort unmanageable.

July 2nd was a day devoted largely to organization and consolidation of both sides. Major John Butler, occupying Fort Wintermute, attended to the provisions and placement of his troops, holding conferences with his subordinates. At Forty Fort, Colonel Denison sent out scouting parties to learn what he could about the enemy. Captain Hewitt, in charge of one of these parties, was shot through the hand but escaped back to the fort. Two others of his party were casualties, having been detected by the Indians as they scouted along the base of the mountain. One of these men was taken prisoner and another was killed and scalped. Later that day, a considerable body of men was sent out to reclaim the dead man's body. Butler's Rangers and Indians lay in concealment and watched this operation silently, taking no actions despite the likelihood that they could have totally destroyed the little task force.

These scouting efforts of the Yankees were fruitful, however, and as of July 2nd, Colonel Denison knew approximately how many of the enemy were out there, and where they were. This statement is supported by a letter from Lieutenant Colonel George Dorrance to Captain John Franklin who was at Shickshinny with about nine men. "We (Captain Franklin and his company) had gone but a short distance when we met an express, Benjamin Harvey, with a letter from Lieutenant Colonel George Dorrance informing me that the Tories and Indians *about 600 in number*, were in possession of Wintermute's fort. That he expected they would attack Kingston next and requested assistance with my company with all possible speed."[181]

At this juncture, July 2nd, 1778, consider what is known concerning the two adversaries, poised for battle. The composition and training of Butler's Rangers is already described. They were an experienced, hardened, thoroughly trained combat unit, ideally prepared for frontier warfare. Their commander, Major John Butler, had been with them from the beginning; he was also experienced and skilled in the type of military tactics employed by his Rangers. As much as any commander of his day, he understood the Indians of his force, spoke their language, and exercised a measure of control over them. His method of approach to the valley, already described, reveals better than average tactical skill and field judgment.

On the other hand, all Yankees were trained to some extent in the use of firearms. As long ago as June of 1774 the General Assembly of Connecticut had ordered one company of militia for each district and had instructed then Captain Zebulon Butler to go to the several districts to help organize each company.[182] Later, these companies were ordered to form the 24th Regiment of Connecticut militia, with Colonel Zebulon Butler in command, assisted by Lieutenant Colonel Nathan Denison. All males sixteen to fifty years of age were required to bear arms. Every soldier and household was required to be provided with and have in continual readiness a well fixed firelock. Training days for the militia were prescribed and required, as well as an annual muster of arms.[183]

The troop dispositions of July 2nd suggest that it was the intent to defend each fort separately, each one having its own garrison and its own refugee families to protect. Of course, this was the thinking of the community at the time it ordered the construction and readying of the forts for defense of the settlements in 1776. There is no evidence of any other tactical plan.

Most of the men, including the chain of command, had had no combat experience, except for the battle of Rampart Rocks. Even the few soldiers on hand from Washington's army had not faced a combat unit designed for "Indian" style tactics. Colonel Zebulon Butler had been stationed at West Point, returning to the valley only a few days before he was asked to take command. Since he became commander of the Valley's defenders, dispersed among their separate forts, the day before the actual battle, he had no opportunity to train his men and to know their capabilities. He had no time to develop a combat team appropriate to the needs of the movement.

Events were to move swiftly. On July 2nd the small garrison at Jenkins Fort surrendered, and Wintermute's Fort became the headquarters of the invading force. Last minute attempts were made to collect all available defenders at the forts at Wilkes-Barre, Forty Fort and Pittston. But the Pittston fort was cut off from the others by Rangers, and it soon surrendered along with its garrison of forty or more armed men. Forts Jenkins, Wintermute and Pittston were taken without struggle.[184] In each case the terms of surrender were the same: Yielding the fort with all its stores, arms and ammunition, public or private, to Major John Butler; and agreeing that the garrison would not further bear arms during the present conflict. In return, Major Butler promised that men, women and children "shall not be hurt either by Indians or Rangers."[185]

Settlers Debate Tactics

Early on the morning of July 3rd, a flag of truce and three emissaries arrived at Forty Fort. The truce party, sent by Major John Butler, consisted of Daniel Ingersoll (a Yankee prisoner taken at the surrender of Fort Wintermute), an Indian, and one of the Rangers. The conditions of surrender were similar to those at the Jenkins and Pittston forts, but specified that all the Continental officers and soldiers on the ground must be turned over to the invaders as prisoners of war. [186]

Colonel Denison, commanding Forty Fort, refused to surrender, but coupled his refusal with a request for time to consult with Colonel Zebulon Butler, who was in Wilkes-Barre, and other officers not immediately present. In considering the proffered flag of truce, several items of importance had to be involved. It was about that time that Lieutenant Timothy Pierce, of Captain Spaulding's Independent Company, arrived on the scene with news that this company would arrive at Forty Fort about Sunday, July 5th. Also, on the way with help was Captain John Franklin with his company, a group of men largely from Salem Township (now lying between the communities of Shickshinny and Berwick). An urgent message had also been carried by Benjamin Harvey to Captain Clingman, with ninety men, located near Fishing Creek. The message was that "the Tories and Indians, about 600 in number, were in possession of Wintermute's Fort; that he expected they would attack Kingston next and requested assistance...with all possible speed."[187] Clingman did not come, as affairs developed, but Colonel Butler and Colonel Denison thought he might. Actually, Clingman's company was of Pennsylvanians with deep feelings against the Connecticut settlers, but it was thought that they might come out of a sense of humanity. Had all these forces arrived, there would have been added perhaps another 250 fighting men to help with the defense against the Indians and Rangers.

On July 3, at the request of Lieutenant Colonel Denison and fellow officers, an urgent message was sent to Fort Wilkes-Barre , requesting that Colonel Zebulon Butler cross the river and at once assume command of the force gathered at Forty Fort.[188] On two occasions that same day, after his arrival at Forty Fort, Colonel Butler sent out a flag of truce requesting a further meeting to discuss terms, by this delay hoping to allow more time for the arrival of reinforcements. But the bearers of the flag were, on both occasions, fired upon by enemy scouts and returned in haste to Forty Fort without accomplishing their mission. Other scouts were dispatched with orders to determine the strength and disposition of the enemy, but these parties were fired upon, taken prisoner, or otherwise disposed of.

Colonel Denison was fearful of imminent attack upon Forty Fort and strongly supported any measure likely to delay such an attack. Mention is made by Harvey that he was unable to form a satisfactory estimate as to the number of the invaders. But his message to Captain Clingman and the report of Captain Hewitt's scouting party of June 2nd both allude to an invading party of a large body of men, in the first instance, about 600 in number, and in the second a *large* party of the enemy. Intelligence already at hand certainly indicated that a large force of the enemy was approaching.

Heightening the sense of panic was further information that the enemy were burning all the settlements above, and collecting all the cattle within their reach—it was apprehended that they would not risk an attack upon Kingston but would burn, plunder and destroy all the upper settlements. Some of the officers proposed going to the attack, leaving the fort, and taking the enemy on their own ground.

Much has been written about the debate at Forty Fort which concluded in favor of attack. It appears that surrender of the fort was truly unthinkable. Miner[189] states, "the valley would be destroyed piecemeal...our little army could not be kept long together. Unless led to action each man would fly to the protection of his own family...to attack and defeat the enemy was the only hope of salvation for the settlements."

Several descriptions of the council of war at Forty Fort can be found in histories already cited in this narrative. Chapman[190] states: "The debates in this council of war are said to have been conducted with much warmth and animation. The ultimate determination was one on which depended the lives of the garrison and the safety of the settlement. On one side it was contended that their enemies were daily increasing in numbers, that they would plunder the settlement of all kinds of property and would accumulate the means of carrying on the war while they themselves would become weaker; that the harvest would soon be ripe, and would be gathered or destroyed by their enemies, and all their means of sustenance during the succeeding winter would fail; that probably all their messengers (for help) were killed, and as there had been more than sufficient time and no assistance arrived, they would probably receive none and consequently now was the proper time to make the attack. On the other side it was argued that probably some or all the messengers may have arrived at headquarters, but absence of the Commander-in-Chief may have produced delay, that one or two weeks more may bring the desired assistance, and that to attack the enemy, superior as they were in number, out of the limits of their own fort, would produce almost certain destruction to the settlement and themselves, and captivity and slavery, perhaps torture, to their wives and children."

Lazarus Stewart Challenges Colonel Butler

The debate became very heated, with much passion on both sides. Those in command favored remaining at the fort and using it as a pivot of defense. The younger men wanted to launch the attack at once, and their enthusiasm was fanned by the fiery words of Lazarus Stewart, who at the time was a private in Captain M'Kerachan's Hanover Company. Stewart charged cowardice against all who opposed advancing, "particularly against Lieutenant Colonel Butler, who was against an advance; he (Stewart) threatened to report him as a coward to headquarters."[191] The Hanover Company became mutinous and Captain M'Kerachan thought it best to resign. Stewart was elected at once to command the Company. At one point, Lieutenant Colonel Denison ordered Stewart placed under arrest for disorderly conduct.

Stewart's actions were quite consistent with his life story, replete with daring escapades. Harvey states that Stewart "possessed more military knowledge and experience—particularly concerning Indian warfare—than any other officers with the exception of Lieutenant Colonel Butler, Captain Robert Durkee and Captain Samuel Ransom."[192] It should be noted that Stewart was not an officer until this revolt of the Hanover Company against its regularly appointed Captains. Pearce dedicated several pages to his study of Stewart's life and notes that he possessed a strong and active body with a daring and enterprising spirit.[193] He had been in command of a company of young men in the forces of General Braddock during the French and Indian War, and seems likely to have been among those caught in a destructive ambush near Fort Duquesne. Braddock had about 2,200 men, roughly three times as many as did the French and Indians. At the battle, the Indians flanked the column on either side and pelted them from every tree and log. Brewster states that the confused and bewildered mass of men were mowed down like sickled grain.[194]

Stewart's next military involvement was as leader of the Paxtang Rangers. Because of Indian raids, the people of Paxtang (near Harrisburg) formed themselves into a military corps and placed their pastor, Reverend Mr. Elder, in command. Stewart was then appointed a captain in this militia and subsequently directed its activities. With his rangers he destroyed about a dozen unarmed (but not undefended) Indian prisoners being held captive in a stone work house.

Stewart is also described by Pearce as being with the Pennsylvania militia under Captain Clayton, who went to Wyoming to drive off the settlers following the massacre of 1763. No combat was involved, since the Connecticut settlers who had not been killed during the Indian raid had already fled. We recall that Stewart later commanded the ambush on the east side of the river at the time Plunkett tried to invade and conquer. He was at that time serving under the command of Lieutenant Colonel Zebulon Butler. There is no doubt of the bravery and resourcefulness of this daring man, but his actual combat experience might be considered as somewhat limited when held up for detailed study.

The issue was finally resolved when Lieutenant Colonel Butler agreed to go along with the attack and to continue in overall command. Along with many of the older men he had held out for a fortress defense, but in order to preserve a unified force, compromise was reached.

Thomas Bennet, occupying one of the cabins in the fort, decided to go along as a volunteer but he would proceed no further north than the lower border of Tuttle's Creek (now known as Abraham's Creek), which was about one and a half miles from the fort. Bennet, now fifty-seven years old, had great misgiving over this tactic of attack, believing that such an approach must only lead to ambush by the highly trained and very tough Rangers and Indians.

In those days Tuttle's Creek had a high bank on its south side, and the stream was much larger. Both banks had considerable tree and shrub growth. To the north, the land generally continued its slope downward, becoming a marsh during part of the year. The stream at one point passed through a ravine with precipitous banks on either side. Conceivably, this natural barrier might have been prepared as a line of defense, but the number of available soldiers and the pressure of time gave little chance for such a preparation. Furthermore, the left flank would have extended over flat land to the mountain, and the right flank could run to the river's edge.

Having arrived at Tuttle's Creek, the troops halted for a few hours. Debate as to proper action rekindled, ending with the decision to press forward. Bennet again expressed opposition to any such procedure and decided to walk back to the fort.

Chapman states that Colonel Butler, at this point, sought volunteers who would go forward as scouts to ascertain the situation of the enemy. Abraham Pike and an Irish companion offered their services, and they being the only volunteers, were accepted. The scouts found the enemy in possession of Fort Wintermute carousing in supposed security; but on their return they met two strolling Indians by whom they were fired upon.[195] Harvey describes repeated scouting parties and white flag emissaries dispatched from the Yankees by Lieutenant Colonel Butler[196]. All seem to have been detected, many actually drawing enemy fire. It is apparent that the enemy knew exactly the hour by hour situation of the advancing settlers, whereas Lieutenant Colonel Butler and his small force never had the same level of intelligence from their own scouts.

The Battle of Wyoming

Battle descriptions can be found in detail in the references already cited (Harvey-Smith, Miner, Chapman, Stone, Peck). What happened was a classical ambush by a well concealed enemy, trained for precisely this kind of warfare. About three hundred of the settlers were killed or missing, and of those missing many remained unaccounted for.[197] Officers killed included Lieutenant Colonel George Dorrance, Major Wait Garret, Captains Dethick Hewit, Robert Durkee, Aholab Buck, Asa Wittlesey, Lazarus Stewart, Samuel Ransom, James Bidlack, and others. Timothy Pierce, James Welles, Elijah Shoemaker, Lazarus Stewart, 2nd, Peren Ross, and Asa Stevens—all lieutenants, were also killed. Several of the men were first held as prisoners, then tortured and massacred by the ferocious and uncontrollable Indians. Wild scenes of torture persisted all that night, the smell of burning flesh pervading the valley. This brief description represents what might be considered the American point of view.

The British story of events is somewhat at variance. Cruikshank[198] begins his report with the statement, "The Indians contended they were still the rightful owners of the lands occupied by the Wyoming people. They had protested fruitlessly for more than 28 years against the settlement of the valley." As to the battle itself, Cruikshank states that shortly after noon four or five hundred men were seen advancing along the river. He describes this force as comprising the entire detachment of continental infantry and Wyoming riflemen under Colonel Butler, an experienced veteran, and the greater part of the 24th Regiment of Connecticut militia under Colonel Denison. Lieutenant Caldwell, the Ranger who was assigned to destroy Jenkins Fort, was recalled. By about 4 p.m. the enemy was still about a mile away. Major Butler then ordered Fort Wintermute to be set on fire, whereupon the Americans were seen to push forward rapidly, apparently from a supposition that the British force was retreating. Major Butler then posted his men in "a fine open wood," extending from an impenetrable marsh on his right to the river on his left, the Indians being stationed on the right in six distinct parties; he ordered them to lie perfectly flat on the ground and reserve their fire or any other actions until a signal was given from the Seneca chief. The Indians and Rangers remained silent, permitting the Americans to advance "in line" to within 100 yards, when the Indian chief gave his shrill war whoop. This was followed by a deliberate and deadly volley. Already the Indians had turned the enemy's left flank by creeping along the margin of the marsh, and the militia there gave way in sudden confusion. The Indians darted forward to cut off their retreat and drove them towards the river.

Some weeks after the conflict, Major Butler, in a letter to Colonel Bolton stated "our fire was so close and well directed that the affair was soon over, not lasting above half an hour from the time they gave their first fire till their flight. In this action 227 scalps and only five prisoners were taken. The Indians were so exasperated with their loss at Fort Stanwix last year that it was with difficulty I could save the lives of these few. Colonel Denison...told me they had lost one colonel, two majors, seven captains, thirteen lieutenants, eleven ensigns, and 268 privates."[199] This totalled 302 men, surprisingly close to the approximation made by Chapman, quoted above. Losses on the British side were stated to be one Indian killed, with two Rangers and eight Indians wounded.

Major Butler continues: "By the final capitulation it was agreed that all the forts should be utterly demolished, the continental stores surrendered, and that none of the inhabitants should again bear arms. Prisoners on both sides were to be liberated." Butler further stipulated that "properties taken from the people called Tories up the river be made good, and that they are to remain in peaceable possession of their farms and unmolested in a free trade..." On his part, he promised to use his utmost influence "that the properties of the inhabitants shall be preserved to them." Later he asserted that these conditions were violated by Lieutenant Colonel Denison, who appeared in arms before the year ended. Major Butler concludes his letter with this astonishing statement: "But what gives me the sincerest satisfaction is that I can, with great truth, assure you that in the destruction of the settlement not a single person was hurt except such as were in arms; to these, in truth, the Indians gave no quarter."

On file at the library of the Wyoming Historical Society is a fascinating thesis by Alfonso Stanley Zawadski. [200] He states that "Congress must have had some data to indicate that the Indians were planning an offensive soon or otherwise a deputation would not have been sent to appeal for Indian neutrality. These emissaries must have gathered some intelligence re the Indians, and so Congress must have been aware of the Indian threat to the frontier. In the last analysis Congress was responsible for the tragedy of the battle of Wyoming."

Then there was the report published in the *Annual Register* (London), in which the responsibility for the tragedy of Wyoming is placed on Colonel Zebulon Butler. "It would seem his (Zebulon Butler's) situation and force in that place, that he might have waited at (Forty Fort)...and successfully resisted all the attempts of the enemy....But this man was so wretchedly weak that he suffered himself to...abandon the advantage and security afforded by his fortress, and to devote those under his charge to certain destruction, by exposing them naked to so severe an enemy."[201] The article goes on to state that Colonel Butler marched his men out to protect himself while attempting to hold a parley with the enemy and that he mistakenly marched out into the open field at so great a distance from the fort that he gave up every possibility of the protection which it otherwise afforded.

On the other hand, Lieutenant Colonel Zebulon Butler sent a written report to the Board of War in Philadelphia, dated July 10 and postmarked Gnadenhutten (Fort Allen, presently Lehighton): he had left Wilkes-Barre on July 4th, the day after the battle, arriving at Fort Allen a few days later.[202] In this report he said, in part, "After collecting about 300 of the most spirited of them, including Captain Hewitt's Company, I held a conference with the officers who were all agreed that it was best to attack the enemy before they got any further. We accordingly marched, found their situation, formed a front of the same extension as the enemy's, and attacked, from right to left at the same time. Our men stood the fire well for three or four shots, till some part of the enemy gave way; but, unfortunately for us through some mistake the word 'retreat' was understood from some officer on the left which took so quick that it was not in the power of the officers to form them again, though I believe if they had stood three minutes longer the enemy would have been beaten." He goes on later to say, "What number of the enemy were killed is yet uncertain, though I believe a very considerable number..."

As in most other battles in history, opposing and conflicting views of events appear, according to which side is the narrator. Regardless, the victory of the day belonged to the Rangers and Indians; for the Yankee settlers, the battle was lost.

During the subsequent thirty years, numerous accounts of the battle appeared in print. Charles Botta, the Italian historian, wrote a "History of the War for the Independence of the United States of America," which was translated into English and published in this country in 1820.[203] Many untruths of "fanciful and mythical" nature were to be found in this book. Extracts of this were published in the National Gazette (December 6, 1820) and a copy of this fell into the hands of General Lord Butler, the eldest son of Zebulon Butler, residing at the time in Wilkes-Barre. General Butler then wrote what he considered to be an accurate account of the events of July 3rd and 4th, and his document was attested to by Elijah Blackman, Rufus Bennet, and Matthias Hollenback, all of whom were living survivors in 1820. Those portions relating directly to the battle and the part played by Lieutenant Colonel Zebulon Butler were most likely accurate accounts. They can be accepted as final words on the subject from the American side. General Lord Butler[204] states "In the first place, Colonel Zebulon Butler, at the time spoken of, had not the command of the whole colony....He was a Lieutenant Colonel in Washington's Army, but, happening to be in this part of the country on a furlough, he was requested to give his assistance, and take the command of the men in case it should be necessary to fight....It is not true that Colonel

Zebulon Butler was drawn out of the fort by the lavish promises of his enemy that, if he would consent to a parley in the open field, the siege would be raised, and everything accommodated. Nor is it true that he marched out for *that* purpose, and from motives of caution took with him 400 men, well armed. The fact is, the only conference he marched out to was a battle; the only parley he expected was the point of the bayonet.

The whole number of men under his command that day was about 350, and it has since been ascertained that the enemy's force amounted to from 1,000 to 1,500. The battle was fought sooner than Colonel Butler wished. He advised delay, hoping to ascertain the force, position and intentions of the enemy, hoping that succor would arrive, and that he then would be able to meet the enemy to more advantage. But as he had no right to the submission of either the officers or their men, he was obliged to forego his own opinion, and to consent to lead them on. Another circumstance obliged him to take this course. There were some brave men among them, who were as rash and imprudent as they were brave, who were determined to fight that day, or leave the fort and return to their homes.

So, far from the Americans having been "surprised" by the British and Indians...had it not been for the imprudence of a few men sent forward as an advance guard, in firing on some Indians whom they discovered setting fire to a house, the enemy themselves would in all probability have been taken by surprise, and obliged to engage under many disadvantages."

Concerning the ambush and Indian torture, Stone[205] has this to say: "Even when most cruel they (Indians) have been practicing the trade of war—always dreadful—as much in conformity to their own images and laws, as have their more civilized antagonists. The white historian has drawn them with the characteristics of demons."

Stone draws attention to the fact that the Indians have had no writers to relate their own side of the story. Every warrior, in shaving his head for battle, was careful to leave the lock of defiance on his crown, as if to say to his enemy—take it if you can. Taking the scalp was, to him, the sign of victory; the stake and torture were identified with his concept of the power of endurance.

The Battle of Wyoming was lost. On the American side, the tactic employed led to defeat. Even with numerical superiority, it is likely that they would have been defeated—just as were the greatly superior forces of General Braddock near Fort Duquesne. The British forces at Wyoming demonstrated superior tactical skill which was enhanced by the intelligence gained by their Indian scouts. Whether a tenacious stand within their fortress would have favored the Americans is totally a matter of conjecture. What seems certain is that a tactical blunder was committed by these brave and courageous men; it was done in desperation and panic, reflecting the lack of careful planning and preparation for what was recognized to be inevitable conflict on this frontier.

The ultimate responsibility for this tragedy rests upon the Congress, which was repeatedly informed of the threatening situation by the settlers and by several officers serving in the Continental Army with homes at Wyoming. There is one other aspect of this affair which seems worth mentioning: the governing body and the governor of Pennsylvania had no warm feelings of support for the Connecticut settlers at Wyoming. In fact, the Pennamites had tried repeatedly to oust them prior to the beginning of the revolution. There would be more such attempts in the years ahead. Such a smouldering animosity could have influenced the Congress and the War Board to reject the many pleas for help, but the War Board had to consider overall troop requirements in this war for independence, of which the battle at Wyoming was but one aspect.

CHAPTER 13

Aftermath of the Battle of Wyoming

Survivors Reassess Situation

When Thomas Bennet arrived back at the fort, he found everyone in a state of alarm. He paced back and forth, reflecting the mood of his companions. His own concern was heightened because his son, Solomon, then age twenty-one, had remained with the advancing soldiers. Bennet was a man of strong will, but he was no stoic; he listened to the musket and rifle fire in the distance, heard it diminish, then cease. He sensed disaster and shouted "our boys will all be cut to pieces."[206]

As evening approached, some surviving fugitives began to straggle into the fort. Colonel Franklin, who was on his march from Huntington, states in his report "...we hastened on with all speed, and found on arriving at Forty Fort that a battle had been fought, and Colonels Butler and Denison, with fifteen or twenty others, had, in their retreat, gained the fort. Colonel Butler tarried there but a very short time, when he crossed the river to Wilkes-Barre."[207]

The night of July 3rd was clear and would ordinarily have been restful at the fort. But alas, the anguish and the grief over lost loved ones mixed with the fear of imminent attack by the savage enemy, and prevented sleep that night. No attack developed.

With the clear dawn of a new day, the surviving women, children and old men were forced to go about the simple tasks of housekeeping within the acre plot of the fort. Reduced now to about three or four hundred persons, no one was allowed to leave without permission of Lieutenant Colonel Denison, who was still in command. There was fresh water to be carried up from the spring, which lay just off the southeast corner of the fort on the river's edge. Provisions were also available in the underground chamber which had been dug out during the previous year when astute leaders anticipated a state of siege. These basics of food and water were enough to sustain the survivors for about two weeks.

Many of these details were attended to by the women, the men rotating a constant lookout and guard through each twenty-four hour period. Most of the latter were the old men of the settlement, plus a few survivors of the massacre who had straggled back to the fort during the evening of July 3rd and the long night that followed.

Thomas Bennet and his wife were fearful that their eldest son, Solomon, had been killed or taken prisoner. As of early morning, July 4, he had not returned. As morning passed into afternoon, a weary and exhausted Solomon suddenly appeared at a gate of the fort. Having been on the right flank of the little army with Captain Bidlack's company, he had fled to the nearby river with savages in hot pursuit. At one point he was nearly captured by a pursuing Indian. He had but a single lead ball left in his pouch, and quickly loaded his gun. With deadly aim, he felled his pursuer, then made a dash for the river. Here he encountered Matthias Hollenback, who had lost his clothing in the melee. He loaned half of his own to Matthias (which half we will never know)—and together they proceeded down river to Wilkes-Barre fort. After resting there overnight, Solomon crossed the river again and walked back to Forty Fort. [208]

Male Bennets Leave Wyoming

That afternoon, the Bennet family held a conference. Peck[209] states, "When it was ascertained that arrangements were in progress for a capitulation, Solomon Bennet said 'I will never give myself up to an Indian.' Mrs. Bennet then demanded, 'What will you do then?' and added 'you must clear out immediately.' Thomas then expressed some doubts as to his own fate, when Mrs. Bennet answered 'You must go too.' Andrew, a lad about 11 years old, began to cry when the mother said with emphasis, 'and you must go too, for if we are all killed, you can do us no good.' Accordingly all three left for Stroudsburg that afternoon."

The trio was not alone. Setting out over the "lower" road through Bear Swamp, "fugitives were flying in every direction to the wilderness, and all was confusion, consternation, and horror. The only hope of safety seemed to be in flight. The several passages through the swamp were thronged."[210] Nevertheless the male Bennets did reach Stroudsburg, remaining there for a few weeks, expecting to meet Mrs. Bennet and the two daughters.

Meanwhile, events back at the fort moved relentlessly toward destruction. The terms of capitulation were drawn up on July 4th, but Colonel Denison delayed signing until the next day. He wanted time to warn all the continental soldiers that they would be required to give themselves over to the Tories as prisoners. As a result, all of them, including Colonel Zebulon Butler, departed from the area at once. The terms of capitulation were, under the circumstances, quite reasonable – the second item stated "the inhabitants are to occupy their farms, peaceably, and the lives of the inhabitants preserved entire and unhurt." It was no doubt because of this statement that many families stayed on in the fort during those trying days.

Capitulation and Destruction

Martha Bennet and her two daughters were among those who hung on, hoping that they would really be permitted to return to their home. The papers of capitulation were signed at 4 p.m. July 5th. The signing took place in the Bennet cabin, which had a small but adequate table adaptable to this purpose. The table was donated years ago to the Wyoming Historical Society.

On that day, Major Butler marched his Indians into the fort in regular order, and, after drilling them a little, dismissed them. No one was molested and they soon departed. But they returned the following day and began several days of plunder and mischief. Colonel Denison resided in the Bennet cabin during these days and on several occasions he remonstrated with Major John Butler over the conduct of his Indians. But Butler had obviously lost control and could do nothing with them.[211]

Peck[212] states "The Indians were now worse than ever. They came into our house, and a stout Indian claimed Colonel Denison's hunting shirt, a very nice one, made of fine forty linen, with a double cape, fringed around the waist. The Colonel objected; but, upon the Indian raising his tomahawk, and mother (Mrs. Bennet) begging him to give it up, he consented. While she was unbuttoning the wristbands the Colonel stepped back, and Polly (Bennet) who sat by me, received a package of money from his pocket. It was the town money, in Continental bills; it afterward did the needy much good."

Peck continues to quote Miss Martha: "Captain Henry, an old Indian who had lived upon terms of intimacy with our family, and who was a prisoner in the fort when it was given up, came in with father's fine broadcloth coat on, which he had taken from the family chest. 'Where old Bennet?' Mother replied 'Gone through the swamp to Stroudsburg.' 'Ah,' says he, 'me old Bennet now. Where Solomon, that good marksman?' 'Gone to Stroudsburg.' 'Where Andrew, the little boy?' The same answer."

Plundering of this nature became a daily experience, and about one week after the battle, smoke began to arise from the burning houses of the settlement. Smoke arose from all quarters at the same time. A party of widows, with Mrs. Bennet, visited the battle ground in an unsuccessful attempt to identify the bodies of their loved ones, but they returned with the everlasting memory of an awful spectacle of the "mangled and wasted bodies of their neighbors, brothers and husbands."

During these few weeks, the Bennets and others had some hope that General Washington would send a relief column of sufficient strength to chastise the Indians and to drive them away. On July 8th, Major Butler rapidly withdrew to Niagara, probably on orders from higher command. With him went the majority of the Indians, but a number of them remained behind to continue the plunder and destruction of the settlements in Wyoming.

Martha Bennet

About this time, Miss Martha Bennet took passage by canoe down the river with Colonel Denison, arriving at Sunbury the next day. There she joined a party of between thirty and forty other fugitives quartered together in a house. Alarmed by the rumor of savage and hostile Indians roving the west branch of the Susquehanna, some of these fugitives prepared to go across the mountains to Fort Penn (Stroudsburg). Miss Bennet accepted an invitation to go with them.

The party took off on foot, with a small cart drawn by a yoke of oxen, carrying some baggage and small children, and providing assistance for the ill. They walked about seventy-five miles, almost all of this through wilderness. Miss Bennet wore through her single pair of shoes and her feet were cut and bruised, leaving blood on the path as she covered the distance. Miss Bennet states "We made ourselves as happy as possible, amusing ourselves with telling stories and singing songs." They encountered no Indians along the way, but did spend one overnight in an abandoned house. "Most of the goods were removed, but they made a supper of bread and milk, and lay down upon sacking bottoms from which the beds had been removed."[213] The party arrived in Stroudsburg after three and one half days of foot travel, weary but relieved.

Mrs. Bennet and Polly Among Last to Leave Wyoming Valley

During this period, Mrs. Bennet and her five-year-old daughter, Polly, remained at the fort. Soon after Miss Martha had left, more and more Indians came in, many of them unfriendly and not trustworthy. They remained completely out of control, daily plundering and burning but not harming any of the inhabitants of the fort.

Finally, about two weeks after the battle, Mrs. Bennet and Polly walked over the mountain in company with Major Pierce and his family. Peck[214] states that, "They were perhaps the last of the settlers who were left." On the other hand Brewster[215] states that "The last to leave Forty Fort were James Sutton and the Lemuel Gustins and their families. They took boards and timbers from deserted cabins and built a large boat which it took them nine days to complete, and upon this embarked with their families and belongings and floated down the river as far as Middletown."

Polly later recalled some of the flight over the mountain. She had to walk the entire distance on foot, there being no beast of burden in the company. "She remembered camping out, or rather lying on the ground under the open heavens, in what has been called the 'Shades of Death.' Hungry and weary they laid themselves upon the bare ground."[216] Most of the refugees leaving Wyoming Valley used the Lower Road, which passed through Solomon's Gap and then northeast along the base of Wilkes-Barre Mountains. About eleven and one-half miles along this path, it entered Bear Swamp and traversed it for about one and one-half miles, crossing Bear Creek midway. Then two and one-quarter miles further it entered the Great

Swamp and crossed it for fifteen miles. The depths of these swamps were alive with huge rattlesnakes, wolves, panthers, wild cats and foxes. In season, and it was then summer, biting and stinging insects were everywhere.

The path was choked at places with fleeing women, children, and an occasional man. Several deaths are said to have occurred from panic, fatigue, hunger and exposure. Miner states[217] "By what sufferings and torture many died, the world will never know." One part of the Great Swamp was particularly dreary and dismal, and, because so many fell and perished in the mire and among the brambles, it was called "The Shades of Death."[218]

What the British Accomplished

The settlement of Wyoming was now abandoned. The valley presented one wild scene of conflagration and ruin. Major Butler's description of his accomplishments includes the following: "On our side we have taken and destroyed eight palisaded forts, and burned about 1,000 dwelling houses, all their mills, etc. We have also killed and drove off about 1,000 head of cattle, and sheep and swine in great number."[219]

Loss of lives for the Americans was not restricted to the active combatants. The loss of possessions was critical, and for most this meant the survivors had nothing left but the clothes they were wearing. In addition, all the town records were lost, including a number of documents describing land ownership.

The British had accomplished the destruction of this frontier settlement, denying the Continental army any of its food production, and laying bare to attack the settlements along the Delaware and those further south along the Susquehanna River. This strategic advantage was never pursued by the enemy, and populous areas east and south of Wyoming were never challenged by British forces. This ultimately allowed the Continental army to concentrate its efforts elsewhere, despite the exposed flank of the western frontier.

CHAPTER 14

Fugitives from the Battle of Wyoming

Stroudsburg Receives the Fugitives

For most of the fugitives from the valley of Wyoming, the first destination of choice was Stroudsburg. The Yankee-Pennamite War had created sharp enmity between the Connecticut settlers and some of their neighboring Pennsylvanians. Stroudsburg, however, was known to be friendly and to favor the Yankees, a fact which no doubt influenced their choice of rendezvous.

The history of Stroudsburg prepared its residents for tolerance to the refugees. The area had been settled originally in 1725 when Nicholas Dupuis built a large stone house in lower Smithfield township. In about 1737, Daniel Brodhead acquired 1,500 acres to the southwest of the Shawnee settlement, and laid out a town over a mile square at the junction of Analomink (Brodhead's) and Pocono Creeks. He called this Dansbury, as a personal memorial. Fifteen years later, this became Stroudsburg. [220]

In 1755, Fort Hamilton was built here and was for a few years garrisoned by Provincial troops. During the French and Indian War the fort was destroyed, and many of the area's inhabitants were driven off or massacred. Some of the survivors settled again in and around ruins of the fort.[221] Ultimately a new fort, Fort Penn, was erected and by 1775 there was a garrison of 127 men under Captain Jacob Stroud, who was sympathetic to the land claims of the Connecticut settlers.[222]

When the fugitives from the battle of Wyoming straggled into town, there was widespread sympathy and concern made manifest by the offering of food and shelter by the inhabitants. But Fort Penn and Stroudsburg were also frontier posts, now made even more vulnerable to invasion from the north through the byway of the Delaware River. Consternation and fear spread through the community. The commander of Fort Penn, Captain Alexander Patterson, lent his voice to the growing pleas for adequate reinforcements as well as for a new defense plan for his exposed frontier.

Among the early fugitives to reach Stroudsburg were Thomas Bennet and his two sons. Departing Wyoming on July 4th, they fled directly to Stroudsburg, very likely arriving in that area no later than July 8th. The Bennet family had decided to attempt a rendezvous here and the male members would await the arrival of Martha Bennet and her two daughters.

Stroudsburg was also to be the rendezvous for Lieutenant Colonel Zebulon Butler and Captain Spaulding. Spaulding had been able to reach a point within thirteen miles of Wyoming by July 4th, the day after the battle. From his advanced scouts, he learned of the defeat of the settlers and the widespread destruction of the settlement. Perceiving that his single company of men could do nothing to relieve the situation, he marched his men rapidly to Stroudsburg.[223]

Lieutenant Colonel Butler departed Wyoming on July 4th and arrived at Fort Allen, Gnadenhutten, a few days later. A letter arrived from Colonel Timothy Pickering of the War Board in Philadelphia, under date of July 15, 1778, advising Colonel Butler to take what troops he had and march to join Captain Spaulding at Stroudsburg.[224] Upon receipt of this note, he moved at once to Fort Penn, where he took command of Spaulding's Westmoreland Independent Company, as well as such of the Westmoreland Militia who came that way on their flight from Wyoming Valley.

Claim to Wyoming Again at Issue

There was great apprehension among the surviving Connecticut men that the Wyoming lands would be confiscated by the Pennamites. The common sentiment is seen in the closing note of a letter written July 28, 1778, by Colonel Nathan Denison: "I find that there is numbers of people in this state (Pennsylvania) desire to take advantage of our distressed situation to get possession of our settlement, which I think cannot be allowed of ..."[225] It was during this same period, soon after the arrival of Major Pierce's Company of fugitives, that Mrs. Bennet heard a young Philadelphia lawyer uttering terrible threats against the Yankees, declaring "that he would go to

Wyoming with a Company, and a Yankee should not set foot upon the ground."[226]

These concerns over possession were based not only upon local gossip and rumor. The power and influence of the Pennamites is revealed in an official communication dated August 7, 1778, from the Supreme Executive Council to the Pennsylvania Assembly, as follows: "The late fatal catastrophe which has befallen the Connecticut settlers on the river Susquehanna, deplorable as it is, recollects the disputed footing on which these sufferers stood. Compassion for them, as well as justice to this state, require that they be reminded of the precarious nature of their tenure, before they reassemble themselves."[227]

Despite these concerns over possession, the War Board came under considerable pressure to do something for the protection of this extensive and vulnerable frontier. Much of this pressure came from prestigious Pennsylvanians, an example of which is a letter of August 24, 1778, from Robert Levers, Esquire, of Easton, to The Supreme Executive Council, stating in part: "The county of Wyoming, when settled, formed a good barrier for a considerable part of the interior settlements of Northampton County, and for some part of Northumberland.... If I may presume to deliver my sentiments with freedom and without offense, there seems to be a necessity for supporting the post at Wyoming for the preservation of the interior of the country; for if Wyoming should become a rendezvous for the enemy, the country within will be everlastingly in danger, and the least alarm throw all in confusion. But as the late great settlement of Wyoming is now destroyed by the devastations and depredations of the Tories and Indians, an important question will arise, wherein the interest and peace of the several states may be involved."[228]

During this period, the War Board had put together an overall plan for the defense of this frontier. The chief points of this plan were: to send a regiment under Colonel Hartley to Sunbury, where a fresh Indian attack was anticipated; to charge Lieutenant Colonel Butler with responsibility to gather as many men as possible, to provide them with arms and ammunition, and to proceed to Wilkes-Barre as soon as possible; to develop a larger body of troops for a punitive expedition against the enemy in western New York State.

Yankees Return to Wyoming

By late July, a total force of 113 men assembled under Lieutenant Colonel Butler, comprising seventy-eight men of Captain Spaulding's Company and thirty-four men from the militia under the immediate command of Dr. William Hooker Smith. All of these men had been part of the Connecticut settlement and were eager for the opportunity to return to what had been their homes. Recognizing the need for an immediate return to Wyoming, the War Board decided to use this Yankee force, because it knew the territory and it could be relied upon to hold the post at Wyoming, regardless of hardship. The War Board's need to use this Yankee force exceeded whatever sentiment there was to deny the Wyoming lands to them.

Providing these men with arms, ammunition, clothing and food was more difficult than giving the orders to proceed. On July 30, 1778, Colonel Denison sent a letter to Colonel Butler while still at Fort Penn; which is quoted in part: "I applied to Colonel Stroud this morning for arms and ammunition for our people. He replied that he had not more than one hundred or one hundred and fifty of led in stoar but expected a waggenload of ammunition from Allentown soon; so that we need not expected to be supplyed from this stoar; as to arms he says he has about one hundred which he had from Colonel Hooper and wants direction of them..." Colonel Denison later remarks "There is a scheem on foot for the Pennsilvaney People to git Possession of our settlement."[229]

Lieutenant Colonel Butler led his men out of Stroudsburg on August 2nd. Thomas and Solomon Bennet were both members of this task force, with young Andrew following along with his father. The march was toilsome but the season of the year favored rapid progress. Butler was careful to provide constant scouting to avoid ambush by the savages. On August 4th, the party halted at Bullock's abandoned farmhouse, about nine miles from the valley. Up to this point, they had encountered no Indians. In order to secure his entry into the valley, Lieutenant Colonel Butler sent forward two small detachments to reconnoiter—one under command of Bennet's friend, Matthias Hollenback, and the other under the command of Lieutenant John Jenkins, Jr. Hollenback's group moved to the south, entering the valley near Nanticoke Falls. They flushed a small party of Indians, wounding one and chasing the others into the woods. One of the men captured and salvaged an abandoned canoe; without further opposition Hollenback's party marched north to Wilkes-Barre. Lieutenant Jenkins' party marched from Bullock's north to the mouth of the Lackawanna River, then turned down river toward Wilkes-Barre. They also discovered a small party of Indians who fled rapidly into the woods.

On August 4th, the two scouting groups met the main body of Lieutenant Colonel Butler's command in the ruins of what had been Wilkes-Barre. Evening was approaching and a temporary camp with posted guards had to suffice. In the morning, a large and intact log house was discovered on the east side of Main street, below Northampton. This became headquarters and within a few days was surrounded by a palisade of pickets.

Female Bennets Flee for Safety

It was during this same period that Martha Bennet and her two daughters left Stroudsburg to go to Goshen, New York, where the Bennets had many friends. Here they took up residence with a Captain John Bull, an old gray-headed man with a large family.[230] Mrs. Bennet busied herself with the spinning wheel, doing two days' work in one, while Martha hired out doing housework for fifty cents a week. They made much needed clothes, some of which they sold, while others they sent to Wyoming for Thomas and the two boys.

Early in the spring of 1779, Mrs. Bennet and her daughters went to Bethlehem, Connecticut, where lived her brother, Samuel Jackson. The Bennets had several area friends of longstanding in this small village about ten miles south of Litchfield. This trip was facilitated by the generous help of Captain Bull, who sent his horse part of the way. Each member of the party took a turn riding this horse while the others walked. They remained in the Litchfield area until their return to Wyoming in the early part of 1780, by which time they had accumulated some savings set aside from weekly earnings.

CHAPTER 15

Yankees Return to Wyoming

Holding the detachment together

The return of Lieutenant Colonel Butler's detachment to Wilkes-Barre the evening of August 4, 1778, ushered in a period of great hardship for the settlement. Of this period Brewster[231] states "...there is little to record except a number of atrocious murders and the grim determination of the surviving settlers to return to the fertile lands." This was indeed one of the most critical periods to be experienced by these same settlers, as is revealed in the following extract from the "Orderly Book" of Lieutenant Colonel Butler dated August 7, 1778: "Our present situation appears rather dangerous and alarming, and the little remaining prospect of our crops depends on our maintaining this Post and keeping possession of the country, therefore every person will consider himself under the strongest tie and obligation to do his utmost in the defense of the place against the common enemy. And as it is impossible that we can make ourselves formidable in any degree without submitting ourselves to good order and discipline, therefore the martial law is to be strictly adhered to, and obeyed as well by the militia as (by the) continental troops and all who join the detachment under the command of Colonel Butler.

"The previous practice of strolling about in small parties, and absenting themselves without leave, is not only hurtful to good order but dangerous; therefore, the Colonel forbids it in the most strongest manner. And because complaints have been exhibited that some evil persons have been plundering and making wastes of what little private property has escaped the merciless hands of our common enemy, the Colonel forbids, in the most positive manner, any kind of plundering or making waste of property—as killing sheep, swine, or poultry; or in any manner injuring the interest of any man...

"For the future the guard is to be relieved at 6 o'clock in the morning, and the roll is to be called twice a day, viz: morning and evening. It is expected that the officers will be particularly attentive to see that the above order be complied with...all who are found guilty of the break of this order may expect to suffer the consequences of martial law in their cases."[232]

Discipline was maintained with care, the punishment of infractions meted out where needed. Absenteeism, drunkeness, gambling, killing and destroying livestock, slovenliness—all occurred frequently enough to warrant specific orders from Colonel Butler. Punishment varied. Reduction in rank, lashes to the bare back, and standing several minutes on a sharp picket with bare feet, are all described in these orders. All punishment was carried out at evening retreat, before the entire detachment.

The detachment was a mixture of soldiers and settlers, the latter enrolled in the militia comprising sixty or seventy men. The militia was well armed and was employed in securing the crops, gathering livestock, gathering firewood, and erecting temporary shelters. Small groups of armed men performed these and other general work assignments for the detachment, always reporting back to the camp headquarters at day's end. Several of these were older men belonging to the Alarm List of the 24th Connecticut Regiment formed in Wyoming by the settlers. Some, like Thomas Bennet, cared for crops and livestock of their own, and generally tried to create living quarters for the return of their families.

During the early weeks of the "return," the only soldiers kept at the post were from Captain Spaulding's Company, consisting of seventy-eight men including eleven officers. As of August 14, Colonel Butler[233] states, "We have sixty or seventy of the militia, this place well armed. I expect more daily, but they are employed in securing the crops, so that I have only Captain Spaulding's Company to do all the scouting and guarding..." This force was augmented in late August by the arrival of ninety-one men from Easton, commanded by Captain George Bush—detached from the regiment of Colonel Hartley, at that time stationed in Sunbury.

Colonel Hartley's Expedition

The force assembled at Camp Westmoreland was placed under the overall command of Colonel Thomas Hartley, but for the most part Colonel Butler was allowed a considerable amount of independence during the ensuing fall and winter. However, on September 13th, Butler was ordered to supply a detachment of 150 men to march with Colonel Hartley on an expedition into what is now Bradford County, making a circuit of nearly 300 miles. Colonel Hartley described this expedition in his narrative report to Congress, excerpts of which follow: "...the troops met at Muncy Fort on 18th September, and they amounted to only about 200 rank and file ....On the morning of the 21st, at 4 o'clock, we marched carrying twelve days' provisions. We met with great rains and prodigious swamps, mountains, defiles, etc. We waded or swam the river Lycoming upwards of twenty times. In lonely woods and groves we found the haunts and lurking places of the savage murderers who had desolated our frontier. We saw the huts where they had dressed and dried the scalps of the helpless women and children who had fell in their hands..."[234]

Hartley's Expedition had a limited success. Colonel Hartley states "Considering our number we pushed our good fortune as far as we dare, we gave present relief to the frontiers and turned back the barbarians from deluging our country with the blood of helpless mothers and infants. They are a strange enemy, they shun danger when among us, but near their own country they fight brave..."

Colonel Hartley returned to Wilkes-Barre on October 1, 1778. His men had a most arduous and exhausting experience. They had faced the enemy on several occasions and "behaved well to a man." Their arms were simple, consisting of muskets and bayonets, not likely to yield accuracy of fire. According to Hartley his men were no great marksmen and were awkward at woods fighting. After the distribution and sale of some plunder, Colonel Hartley and his immediate command left for Sunbury on October 3rd, leaving Lieutenant Colonel Butler once again commanding officer at Wilkes-Barre. In his narrative, quoted above, Hartley concluded as follows: "...I would respectfully propose that Congress would be pleased to send a Connecticut regiment to garrison Wyoming as soon as possible. It is but 120 miles from Fishkill... I have given all the support in my power to that post, but if troops are not immediately sent there settlements will be destroyed in detail. I left one half of my detachment there with five of my own officers..."

The detachment at Wyoming grew slowly after October and November 1778. The work performed fell into several categories other than guard duty and daily scouting. The men had to be self sufficient, and thus there was a constant forage for provisions. Scattered domestic animals roamed the valley after the massacre, and running these down was a daily task. Pigs, sheep, cattle and horses were found and fenced. Some of these were slaughtered to provide edible meat. Some wild game and fish supplemented this domestic supply. There were scattered areas of rye grain needing harvesting. Good fresh water was in constant supply from the numerous springs. On October 3rd, Colonel Butler appointed his seventeen year old son, Lord Butler, to be quartermaster. Mason Fitch Alden was appointed forage master. These two men soon instilled a sense of order into the gathering and sharing of provisions.[235]

In a series of letters to the Board of War, Colonel Butler expressed great need for clothing, flour, salt and medicines, plus a man to perform as a physician. His letter of October 30, 1778, as follows: "...I think if they (Indians) should come we have such a fortification that with some more ammunition we can defend against large bodies...(I) should be very glad that there might be an order (from the War Board) for (necessities) to be forwarded as soon as possible and as there is some expense for forage the horses...should be glad that Captain Spalding might have liberty to purchase some necessary clothing for myself and the other officers in the Continental store and that he might be furnished with sufficient orders for clothing for the troops as there is not any to be had hear..."[236]

The overall health of the detachment and of the few settlers was good. There were no outbreaks of life threatening disease. Dysentery and respiratory infections were common afflictions, but medicine was scarce and non-specific. Trained physicians were a rarity during the American Revolution, but fortunately in the Wyoming detachment was Captain William Hooker Smith, a physician by training, also in command of a company of militia. His presence may have helped to maintain cleanliness, reasonable nutrition, and proper encampment, all advocated by Benjamin Rush as preventive measures for troops in the field.[237]

Construction of a New Fort

The construction of a new fort was begun October 3, 1778, the site chosen being on about 1/2 acre of ground between the western end of present Northampton Street and the river. This new fort was "built by laying two rows of logs horizontally, four feet apart and filling the entire space between with earth, well tamped down. The solid wall - six or more feet in thickness was carried to a height of seven feet, and all around the inside of the square enclosure...a platform or bench was built, standing upon which the occupants of the fort were able to deliver their fire...All around the outside of the wall a ditch was dug, and beyond this was placed an abattis, formed by setting firmly in the ground, in a row, the tops of pitch pine trees with their (sharpened) boughs pointed outwards."[238] Embrasures for cannon were added at several points in the wall, and the four corners were rounded for full range of fire. Cabins and barracks were built within the enclosure. All of this work was completed by the end of October 1778.

Indian Raids

Security remained a constant problem for the detachment. During the fall, winter and spring of 1778-1779 there was a gradual return to the area of settlers attempting to create shelters for their families. These were under constant threat of savage attack, and they were vulnerable because the detachment could not provide protection without dangerously depleting the manning of the fort. Between August and December 1778, twenty-three persons were killed and five more were taken prisoners.[239] In each instance, a small band of Indians would lie in ambush and pounce at the settler, then scalp and murder him. Occasionally victims would be in groups of two or three, but usually the victim would be alone and defenseless.

There was one major savage attack in force on March 23, 1779, when roughly 250 Indians attempted to overwhelm the new fort. With fire from small arms and from the cannon, the settlers repelled this band of Indians without taking serious casualties. This was to be the last Indian attack in force upon this frontier settlement.[240]

Securing the Outpost

As spring approached, news spread that General Washington was planning a major offensive against the Iroquois, using the settlement at Wyoming as the base. The detachment and settlers felt great relief that help in strength would at last arrive. They had performed a most important function, holding the little outpost secure during this critical fall and winter of 1778-1779. Arriving at the deserted settlement one month after the savage battle of Wyoming, they had successfully reestablished an enduring presence. Most of those men on the site were Connecticut settlers and soldiers, a fact to become of significance in the contest for land claims a few years ahead.

CHAPTER 16
The Sullivan Expedition

General John Sullivan

A punitive military expedition against the Indians had been under consideration by General Washington for several months. On March 6, 1779, Washington wrote to General John Sullivan from his headquarters at Middlebrook, New Jersey: "Congress having determined upon an expedition of an extensive nature against the hostile tribes of the Indians of the Six Nations, the command is offered to Major General Gates as senior officer; but, should he decline, it is my wish it should devolve upon you...."[241] Gates did not accept this assignment; it then went to General Sullivan.

Sullivan, then age forty, was considered an able general by Washington. "Brave, energetic, resourceful, the fiery Sullivan ...brought to his posts in the Army a keen desire to be of service. His failures during the war—and they were not inconsiderable—came more from bad luck than from incompetency."[242] He had failed at Long Island and at Brandywine, but had been a great success at the brilliant victories of Trenton and Princeton. His intense desire to be a success had frequently made him pester his superiors for more troops and supplies when they were really not needed or not available. He liked to brag about his accomplishments—a trait which caused offense among some of his peers. Sullivan's steadfast loyalty to the patriots' cause and undying devotion to General Washington created a bond which endeared him to the latter. Washington wanted a young and vigorous leader who could conduct his command to fit the stealthful tactics of the Indian warriors. His choice of Sullivan was to prove to be well taken.

Upon receipt of Washington's letter, Sullivan hastened to headquarters to develop the plan of attack. They discussed mission and tactics, paths to be taken, quality and number of troops, and the critical matter of supplies, always constricted and deficient. Washington had already collected a number of maps and scouting reports, which he turned over to Sullivan.

The immediate problems facing them were to determine which route the army would take to enter the land of the Six Nations, and the best way to move a large army, well supplied, into a wilderness. Washington wanted the main thrust to go along the Susquehanna River by way of Tioga, since this was the most direct and shortest route. It also had the advantage of providing a large waterway to transport much needed supplies. Sullivan's first reaction was to send the main body of 4,000 men into the Indian country by the Mohawk Valley, thus cutting off and encircling the body of Indians. By the next morning, he had decided to use the Susquehanna because of the greater ease of moving supplies along this route.

It was decided to rendezvous at Easton and to proceed from this point over the mountainous path to Wyoming. At the time, two roads had been developed. Colonel Zebulon Butler described them as follows: "As to the road to the Minisink. The upper "road" is from this garrison (at Wilkes-Barre) to Lackawanna, by the Susquehanna, nine miles to a large flat, deserted by our people; ten miles to Capouse Large Meadows and several stacks of grain—except it is burnt very lately; 23 miles to Lackaway, to a settlement deserted, but I believe forage plenty; 14 miles to Shohola, a settlement, large meadows and I believe, hay plenty; 14 miles to Well's Ferry (Dingman's?), opposite Captain Chamber on Delaware. The "lower road" 158 miles to Bullock's—house deserted by owner, small meadows, no forage; 27 miles to Larned's—some improvements but much eat out by travellers; 8 miles to Colonel Stroud's; 37 miles to Well's Ferry, on the west side of Delaware...The "upper road" has been much used with carts and waggons, and the lower road has not been used with carriages at all."[243]

With Easton as the point of departure, the more direct route was the lower road, and this would require considerable work before it could be used as a military conduit for troops, and their supporting train of artillery, baggage and supplies.

Roughly 500 men were assigned the work of building the "Sullivan Road" beginning in the middle of May. The sixty-five and one-half miles of road from Easton to Fort Wyoming

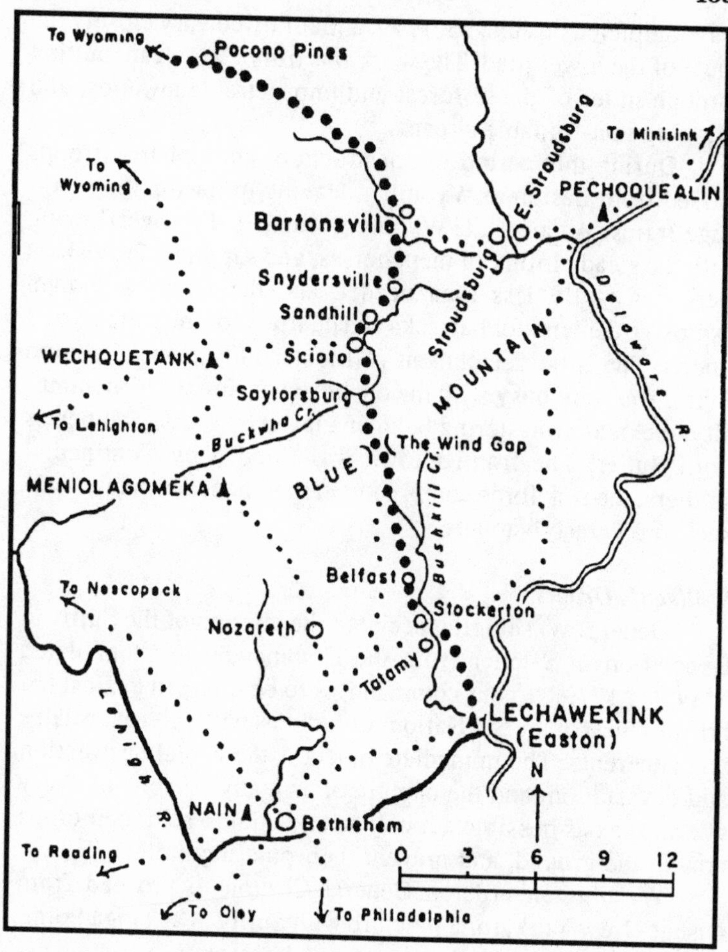

Map showing a portion of Sullivan's Road from Easton to Pocono Pines. With permission from Paul A. Wallace, *Indian Paths of Pennsylvania*, p. 157

For a detailed map of the Sullivan Road, see Map 48 in the collections of the Wyoming Historical and Geological Society. It was drawn by Lt. Benjamin Lodge in 1779 but is not reproducible.

was completed on June 13, 1779, and followed very closely the route of the lower road. The work was truly Herculean, cutting through miles of dense forest and impenetrable swamps, and bridging non-fordable streams. [244]

During this period of construction, units of foot troops passed from Easton to Wyoming, leaving in Easton their baggage trains. As a result, Wyoming was filled to overflowing with the steady influx of men, horses, and supplies. Provisions were constantly less than needed and there was a sudden explosive demand for barracks and quarters for the officers and troops. The little detachment of Lieutenant Colonel Zebulon Butler was kept busy with the onsite expansion of the community, the quartermastering being managed by the detachment's Lord Butler. The frontier town was flooded by Continental soldiers, the task force comprising Frenchmen, Germans, Yankees and Pennsylvanians.

Sullivan's Orders

General Washington declared the mission of the Sullivan Expedition in a letter from the Commander-in-Chief dated May 31, 1779: "(Your command) is to be directed against the hostile tribes of the Six Nations of Indians, with their associates and adherents. The immediate object is their total destruction and devastation, and the capture of as many persons of every age and sex as possible. (It will be essential to ruin their crops now in the ground, and prevent their planting more.)"[245]

Washington ordered General Clinton to proceed from Otsego, New York, for a juncture with Sullivan at Tioga Point. His mission would be the same—total destruction and devastation with the capture of as many persons as possible.

As to tactics Washington advised a posture of aggressive attack accompanied by shouting and whooping, using bayonets wherever possible. He also instructed Sullivan to use an "extraordinary degree of vigilance and caution to guard against surprises from an adversary so secret, desultory, and rapid as the Indians." He was cautioned to move his troops as swiftly as possible, losing no time transporting heavy and cumbersome equipment. Depots of unnecessary equipment were to be left behind at appropriate places.

For this mission, it was thought that roughly 3,000 troops would be needed. Early in April, General Washington assigned to this task the German Regiment, Armands Corps, Captain Schott's Corps, and what Pennsylvanians could be spared. These were all soldiers of the Continental Line, combat veterans hardened to field maneuvers. No militia was included. The troops were from Maryland, New Jersey and Pennsylvania, some of the latter likely to bear some prejudice against the Connecticut people already on site. In this regard President Reed of Pennsylvania wrote to Colonel Samuel Hunter: "...We have now only to add that, as it is a time of common danger, we would recommend to you to cultivate harmony and a good understanding with the people at Wyoming, leaving our unhappy disputes in that quarter to be settled as peace and more favorable circumstances will permit."[246]

When the first troops arrived at Wyoming they found desolation, burned and ruined houses, and many fatherless children and orphans. Gardens and fields were overgrown with weeds and brushes, the overall scene one of melancholy. The river was crystal clear, the land exceedingly fertile, the climate cool and temperate.

The scene was abruptly changed to accommodate the soldiers and their supplies. With feverish activity, a number of barracks and new log houses were built. Horse sheds, warehouses, a large bake house and several smoke houses were constructed in a matter of a few weeks. Most of this encampment was on the east side of the river (now Wilkes-Barre), but General Poor's command was on the west side at Forty Fort.

Supplying the Expedition Forces

Supplying this body became an intense and serious operation. Some of the needed material came from Easton over the Sullivan Road. A large volume came up the river from Sunbury, transported in large bateux in fleets of thirty or more. By July 24th, a fleet of 134 boats loaded with provisions of all kinds had been assembled. These had been laboriously poled upstream to Wilkes-Barre by at least two polemen per boat, each fleet escorted by a protective detachment of soldiers advancing along shore in advance of the main body of vessels. Flour, meat, and ammunition were funneled in this fashion from supply points downriver.

Some resistance to providing supply was manifest from Pennsylvanians down river. "Many people in Pennsylvania had opposed the Expedition from the first .... The Pennamite party ...did not hesitate to express their dissatisfaction...that the Indians should keep the (hated intruders) out of the disputed territory until the war was over. This opposition began to show itself...in the lack of hearty cooperation and the failure to furnish either their quota of men or supplies for the Army."[247]

Brief Interlude

As is the style of troops in bivouac, a social life developed over the several weeks devoted to building up adequate stores, livestock, pack horses and provisions. Numerous regimental and brigade parties were held, with dinners, dancing on the green, and sundry games. Some of the men enjoyed several days of good fishing in the river, where swimming and bathing were also available and other military duties were carried out daily. Hunting was discouraged because of the widespread but sparse habitation.

One elaborate entertainment occurred on July 5th at Forty Fort. "General Poor extended a general invitation to officers of his brigade to be present, and also invited a number of officers from other commands...several of the principal inhabitants of Wilkes-Barre were there by invitation. Eighty-seven gentlemen in all attended, and a bountiful dinner was served in a booth about eighty feet long, constructed of spruce and hemlock bushes and having a marquee pitched at either end. A number of good songs were sung and the day was spent in mirth and jollity." [248] In all, thirteen separate toasts were drunk.

Gradually, the stores and supplies were assembled. Neither troop strength nor supplies were ever adequate in the opinion of General Sullivan, but he came under great pressure to launch his expedition, as ferocious Indian activities were reported to the north of his encampment. On July 24th he gave the order to be in readiness to move out: "The commissaries and quarter masters to have everything in perfect readiness as no excuse will be permitted for delay."[249] The order specified the disposition of about 2,000 pack horses, the pack men to be drawn in part from the wagoneers—all wagons to be left behind. In addition to the pack horses there were over 700 beef cattle and a large fleet of boats loaded with the artillery and stores. Actual departure took place on July 31st at noon, amidst much celebration. Lieutenant Colonel Butler was left in command of a small detachment to guard the settlement.

Details of the Sullivan expedition are available in several historical reviews, especially in Harvey (II, 1205-1220) and Whittemore's history of the expedition. Generals Sullivan and Clinton accomplished the mission of devastation given them by General Washington. The two forces joined at Tioga Point on August 22nd. Sullivan led his expedition as far as Genesee Castle, destroying all towns and crops along the way. The battle of Newtown was the sole conflict involving the entire army, and few casualties were inflicted upon the hastily retreating Indians. American casualties of the campaign totalled no more than forty men, and those of the enemy were also light.

Sullivan placed the number of towns destroyed at forty and was sure none remained in the Indian country except one near Genesee Castle. In addition to many vegetable gardens destroyed, the army had ruined about 160,000 bushels of corn.

The returning army arrived at Wyoming on October 7th and encamped on the ground they had previously occupied. The inhabitants gave the heroes a warm welcome and thirteen rounds of salute were fired from the cannon of the fort. On October 8th, a grand feast was provided by Colonel Zebulon Butler and on October 9th Sullivan set out for Easton. A detachment was left to garrison Wyoming. Schott's Corps, Captain Spaulding's Westmoreland Independent Company, the German Regiment, and a few additional troops were ordered to remain under the command of Colonel Zebulon Butler. In late October, the German regiment was ordered to Sunbury to help garrison Fort Augusta. This reduced the Wyoming garrison to less than 200 officers and men, "Comprising Schott's Corps, Spaulding's Company, Lieutenant Obadiah Gore, one sergeant, one corporal and ten men belonging to the 3rd Regiment, and a small body of militia officered by Captain William Hooker Smith and Lieutenant Daniel Gore. Duties devolving upon Colonel Butler, the commandant, made it necessary for him...to afford protection to the returning inhabitants, to guard the approaches to the valley, and to exercise a surveillance over an extensive range of country."[250]

Creation of an Overland Corridor

The effects of the Sullivan expedition upon the Wyoming settlement were considerable. The Sullivan Road from Easton to Wilkes-Barre created an important overland corridor for trade with the growing communities on the Delaware. In a few years it would become the Wilkes-Barre-Easton turnpike. No doubt many years would have passed before the creation of such a road, were it not for its military necessity in 1779.

The massive devastation of the Indian homelands would have a long term effect upon the ability of the Indians to mount any large scale offensive. However, savage raids by bands of desperate Iroquois would continue for the next few years. A panorama of vast opportunities for settlement of beckoning new land was spread before the men of the expedition, and many would return after the war to choose and to locate home sites. Opportunities for land speculators would be widely advertised by word of mouth from the many soldiers and their officers. The complexion of the Wyoming settlement would never again have the unity and ethnicity of the Connecticut Congregationalists, and very gradually, the Connecticut claims would come under increasing challenge.

Finally, the robust social and recreational indulgences of a few thousand troops in bivouac on the Wyoming lands along the Susquehanna disturbed and challenged the simple, conservative ways of the settlers. Such a flame of excitement left a new sense of life's directions upon many of the inhabitants, so that subtle changes began to appear in their activities.

CHAPTER 17

Reestablishing Life in Wyoming Valley

The Wyoming Detachment of the Sullivan Campaign

Thomas, Solomon, and Andrew Bennet participated in all the activities of Colonel Butler's detachment during the lonely and busy period beginning with the return after the massacre, and continuing through the occupancy and passage of the Sullivan Expedition. They performed as guards, scouts and patrols. All attempts at farming were done with a guard detail and the Bennets were never careless as they went about their daily assignments.

Following the departure of the bulk of Sullivan's troops in October 1779, Thomas Bennet began to look around for some kind of shelter. He wanted to send for his wife and daughters but knew they would not return to the valley unless the threat of further Indian raids was reduced or eliminated. Along with other inhabitants, Bennet thought the completion of Sullivan's destruction of the lands of the Iroquois would assure a new degree of safety to the frontier settlement. He found an unused barracks on the west side of the river just opposite Wilkes-Barre and began to improve this in the fall of 1779.

Severe Winter of 1779-80

All construction efforts and nearly all overland travel was completely arrested during the winter of 1779-1780 because of extremely severe weather. The snow began to fall about the 10th of November, 1779, and continued almost every day till the middle of the ensuing March. In the woods and other sheltered places it lay for many weeks at least four feet upon the level. The weather was intensely cold during the greater part of that period, and harbors, rivers, creeks and brooks were all frozen over. But the *great* snowstorm began on January 3, 1780. This storm was accompanied by very high winds and blizzard conditions and lasted for several days. Six feet of snow was the general rule, roads were impassable, and all supplies were cut off. All travel was on foot by snowshoes. Just surviving this winter was a challenge to the detachment at the fort and to the inhabitants scattered over the valley. [251]

Early in 1780, Colonel Butler began to exert efforts to increase the garrison at Fort Wyoming, anticipating the recurrence of Indian raids and recognizing that his 120 officers and men were inadequate to fulfill their responsibilities. Failing in his attempts to obtain any help from the Continental Army, he appointed Captain John Franklin to enlist a company of militia from inhabitants of the town of Westmoreland. Franklin shortly organized a company of seventy-four officers and men. The detachment then comprised sixty men of Captain Spaulding's Continental Company, about fifty men of Captain Schott's Corps, detached from Sullivan's Army, thirteen men from the 3rd Connecticut Regiment, and the seventy-five officers and men of Captain Franklin's new militia. [252] Thomas, Solomon and Andrew Bennet joined the new militia and during the spring of 1780 were fully occupied.

Bennet Women Return to Wyoming

During the summer the male Bennets were able to improve the barracks to accommodate the entire Bennet family. In the fall, Thomas felt prepared to have his wife and daughters rejoin him at Wyoming, and sent Solomon to Connecticut, hoping to persuade Martha that it was safe to return.

In the fall, Solomon Bennet arrived in Litchfield with a horse and persuaded his mother and two sisters to accompany him back to "their loved and much desired Wyoming home." [253] Martha decided to take a sloop from Canaan up the Hudson to Newburg, thus avoiding some of the overland trip. Mrs. Bennet and Polly took turns riding on the horse and in due time the little party reassembled at Newburg. They then went on to Goshen, passing General Washington's encampment on the way. At Goshen they purchased a yoke of oxen and a cart, upon which they loaded the accumulated fruits of their earnings. They proceeded to Stroudsburg where they took the new road built by Sullivan's army. The going was tough and slow but they finally arrived intact at Wyoming, the family reuniting after a separation of nearly two years.

The Bennets found their barracks home comfortable. They had an abundance of corn and garden vegetables, but flour was scarce. The grist mills had been destroyed and were not yet rebuilt, so it was necessary to resort to the hominey block, a hollowed out trunk of a large tree. The corn would be placed in the hollow and then crushed with a pestle hung upon a spring pole. Several families would share the use of this primitive mill, and often an individual would be obliged to wait for a turn at the block. Of course, the garrison had a supply of flour under the control of the commissary, William Stout. It was tightly held for the use of the men of the garrison and could not be bought by the settlers of now about thirty families. "...yet Miss Martha Bennet being skillful in fine knitting and working lace, could procure it for her work. By knitting a pair of stockings and a pair of gloves for the commissary, and working a lace cap and some silk lace to trim a cloak for his lady, she procured one hundred pounds of flour." [254]

Miss Bennet was kept very busy, often working until 1 or 2 o'clock in the morning, doing most of the spinning and knitting by the light of burning pine in the fireplace. During daylight hours the ladies were busy with their housework and with gathering and preparing food for both immediate and later use. Miss Martha was a key agent in supplying the necessaries of life to the family, such as by knitting a lace cap for old Mrs. McClure in exchange for three pigs which the men slaughtered for the family larder.

Life during this period continued to relate closely to the fort and its garrison. In constant fear of Indian raids they welcomed the evening cry of the sentinels that *All's well!* Relationships were built up between the soldiers and young ladies of the community.

Thomas and Andrew Bennet taken captive by the Indians

Concerning this period, Miner[255] states: "The sense of serenity and repose, so welcome to the wearied settlers ... they were not long permitted to cherish. Effectual as the punishment of the savages seemed, instead of subduing, it only appeared to have exacerbated their thirst for revenge."

One of the first families to experience the fury of the savage spirit was that of Bennet. Being unable to procure any land to work under cover of the fort at Wilkes-Barre, he decided to work some of his own above Forty Fort. On the 27th of March, 1780, he began plowing with a team of oxen. His youngest son, Andrew, rode upon the horse. At the edge of the clearing, the horse shied and Mr. Bennet suspected danger. When they came around the next time, four Indians jumped from the bushes, seizing father and son. The Indians hurried off with their prisoners. After a short distance, they met two more Indians with Lemmeus Hammond as a third prisoner. The party took an old war path over the mountain.

When Mr. Bennet did not come home by sundown, Mrs. Bennet alerted the fort and wanted a search party to depart at once. However, the command thought it prudent to wait until the following day when they would have the advantage of light. The next morning a company left the fort in pursuit. They found the oxen and the horse and discovered the Indians' track. This they followed to the top of the mountain, but finding nothing else they returned to the fort. [256]

Meanwhile, the Indians hurried on with their prisoners. That night they lodged near the foot of what is now Cummings Pond. The next day they proceeded on to Bowman's Creek and when they entered into the "green woods" they found the snow "waist band" deep. The travelling was at times most arduous, especially for a man of years. At this point they crossed the Susquehanna and pushed on toward Meshoppen. "In the afternoon of this day they met a party of about thirty Indians headed by a Tory named Moses Mount, who were on their way to pillage and devastate some of the frontier settlements. Mount and one of the Indians eagerly questioned Bennet as to the state of the garrison at Wyoming, the number of inhabitants in the valley, etc. He informed the leaders of the war party that there were 300 fighting men in the fort at Wilkes-Barre, that they were well armed and provisioned, that they had a cannon, and that the settlers had all taken refuge there. The war party then concluded that they would strike the river below the valley, and they went on their way; but first they told Bennet and Hammond that there were 500 Indians from Fort Niagara already out on the war-path, and that a party equally as large...was coming on after them; that Brant, with one party, had gone to the Mohawk River; that a second party had gone to the Minisinks; and a third party to the west branch of the Susquehanna." [257]

Settlers Escape

On the evening of March 28th, the party of Indians with its three captives from Wyoming built a fire with the aid of Thomas Bennet, who, being an elderly man somewhat afflicted with rheumatism, was least feared, and was permitted to go unbound. From a few words dropped by one of the Indians, Mr. Bennet drew the inference that it was their design to murder him and his fellow captives. "Whispering to Hammond, when the Indians had gone to a nearby spring to satisfy their thirst, a plan of escape was concerted." [258]

The forced march had tired the Indians and they rapidly fell off to sleep around the warming fire. Hammond and young Andrew Bennet were tied down between the Indians. Thomas Bennet sat close by tending the fire, apparently considered too old and crippled to be a threat. One elderly Indian took the first watch and he alternately dozed and picked the scanty meat from the head of a deer he was roasting. At the appropriate moment Bennet picked up the guard's spear and by a powerful thrust pierced his body. The Indian let out a groan and fell into the fire. In rapid succession, Bennet released the two other captives. Three of the other Indians were tomahawked before they could get up, and the others fled.

Brewster[259] states: "Just at that moment the only two Indians remaining alive took to their heels, when Mr. Bennet, who could throw a tomahawk with the precision and force of any Indian on the frontier, picked up a tomahawk and let it slip, and it stuck in the back of one of them." Colonel John Butler of "Butler's Rangers" reported this affair as follows: "Scouts have been out during the winter. One party returning with prisoners, through carelessness let them untie themselves at night, so that after killing five Indians they escaped." [260]

The Bennets and Hammond planned their return to take as straight a course as possible through the woods to the Capouse Meadows, avoiding all Indian trails. Enroute they forded the swollen Meshoppen Creek with tremendous effort, thence keeping a course laid out by the veteran hunter and woodsman, Thomas Bennet. With frozen clothes and frostbitten feet ,they crossed the high ridges and deep valleys that lay across their path. On the second day they reached the south side of the mountain range northwest of the Lackawanna River. Very hungry now, they paused to eat wintergreen, then moved rapidly down the side of the mountain to the point where the Lackawanna enters the Susquehanna. From there, they moved on down the valley to the fort at Wilkes-Barre, arriving there six days following their capture. [261]

During those six days, Mrs. Bennet and the children were agonized with suspense and dread. They were all too familiar with the savages' delight in torture of their captives and held out little hope that they would ever set eyes on either Andrew or Thomas again. "In their imaginations, the aged sire and his boy were often seen suffering the most excruciating tortures for hours, and then their bodies left to be devoured by wild beasts."[262] On the sixth day they saw three limping, haggard figures approaching the fort, unrecognizable at first glance. The family's excitement and joy on reunion was beyond expression.

Mr. Hammond and Andrew fully recovered from their ordeal after a few days of good food and some rest in a place of warmth and protection. Thomas was exhausted and required several days to regain his strength. His feet were so dreadfully injured by the frost that several of his toes came off at first joint, and he was obliged to walk with crutches for more than a year, during most of which time he suffered indescribably. But by the following spring he was back working in his fields.

Indian Raids Continue

The Sullivan expedition did not remove the threat of roving Indians. From 1780 to 1783, Indian raids were constant occurrences. In each instance a small number of settlers at some distance from the fort would be caught, subsequently to be murdered, scalped, or taken prisoner. Often, prisoners were marched to Niagara for incarceration; some of these escaped and found their way back to Wyoming. Others survived as prisoners and were released after the war was concluded. With the Wyoming settlement no longer able to protect this frontier, raids became widespread. In 1780, settlers and families were killed or taken prisoner in Forty Fort, Hanover, Nanticoke, Fishing Creek, Capouse, Mahoning, Sugarloaf and Shawnee. In 1781, savage raids were recorded at Sunbury, Tannersville, Lehighton (formerly Fort Allen), Buttonwood, Brinkers, Hanover, Shawnee and Shohola.[263] Terror was everywhere. Scalps were taken until July 1782 when the Indian threat faded.

Hunger and Poverty of the Wyoming Settlers

In Wyoming, the settlers worked the fields close to the fort, reducing much needed crops because of fear of random raids. Food was scarce and the continued conflict created deep-seated poverty. The memorial of January 1783 describes their lot as follows: "Our houses are desolate— many mothers childless—widows and orphans multiplied— our habitations destroyed—and many families reduced to beggary— which exhibits a scene most pitiful and deserving of mercy."[264] In this situation of inadequate food, poor shelters, and constant fear, the health of the community deteriorated. Miner states:[254] "As the preceding winter had been extremely cold, so the summer was marked by an unusual degree of heat. August especially was—panting hot, severe thundershowers being frequent, followed by a close and oppressive atmosphere. The consequence was an autumn of greater sickness than had ever before been experienced. The settlers in Kingston particularly suffered. Calomel, tartar emetic, and Jesuits bark, dispensed by Dr. William H. Smith, with skill, were efficacious, and the number of deaths, though considerable, bore a very small proportion to the great number afflicted."[265]

Regular town meetings began again in the fall of 1780, a major concern being the abatement of taxes levied by the State of Connecticut. The settlers had few material goods and although the harvest was good in quality, it was not adequate for sustenance. A large shipment of provisions coming up the river had been impounded at Sunbury by Pennamites. "This was the first incident which had occurred for three years, exhibiting the smoldering, but by no means extinguished, jealousy that existed on the part of Pennsylvania, towards the Connecticut garrison and settlement."[266] Town meetings debated these and other issues and once again elected selectmen, constable, treasurer, collectors, surveyors of highways, grand jurymen, etc., and resumed the structure of government of Westmoreland consistent with Connecticut law.

The surrender of Cornwallis occurred at Yorktown on October 19, 1781, effectively deciding the contest in favor of the Americans. Cornwallis' surrender convinced the London War Ministry that the United States could not be subdued by force of arms and that the Americans were bound to attain independence. Even so, when Parliament met on February 27,

1782, the King of England urged that the war be prosecuted with renewed vigor. But General Conway, on February 27, 1782, moved in the House of Commons: "That it is the opinion of this House, that a further prosecution of offensive war against America, would, under present circumstances, be the means of weakening the efforts of their country against her European enemies, and tend to increase the mutual enmity so fatal to the interests of both Great Britain and America." On the 4th of March following, Parliament resolved that there would be no further prosecution of offensive war on the continent of North America. [267] Negotiations for peace soon followed.

These events awakened new hope in the hearts of the settlers. Joy at the cessation of the war was mingled with the anticipation of a new found peace—a peace in which there would be freedom from Indian raids and security that somehow the Connecticut lands at Wyoming would be rightfully theirs. The general attitude of the settlement was one of tranquility. "With the cessation of hostilities between Great Britain and the United States, following the surrender of Cornwallis, and with the disappearance of danger from the Indians on the frontier, Connecticut and some other New England states began to send forward to Wyoming considerable numbers of emigrants - men of character and experience and some of means. Unfortunately for Wyoming, however, its troubles did not all come to an end with the cessation of British-American hostilities."[268]

CHAPTER 18

The Second Yankee-Pennamite War

Land Disputes Erupt Again

The State of Pennsylvania looked with displeasure upon the continued presence of a Connecticut settlement at Wyoming, especially now that the inhabitants were returning in great numbers to take possession of their lands. It could not tolerate this colony to exist within its territorial limits, and insisted that this piece of land and its settlers were under the jurisdiction of Pennsylvania.

Harvey-Smith [269] states that fifteen days after the surrender of Cornwallis the Supreme Executive Council of Pennsylvania petitioned Congress to institute a hearing to settle the dispute with Connecticut over the lands "along the east branch of the Susquehanna." The procedure would be that prescribed by the IXth Article of Confederation, the instrument by which the several states were attempting to develop a united government.

Page Smith quotes Article IX [270] "The United States in Congress assembled shall also be the last resort on appeal in all disputes and differences now subsisting or that hereafter may arise between two or more states concerning boundary, jurisdiction, or any other cause whatsoever; which authority shall always be exercised in the manner following. Whenever the legislative or executive authority or lawful agent of any state in controversy with another shall present a petition to Congress stating the matters in questions and praying for a hearing." The article then describes the manner by which arbitration shall occur, creating a commission to review the claim or claims.

Further, "All controversies concerning the private right of soil claimed under different grants of two or more states, whose jurisdictions as they may respect such lands, and the states which passed such grants are adjusted, the said grants or either of them being at the same time claimed to have originated antecedent to such settlement jurisdiction, shall on the petition of either party to the Congress of the United States, be finally determined as near as may be in the same manner as is before prescribed for deciding disputes representing territorial jurisdiction between different states."

Article IX described procedure for jurisdictional and for "right of soil" disputes, but separated the two as different problems. For the Connecticut settlers the first issue was to be the fate of their jurisdiction. Since every effort had been made by them to remain Yankees, was it possible that after all these years of struggle they would become Pennsylvanians?

In response to the petition, congressional representatives from Pennsylvania and Connecticut met in Philadelphia on April 20, 1782, and prepared a list naming sixty-three men drawn from all thirteen states. From this list five men were chosen by Congress, and on August 28, 1782, they were authorized to be a Court of Commissioners to meet at Trenton, New Jersey, on Tuesday, November 12th to hear the arguments of the two states.

After 41 days of trial, the decision was given as follows: "We are of the opinion that Connecticut has no right to the lands in controversy. We are also unanimously of opinion that the jurisdiction and preemption of all the territory lying within the charter of Pennsylvania, and now claimed by the State of Connecticut, do of right belong to the State of Pennsylvania."[271]

Taylor states that during the trial the judges informed participants that only jurisdictional rights could be ruled upon.[272] The judges explained that private soil rights were a separate matter which could be determined only by a separate action under another clause of Article IX. There could not have been sufficient wisdom to satisfy both Connecticut and Pennsylvania. However, positive gain from this trial was that the establishment of political jurisdiction was never successfully challenged after this decision of 1782.

On January 4, 1783, a messenger arrived at Wilkes-Barre informing the settlers that the decision had been made giving Pennsylvania jurisdiction over their territory. The inhabitants gathered at a town meeting, debated the issue, and set forth a memorial to the General Assembly of Pennsylvania in part saying:

"By this adjudication we are under your jurisdiction and protection. We are subjects and free citizens of the State of Pennsylvania, and have now to look up to your honors, as our Fathers, guardians, and protectors—entitled to every tender regard and respect as to justice, equity, liberty and protection.

It is impossible that the magnanimity of a powerful and opulent State will ever condescend to distress an innocent and brave people, that have unsuccessfully struggled against the ills of fortune. We care not under what State we live, if we live protected and happy. We will serve you, we will promote your interests, we will fight your battles, but in mercy, wisdom, goodness, justice, and every great and generous principle, leave us our possessions ." [273]

The inhabitants at Wyoming were initially reassured by the belief that their right of soil had in no way been affected, that the only question so far decided had to do with jurisdiction. This relief was reinforced by the proclamation of President Dickinson of Pennsylvania prohibiting all persons from molesting the Wyoming settlers. The attitude on both sides seemed conciliatory at the outset.

Accepting the jurisdiction of Pennsylvania, the settlers at Wyoming nevertheless were aware of their vulnerability to being dispossessed of their lands. For thirteen years they had struggled under the auspices of the Susquehanna Company. They now found themselves in a free fall, left to manage their own circumstance with no help forthcoming from Connecticut.

On January 6th a meeting of the inhabitants of Wyoming was held at Wilkes-Barre. Captain John Paul Schott was appointed as Agent for the settlers and was immediately dispatched to Philadelphia to petition the Assembly "in a manner as should be thought most proper and beneficial for the inhabitants at Wyoming." [274]

Captain Schott's petition was presented to the General Assembly January 18, 1783. The document reviewed the history of the settlement in detail and with remarkable accuracy. It concluded: "We further pray that a general act of oblivion and indemnity may be passed," in effect guaranteeing to the settlers their possessions, that is, their lands.

At about the same time a large group of the inhabitants, including Thomas Bennet, petitioned the State of New York for land located on the waters of the Susquehanna within that state. Obadiah Gore was dispatched to Kingston, New York, to present the petition to the State Legislature. On Friday, March 21, 1783, the New York State General Assembly passed a resolution that "Obadiah Gore and his associates shall be permitted to locate on any of the waste and unappropriated lands within this state...whenever the Legislature shall determine to grant the lands."[275] Obadiah Gore was authorized, meanwhile, to explore the lands and determine their future choice. The option was never used, events at Wyoming moving from crisis to crisis and occupying the settlers' every moment.

The Continental guard stationed at Wilkes-Barre was recalled and replaced by two Pennsylvania Companies under Captain Schrawder and Captain Robinson. The two companies promptly marched to take possession of Fort Wyoming, renaming it "Fort Dickinson" in honor of the President of the Supreme Executive Council of Pennsylvania. This changing of the guard was made not just to protect the country against the Indians, but more importantly to curb the Connecticut settlers.

In February, in response to Captain Schott's petition, the Pennsylvania Assembly resolved that three commissioners be appointed to proceed to Wilkes-Barre and there to conduct an investigation of the land dispute and to report findings and recommendations back to the Assembly. They were to attempt a final and equitable adjustment of all difficulties. The House elected William Montgomery, Moses McClean, and Joseph Montgomery to serve as Commissioners; they arrived in Wilkes-Barre April 15th, 1783.

The new Commissioners at once requested the names and settlements of the Connecticut people. The settlers, for their part, named a committee to meet with the Commissioners, selecting Judge John Jenkins, Sr., Colonel Nathan Denison, Lieutenant Obadiah Gore, and Lieutenant Samuel Shippard. Also, a committee representing the Pennsylvania land claimers arrived at about the same time, its chairman to be Captain Alexander Patterson of Northampton County.

The driving force for these three groups of men was the struggle for possession of the land. Although the status of the settlers was approaching poverty, the Wyoming lands remained beautiful and fertile. Much of this land had already been cleared even though the constant Indian raids had interfered with its tillage and yield. It was a golden opportunity for the land speculators from Pennsylvania and New Jersey, their interests to be protected by Captain Patterson and his companions.

The committee of settlers returned a list of the first settlers, a list of the then present settlers, and the number of widows and fatherless. On the other hand, the Pennamite Committee, under date of April 22, 1783, sent the commission a letter recommending a *"compromise,"* as follows in part: "We propose to give them leave...for holding their possessions one year from the first day of March next, at the end of which they shall deliver up full possession of the whole. They shall occupy half the lands, mow half the meadows, dwell in the houses they now possess, and cultivate their present gardens; and if they have any opportunity of disposing of their hutts, barns or other buildings, they shall do it, and remove them off at any time between the present day and the first of May 1784. The other half...of the cleared lands and meadows to be possessed by us and our associates and no impediment to be thrown in our way to enjoy....The widows of all those whose husbands were killed by the savages to have a further indulgence of one year after 1st of May 1784."[276]

The commissioners secretly proceeded to divide Wyoming into two townships, Stoke and Shawnee, with two election districts. They held a sham election of four persons for each district for justices of the peace. The same commissioners made their report to the Pennsylvania Assembly in August 1783 and recommended approval of the infamous compromise cited above. Meanwhile, a prior act staying suits of ejectment and trespass against the Connecticut people was rejected. An act was passed giving them waste or unappropriated land in Northampton and Northumberland Counties, providing they would voluntarily relinquish the Wyoming lands on demand.

The settlers now became fully aware that the Pennsylvania troops stationed at Wilkes-Barre were their keepers rather than their protectors. Their previously democratic government became a mixture of civil and military authority in which they were not represented. "The unhappy husbandman saw his cattle driven away, his home on fire, his children robbed of their bread, and his wife and daughters prey to a lawless soldiery." [277]

Captain Patterson Instigates Conflict

In the fall of 1783, Captain Patterson assumed command of the total operation, having received his commission to do so when he was appointed magistrate by the State of Pennsylvania. He took up his quarters at Wilkes-Barre, changing the name of the place to Londonderry.

In August or September, Lieutenant Colonel Zebulon Butler returned to Wilkes-Barre with his new bride. He was shocked and indignant at the treatment the inhabitants suffered, and openly expressed his opinions throughout the community. On the 24th of September he was arrested for high treason and the next day was sent by Patterson under a military guard to the gaol at Sunbury. He was held there for a few days until satisfactory bail could be secured, then was released.

Brewster [278] states that on October 30th Patterson took a company of militia to Plymouth where he seized eleven men, cruelly bound them and drove them to Wilkes-Barre. There they were thrown into the guard house and compelled by the soldiers to lie down in cold filth and mire for several days and then dismissed without trial. "Major Prince Alden, more than 60 years of age and a feeble man, was thus imprisoned and had his staff seized by Captain Christie and burnt."

The winter of 1783-1784 was very severe. In the middle of January 1784, snow fell to a depth of at least four feet in Wyoming Valley and the surrounding country. For several days the thermometer hovered around zero degrees Fahrenheit, causing the river and its tributaries to freeze solidly with ice.

Wagons and sleds of immense weight could be hauled from shore to shore. Chapman states that there was a sudden thaw in March, accompanied by immense quantities of rain on the 13th and 14th of the month.[279] The ice in the river began to break up and the streams all ran with great rapidity. In the river, the ice first gave way at the different rapids and floated down in huge blocks. Several large ice dams were formed so that the river over flowed its banks and "one general inundation overspread the extensive plains of Wyoming. The inhabitants took refuge in the hills...and saw their property exposed to the fury of the waters."

The experience of the Bennet family is told by Peck.[280] "At about 2 o'clock p.m., Colonel Denison and Esquire Myers came riding down the river on horseback. Seeing the families unapprised of their danger, one of them cried out. 'Bennet, what are you about? The ice will soon be upon you in mountains.' Mrs. Bennet had previously been urging her husband to take the family to high ground...He, however, relied securely upon the tradition communicated to him from 'the oldest Indians who said...the water had never been over these flats.'"

So warned, the "old gentleman began to stir about. The big canoe was loaded and went off, carrying the old people and the children. The boys drove the cattle to Swetland Hill, taking along the wagon and horses." They barely escaped. Martha stayed at the house helping to reload the canoe as it ran back and forth between the house and the bank.

Suddenly the ice above gave way with a tremendous roar. Martha states: "in an instant we were in the canoe—I cannot tell how—and were lifted up among the tops of the trees, and surrounded by cakes of strong ice. The boys rowed and I pulled by the limbs of the trees; but in spite of all we could do, we were driven down the stream rapidly. It was now dark, and our people, with lighted torches, came along the bank in the greatest anxiety of mind, frequently calling out, 'where are you?' As we were swept along by the terrible current, and unable to make much headway,...we saw the light following along the bank, and occasionally heard our friends shout out...We struggled for life, and at 11 or 12 o'clock we reached the shore. Uriah Stevens sprung (from the canoe) upon a log which lay by the shore, and thence upon the ground. I followed him, but the moment I struck the log it rolled, and I was plunged under the water. I was fortunate enough to rise within reach of the young man, and he pulled me out. Solomon, (still) in the canoe, was then driven out among the ice, and it was an hour or more before he reached the shore. My clothes were frozen on me, and I was badly chilled. I was obliged to walk half a mile...before I could get to the fire."

Houses, barns, fences, flocks of sheep, droves of pigs, herds of cattle, stacks of hay and grain, were swept away by the deluge, never to be seen again. There was in general a great scarcity of provisions. At Fort Dickinson, Wilkes-Barre, under date of March 20, 1784, (five days after the great ice flood) Major James Moore wrote to President Dickinson, at Philadelphia, in part as follows: "The people in this country have suffered exceedingly by the late fresh; not less than 150 houses have been carried away. The grain is principally lost and a very considerable part of the cattle drowned. The water was thirty feet above low water mark....The water was so high in the garrison that some of the ammunition was injured."[281] President Dickinson wrote to the General Assembly on March 31st as follows: "Gentlemen,—The late inundation having reduced many of the inhabitants of Wyoming to great distress, we should be glad your honorable house would make some immediate provision for their relief."[282] Miner adds that the Assembly was under too deep a prejudice from the land speculators, who successfully lobbied against giving any aid to the settlers!

The settlers had expected to fill their larders with shad in early April when the annual run would surge up the river from the Chesapeake Bay. However, Captain Patterson ordered the seines to be confiscated—anyone caught fishing would be arrested and thrown into jail. Members of the garrison began plundering the inhabitants, taking from them what little provisions they had left, slaughtering any cattle, sheep or swine which had escaped the flood.

Colonel John Franklin Seeks Congressional Help

In April a new petition was prepared at Wilkes-Barre by Colonels Butler and Denison, and others, pleading for help from the Congress. This petition stated, in part: "The land claimants...are at this present time introducing a banditti of men, together with the soldiers, to take our lands and possessions by force...they are pulling down our fences, laying our fields and grain open to the wide world, fencing across our highways, securing our wells of water from our houses, enclosing our gardens and home lots for their own use...Many of our houses, lots, wells and gardens lie near the garrison and under cover of their cannons; by which means we are continually receiving the greatest abuses and insults from some of the justices as well as from the officers and soldiers."[283] The petition was carried to Congress by Colonel John Franklin.

The settlers were bewildered and, for a time, disorganized; without determined leadership their agents were easily rejected, particularly since they were deprived of the usual legal pathways to which they had long been accustomed. "But their desperation brought forth their great and thenceforth acknowledged leader," Colonel John Franklin.[284]

Franklin, a very impressive man, was six feet four inches tall, square shouldered, and a massive man of gigantic strength. He possessed a marvelous memory and had a rare gift of keen analysis. Of great courage, he was absolutely incorruptible. Of all the leaders of the Connecticut settlers, his intellect and most persevering energy ideally equipped him to lead the settlers through the perilous times ahead. His copious journals, sketches, and memorials have provided historians with invaluable resource material.

Beginning in December 1783, before the ice floods, a series of petitions was delivered to Congress by Colonel Franklin, generally pleading for a fair hearing regarding the settlers' right of soil. Committees of investigation had been appointed, but their reports were tabled, referred to committee, or otherwise silenced through the influence of the land speculators.

Quickly identified by Patterson as a trouble maker, Colonel Franklin was arrested. Patterson had him appear before George Bayard, Justice of the Supreme Court, expecting that he would be transferred to Sunbury and jailed without bail. Thus Patterson would rid himself of Franklin's "obnoxious presence." However, Franklin was admitted to bail and was able to continue his unceasing efforts for the settlers. His personal magnetism was responsible for breaking down Pennamite opposition in many quarters, and it was largely as a result of his persuasion that the Pennsylvania Assembly directed the Executive Council to discharge the garrison at Wyoming in June.

Meanwhile, Patterson became increasingly incensed that the settlers were holding private meetings and he suspected that they were about to create some organized opposition to the land grabbers for whom he worked. During April and May, following the ice flood, "Patterson's forces at Wyoming were augmented by a force of ruffians from New Jersey, under a certain William McDaniel, who, according to Franklin, was a well known villain and Tory, once condemned to execution, who saved his neck by turning informer."[285]

Settlers Expelled

On May 12th, 13th and 14th the soldiers of the garrison were sent forth in detachments with orders to seize about 150 of the most prominent and objectionable Yankee families and to destroy their homes. One group of soldiers marched up to

Abraham's Plains, in Exeter, and swept down river, driving out settlers of the west side. Regardless of age, sex, or infirmity they were herded to a collecting point at Wilkes-Barre and were then forced to march up river to Capouse Meadows.

Thomas Bennet had just moved his family into his new home and had just begun to recover from the effects of the ice flood when the expulsion by force was imposed upon the Connecticut settlers. Miss Martha recalled that many families were driven from their houses; among them were the widows Shoemaker and Lee, near neighbors to Mr. Bennet. Pleading helplessness, they were nevertheless forced to go along with the rest, and take the long march through the wilderness.

Before leaving, the two widows left their heavy chest and some other items with Mrs. Bennet, who had decided to stay with the house. She had never yet left the valley for the Pennamites and swore that she never would. Thomas Bennet was forced to leave, although walking any distance caused pain in his feet. The soldiers picked up Esquire Myers, Giles Slocum, and many others. The group of settlers made a last minute appeal to leave the valley over the improved lower road, but to no avail. The pitiful assembly had to use the upper road out of Capouse, which had little maintenance, no improvement, and had by 1784 been largely abandoned.

At Capouse, Myers and Slocum escaped, but the great majority had no remedy but to submit to their fate. Thomas Bennet made his escape, taking Colonel Denison with him. Together they walked up river to Wyalusing, where the old gentleman remained for several days.

Of the fugitives, Miner says, [286] "About five hundred men, women and children with scarce provisions to sustain life, plodded their weary way mostly on foot, the road being impassable for wagons; mothers carrying their infants, and pregnant women literally waded streams, the water reaching to their armpits, and at night slept on the naked earth. ... Little children, tired with traveling, crying to their mothers for bread, which they had not to give them, sunk from exhaustion into stillness and slumber. ... Several of these unhappy sufferers died in the wilderness, others were taken sick from excessive fatigue, and expired. Some after reaching the settlement."

Mrs. Bennet's Private War

Back at the Valley of Wyoming, Mrs. Bennet was involved with her own private war. Miss Martha, Andrew and Polly remained with mother; Solomon's whereabouts is not documented.

A soldier named Van Horn approached Mrs. Bennet, ordering an accompanying wagoneer to carry off her goods. Van Horn ordered Mrs. Bennet to clear out, but with pitchfork in hand, she flatly refused to budge. She said she was in her own house and would not leave it for him or anybody else. Van Horn was startled. He then ordered Andrew and Miss Martha to load the wagon, an order which they promptly refused to render.

"Some of the men accompanying Van Horn went to the corn house, where there was a quantity of corn; but mother seized a hoe, and presenting herself before the door, declared she would knock the first man down who touched an ear of corn. They looked astonished and left her."[287]

A group of "Yankee boys" appeared on the scene and so alarmed the soldiers that they left in a hurry. As they did so, they ordered Mrs. Bennet to be ready to leave the following morning. The Yankees helped the Bennets restore order and return their things to their appropriate places. The Pennamites never returned and gave Mrs. Bennet no further trouble.

Chapman states[288]: "Acts of violence, productive of so much misery, caused sympathies to arise, which could not be disregarded by the State of Pennsylvania, and the General Assembly appointed Jonas Hartzel, Robert Brown, and Jacob Stroud, Commissioners,...to go to Wyoming to examine the conduct of the Pennsylvania officers and in general to report on the state of affairs of the settlement. As a result of their report, the garrison of troops was discharged on June 13th. Captain Patterson resigned as Justice of the Peace, and as Justice of the Court of Common Pleas of Northumberland County.

Patterson's point of view was set forth in a letter he addressed to the Judges of the Supreme Court at Sunbury dated May 30, 1784. This letter stated, in part: "It now only remains that your honors do obtain the proper information and causes which have produced the present commotions, and that prudent and wise measures be adopted to stop the impending calamities that threaten this large tract of country. You will no doubt hear that great outrages have been committed by the Pennsylvanians against the Connecticut claimants, in violation of law and good government; but I trust it will be made to appear that the measures taken, though not strictly consonant with the letter of the law, were the result of absolute necessity, and dictated solely by the principles of self-preservation....

The Pennsylvanians who had come into this country in great numbers found that the lands they had so long since bought and suffered for were generally clear of houses or fences. They therefore fell to work to improve, and in a peaceable manner endeavored to re-possess themselves of their property, which was wrested from them many years ago by lawless banditti. The malcontents betook themselves to their ancient resources (that of arms) and threatened the Pennsylvanians in a daring and outrageous manner. All hopes of peace being vanished, it was adjudged the most prudent step to seize a favorable moment and disarm the most violent of the intruders; upon which notice was given them to move off their effects and families." [289]

The closing paragraph of this letter illustrated the confusion of interpretation of the Trenton decree made under the Articles of Confederation. It stated, "the Pennsylvanians conceive that the determination of the Congressional Court at Trenton, touching the jurisdiction and preemption of this country, was final and decisive, and that further preemptions to tryal upon the subject was in too great a degree tampering with their patience and property; and they are determined to defend it against any pretensions or people claiming under the State of Connecticut. ...

"The justices at Sunbury, reviewing the reports and testimonies of the Connecticut settlers, sent a letter to President Dickinson reading in part: "We are exceedingly sorry that there is occasion to transmit to Council evidence of so disagreeable a nature as they will be furnished with by the enclosed letters and deposition; but conceiving it to be of the first moment to government, and being called on officially for the purpose, it becomes our indispensable duty....We are altogether at a loss to account for the outrageous conduct of the soldiery (at Wyoming)—the civil officers being intromitted, and confined under a close military guard, for serving the processes of the Commonwealth. The garrison, instead of enforcing civil authority, set it at defiance, and placed themselves above the laws.

"Lawrence Myers, from whom two letters have been received by the High Sheriff (Frederick Antes) and herewith forwarded, is the sub-sheriff. The complexion of those letters will (independent of anything else) enable Council to form an idea how far Civil Officers can act with effect in their several departments...in order that a timely provision may be made for the injured and oppressed citizens in that part of the state, and the dignity of the government supported and maintained."[290]

Patterson Leads Pennamites

Patterson now set about hiring several members of the discharged garrison to serve as an unofficial force for and in behalf of Pennamite land claimers. Meanwhile the inhabitants were invited to return to their dwellings by public proclamation and they were promised protection by the civil government. To assure their safety, Henry Antes, Sheriff of Northumberland, went to Wyoming, hoping to restore law and order.

Some of the settlers returned only to find their homes and farms in the possession of others, and to see that the Sheriff was powerless against the strong willed Patterson and his henchmen. Denied their habitation, the settlers established a camp on Wilkes-Barre mountain in a cave under a shelf of protecting rock, and there they remained until July 3rd, when they moved to a site above Forty Fort. There they occupied four log houses close by Abraham's (Tuttle's) Creek, which they fortified and used as headquarters for several months.[291]

Several factors contributed to perpetuation of civil war in northeast Pennsylvania. The Pennsylvania Constitution of 1776 created a single house legislature with a practically powerless Presidency. Many legislators were themselves land speculators, or were easily influenced by powerful lobbyists. The system permitted and even encouraged reversal of decisions from one session to the next. John Adams remarked:[292] "Pennsylvania will be divided and weakened and rendered much less vigorous in the cause by the wretched ideas of government which prevail in the minds of many people in it." The unicameral government was unable to resolve the issue of land ownership despite repeated appeals by both parties in the conflict.

Furthermore, the Continental Congress established under the Articles of Confederation was simply a committee of the states, and while it could and did pass resolutions, there was no executive to enforce them. After the Revolution there were many decisive factors preventing unity and the several states had not yet become a nation. Slavery, commerce, land claims, and ethnic differences combined to promote jealousy and misunderstanding. Page Smith quotes Josiah Tucker, Dean of Gloucester Cathedral: [293]"As to the future grandeur of America, and its being a rising empire under one head, whether republican or monarchical, it is one of the idlest and most visionary nations that was ever conceived even by writers of romance ... The mutual antipathies and diverse interests of the Americans, their differences of government, habitudes, and manners, indicate that they will have no center of union and no common interest. They never can be united into one compact empire under any species of government whatever; a disunited people to the end of time, suspicious and distrustful of each other, they will be divided... into little commonwealths..."

Appeals to such a body as the Continental Congress had little chance for reaching a firm decision. Attendance by the states' delegates was irregular and uncertain, a quorum frequently being impossible. Even if a proclamation were made, there was no executive to carry it out. Congress could proclaim anything but do nothing.[294] It was wholly dependent upon the states willingness to comply with its requisitions.

The commerce of the states declined considerably after the Revolution. Many of the leading merchants had been Loyalists and had left the country. Ninety percent of the population was made up of subsistence farmers, with small cash crops on the side. Some states suffered more than others. Connecticut and Rhode Island were particularly in an economic slump. Any pathway leading to quick profit was likely to be stampeded, and such was the opportunity for land speculation. The Wyoming lands were particularly attractive, gaining speculators from New York, New Jersey, Pennsylvania and Connecticut.

Fanning the Strife

All of these factors tended to fan the strife in northeast Pennsylvania and to cause it to endure all too long. For the Connecticut settlers it was a bewildering milieu. Families were ruined, lives were destroyed, fortunes were made and lost. Many of these settlers held steady in the storm and managed to survive intact.

The lines were now drawn for open conflict. The Pennamites were concentrated at Fort Dickinson in Wilkes-Barre, while the Yankees had consolidated their position in Forty Fort, just north of Abraham's Creek. From these points each party wauld sally forth to attack and to raid, each establishing an area of dominance. Homes in Forty Fort located near Yankee headquarters were protected by the small concentration at their fortification, which they named Fort Defence. Similarly, houses and farms close to Wilkes-Barre became controlled by the Pennamites. Captain Patterson commanded the latter, and Colonel John Franklin led the Yankees.

Obtaining provisions and ammunition became a first priority. Nearby farms in upper Forty Fort helped support the Yankees and a supply line relayed through these farms to funnel material to Fort Defence. The number of armed Yankees grew to about seventy, and with this growth there was increased burden on the supply train.

The Yankees had knowledge of some grain in the neighborhood of Plymouth and organized a small raiding force of about thirty men to gather the ripening harvest. Miner states[295] "Armed and prepared for labor or war, on the 20th of July they were marching from Kingston to Shawnee, when on Ross' Hill they met a larger party of Patterson's new levies, who opened fire upon the Yankees" (from ambush). Two Yankees, Elisha Garrett and Chester Pierce, were killed in this action, an event which both saddened and enraged the settlers, provoking a general rally of support for their cause.

Confrontation

On July 22nd, Colonel Franklin dispatched a messenger to Colonel Patterson that any Pennamite in the valley was at liberty to leave the area to escape possible injury; many Pennamite farmers fled to Fort Dickinson, but few if any actually departed from the valley. Later that same day Colonel Franklin led a force of sixty-two Yankees down the west side of the river, flushing out and dispossessing every Pennamite family. Several of these homes had been occupied by Yankee settlers a few months previously. Crossing over to Nanticoke, Franklin turned up river, driving all settlers before him toward the fort. Anyone not holding under the Connecticut claim was abruptly dispossesed.

The Yankee force surrounded the fort and its outposts, and proceeded north to Mill Creek, where they took the only functioning grist mill in the valley. Fort Dickinson was protected by a garrison of about 100 armed men, and maintained four cannons with no ammunition. During the siege, a fire broke out and consumed at least twenty-three homes near the fort. The Yankees steadily closed in on the fort, digging entrenchments from which they were able to silence the garrison. On July 27th Colonel Franklin sent a letter to those in the fort, demanding an immediate surrender of the garrison. Miner states,[296] "The summons was received with scorn." A vigorous but unsuccessful attack was made on the fort, several lives were lost on both sides but the Yankees were compelled to retire and took up their former positions at Forty Fort.

Young Martha's Personal Loss

On Sunday, July 25th, "Big William" Smith was shot and killed while attempting to obtain water from the river. At age twenty-five, he had been a vigorous participant in the Yankee raiding force, and a very close friend of the Bennets. In fact, he and Martha Bennet, now twenty-one years old, were lovers and had announced an intention to be married. Peck states:[297] "Miss Bennet was disconsolate, and for a considerable time thought to spend her life in a state of celibacy." The death of Smith created a deep grief among the settlers, and inflicted an incurable wound upon the hearts of a large and respectable circle of relations and friends.

Learning of the armed hostilities taking place in Wyoming, the Supreme Executive Council in Philadelphia ordered "that the lieutenant of the county of Northampton be directed immediately to draw forth a detachment of three hundred infantry and twelve or fifteen light dragoons, properly officered and equipped, from the militia of said county."[298] These forces were to proceed to Wyoming under the direction of the Honorable John Boyd and Lieutenant Colonel John Armstrong. At the same time the sheriff of Northumberland County was to proceed from Sunbury to Wyoming with a civil posse, to represent the state's civil authority. The entire plan was to be under the direction of Boyd and Armstrong.

An advanced company of this militia set out from Easton over the Sullivan trail to Wyoming. The commander of this company, Captain McDonald, sent a letter to Fort Dickinson, intending to alert Captain Armstrong of his approach. The letter was intercepted by the Yankee patrol before it could reach Fort Dickinson. At an urgent meeting of the Yankees, it was decided to dispatch Captain John Swift and forty or more men "to watch the movements of the band of ruffians from New Jersey and elsewhere."[299]

On the same day that Sheriff Antes and the magistrates arrived in Wyoming from Sunbury, Captain Swift met the advanced party of Pennamites from Northampton County at Locust Hill, about three miles east of Stoddartsville, and a short battle ensued. On the morning of August 2nd, between 9 and 10 o'clock, Swift stealthily advanced his men through the woods to within a short distance of the campsite of the Pennamites. Unobserved and concealed, the Yankees found the enemy lying and sitting about under the trees, totally unsuspecting any confrontation. The Yankees opened fire, killing Jacob Everett and wounding several of the Pennamites. The latter then successfully defended their position with returning fire from the house and woods, whereupon Swift and his men withdrew and returned to Wyoming.

In early August, Sheriff Antes and his party attempted to have both sides surrender their arms, preparatory to a negotiated settlement of the land claims in question.

In a letter of August 6th, the magistrates state, in part:[300] "(We) yesterday made a demand of the Connecticut party of a surrender of their arms, and submission to the laws of this State, which they complied with...We also made a demand of the same nature, of the party in the garrison but have received no direct, but an evasive answer...we believe that a due execution of the laws will be the most effectual means to quiet the Country; as to the pretended titles of the Connecticut party, we have nothing to fear, and are convinced that had it not been through the cruel and irregular conduct of our people, the peace might have been established long since."

On August 7th, the magistrates wrote to the president of the Supreme Council as follows, in part: "...we have dispersed the Connecticut party; but our own people we cannot...therefore we think it our indispensable duty to request you to come forward with the militia with as much dispatch as possible."

Yankee Desperation

The Connecticut people were given back their arms and at once concentrated their forces at Fort Defence. More than ever they were united in spirit and purpose, determined to defend themselves by arms where civil authority had failed.

On August 8th, the Northampton militia under Armstrong and Boyd arrived at Wyoming, where they found the Northumberland magistrates plus some troops. Armstrong now had a command of about 400 men. Miner states:[301] "A proclamation was immediately issued, declaring that they came in the name of the Commonwealth, as commissioners of peace, to repress violence from whatever quarter, to establish order, and restore the reign of law; demanding an immediate cessation of hostilities, and the surrender of their arms by both parties, promising impartial justice and protection."

On August 9th Armstrong and Boyd requested all the Connecticut party to assemble under arms, explaining that they had already disarmed Patterson and his party, and that they now wished the Yankees to do the same. As requested Colonel Franklin delivered to Armstrong and Boyd a list of the Yankees who had borne arms during the recent series of confrontations. This included eighty-two names. No member of the family of Thomas Bennet appeared on this list.

Yankees Deceived

The next day, Colonel Franklin led his men to the place designated by Armstrong. Immediately upon the grounding of arms, the Yankees were surrounded by the militia and were made prisoners. Shortly thereafter they were placed under the armed guard of the Pennamites of the garrison, who obviously had not been disarmed by Armstrong. This act of perfidy and deceit would forever remove from Colonel Franklin any element of trust in the Pennsylvania people or their government, and it would rekindle the interest and activity of the dormant Susquehanna Company.

Thirty Yankees who had been with Swift at Locust Hill were confined in the house of Giles Slocum, which was full of excrement and all manner of filth, having previously been occupied by a large number of Patterson's men during the siege of the fort. The thirty men were charged with murder, and were marched under irons and an armed guard to the jail at Easton.

Harvey states:[302] "The prisoners, still handcuffed, were formed in column of twos, and between each two were placed the same number of militia men. All were bound together by a long rope running from the head to the rear of the column, and they were flanked on both sides by a strong guard of armed militia, with bayonets fixed." Colonel Armstrong ordered that the whole body of prisoners would be executed if any one of them attempted his escape.

Forty-six men not at Locust Hill were confined in the house of Colonel Butler for nine days. They were then marched down river to the Sunbury jail, where they received more friendly treatment under the guiding hand of Sheriff Antes. These men were all released under bail on August 30, 1784, and returned to Wyoming Valley as soon as possible.

Those who were sent to Easton "were confined in one large apartment...until the 17th of September. On that day the assistant keeper of the prison came to the apartment as usual to furnish supplies, when one of the prisoners...seized him by the neck, and forcing the keys from his hand, knocked him down with them...and all the prisoners made their escape." [303]

Patterson's Success

During this same period, Armstrong and Boyd swept up and down the valley, removing and dispossessing as many of the Yankees as possible. The Bennet farm and house remained untouched. Many of the Yankees fled and established a new rendezvous at Bowmans Creek, about twenty-six miles upriver from Wilkes-Barre. Acting under the influence of land speculators, and consistent with the policy of Patterson, Colonel Armstrong's conquest now seemed complete. He had dispossessed by fraud and by force the Yankee settlers from the rich and fertile lands of Wyoming. The Pennamites took over the farms and the fields of ripening grain. Patterson left the area for Philadelphia to report his success.

Council of Censures Ineffective

The Constitution of Pennsylvania required election of a Council of Censures every seven years, charged with evaluation of the performance of the legislative and executive branches of the state government. Meeting on September 9th, the Council ordered the General Assembly to turn over all documents relating to the affairs at Wyoming. The Assembly ignored the request of Council, whereupon on September 11th the latter issued a scathing denunciation of the Pennamite activities against the Wyoming settlers, and ordered it to be printed for distribution. This statement concluded in part as follows "we lament that our government have in this business manifested little wisdom and foresight; nor have acted as the guardians of the rights of the people committed to their care. Impressed with the multiplied evils which have sprung from the imprudent management of this business, we hold it up to censure, to prevent, if possible, further instances of bad government which might convulse and distract our new-formed Nation."[304]

The action of the Council of Censures had no influence on the General Assembly. However, the report of the Council of Censures was a symptom of the spirit of sympathy now developing in favor of the settlers and in opposition to the actions of Armstrong and Boyd. Over time this would be an "important influence on the course of policy pursued." [305]

Meanwhile, a few hours after Armstrong left Wyoming for Philadelphia, a party of the Yankees attacked the Pennamites remaining at Fort Dickinson. They broke into one of the storehouses and secured much needed ammunition and some of the rifles which had been taken from them in the preceding August. This action lasted a few days and losses were taken on both sides. Captain Franklin, Captain John Swift and a few other Yankees were severely wounded; two others were killed in this brief siege, whereupon the attack force withdrew and retired to Fort Defence.

Sentiment Changing

Armstrong, learning of this event, asked the Assembly to authorize the activation of a Bucks County militia to accompany him back to Wyoming. The Lieutenant of Bucks County was instructed to raise four of his companies to report for this special assignment. On August 10, 1784, Lieutenant Francis Murray wrote the following to Adjutant General Armstrong: "But when the companies arrived I found it dangerous for any man to say he was willing to turn out, either in his own company or as a volunteer. That any man that did so was in danger of being beat by the others. I then gave orders to the different Captains...to call forth as many men as I then named to them out of the fifth and sixth classes of their companies, as amounted to the number wanted. The Captains obeyed the orders so far as they were able, called for the persons by name but were not able to parade even one man!"[306]

The Supreme Executive Council of Pennsylvania now ordered the arrest of twenty-three named Yankees and offered a reward to any person leading to their apprehension. The Yankees back at Wyoming, learning of the arrest warrant and the likelihood of a new Pennamite militia descending upon them, decided to appeal once again to Connecticut for help. They prepared a memorial signed by their wounded commander, Captain John Franklin. This was delivered to Eliphalet Dyer and Samuel Gray, who were active members of the Susquehanna Company.

Yankees Appeal to Connecticut Assembly

This memorial reviewed the history of the Connecticut settlement in Wyoming and of the previous struggle against both the Indians and the Pennamites. In its closing paragraphs there was this statement: "your memorialists are now reduced to about 2,000 souls..., the principal party which are women and children, now scattered in the woods, with only hutts of bark and thatch to cover them from the inclemency of the approaching winter, and their enemy in full possession of their houses, farms, crops and other property and they starving with hunger and cold, and have nowhere to look for protection (but) to their parent State."[307] The authors then plead for aid in countering their adversaries.

Dyer presented this request in all its detail to the Connecticut Assembly, which passed a resolution urging that the settlers pursue their application to the Continental Congress for a trial of their right of soil and dispossession under the 9th Article of Confederation. The Assembly promised its support in their application and in the trial, and instructed its delegates to Congress to present a description of the sufferings and needs of the Yankee settlers at Wyoming. Out of this came also a general remonstrance from the Connecticut Assembly to the State of Pennsylvania.

Meanwhile, Brigadier General Armstrong was able to gather forty militiamen from Bucks County and marched them into Wilkes-Barre on October 17, 1784. He met reinforcements there under the command of Captain Patterson, still occupying Fort Dickinson. On the other side of the forthcoming conflict the Yankees had brought together at Fort Defence a number of men who had been stationed at Bowman's Creek plus others scattered over the valley.

Ammunition was in short supply at the Yankee stronghold. Miss Bennet states:[308] "The boys at the widow Brockway's (Fort Defence) had nearly exhausted their powder. Word of this came to Colonel Franklin but it was a difficult matter to convey across the river the needed supply. Mrs. Kennedy—an old lady called Mother Kennedy—volunteered to convey the powder to the place where it was wanted. She tied it around her waist, under her dress, and brought it to Mr. Bennet's whence it soon found its way to the Widow Brockway's."

The next day, October 18th, Armstrong led about 130 Pennamites to Fort Defence and surrounded it. Miss Bennet continues "a large company, under the command of Captain Bolin, a fine-looking man, crossed the river from Wilkes-Barre and marched up toward the headquarters of the boys. The Captain called at Mr. Bennet's, and asked for a drink of water. Miss Bennet heard him, with a great swell, say, 'I'll dislodge them.' They moved on toward Widow Brockway's; there were four houses there, built of hewed logs, so situated and provided with loop holes as to constitute a formidable fortification."

Captain Franklin's Oath

Martha Bennet was anxious for the result of this attack. She went around the corner of the Bennet house, watched and listened. A brisk exchange of fire occurred, in which Captain Bolin was killed. Miner states that the action was sharply contested on both sides for an hour, after which the attacking party retired, carrying several wounded to the rear. "Captain Franklin seized the rifle of his friend William Jackson, bloody from his wound, and calling his companions in suffering around, swore here on a solemn oath that he would never lay down his arms until death should arrest his hand, or Patterson and Armstrong be expelled from Wyoming and the people be restored to their right of possession, and a legal trial guaranteed to every citizen by the constitution, by Justice and by Law."[309] Franklin devoted the next several years to the task he set for himself on this October 18th, 1784.

This brief assault upon the Yankees at Fort Defence was to be the watershed of the war. In effect, the Pennamites' failure to break their foe despite a numerical superiority of almost two to one seems to have persuaded their leaders that further armed contest would not solve the issue. Armstrong subsequently described this little battle as follows: "In a little recounter which took place a day or two ago and which was brought on by an attempt to cover the labors of some poor people. ...The insurgents sustained some losses and were driven into a cluster of log houses, which my leading platoon—mistaking their orders—attempted to storm, but without effect. In this affair I had two men slightly wounded. I need scarcely observe to your Excellency that four log houses so constructed as to flank each other, became a very formidable post, and set all attempts of near musquetry at defiance. I had no cannon, and the only alternative left me—a close investment—became impractical from want of numbers. I was obliged, therefore, to relinquish the position I had taken, and with it the happy prospect of exterminating this banditti at once."[310]

Yankees Destroy Fort Dickinson

During the next few days, each side conducted raids, but it became evident to Armstrong that without more men and more effective arms, he could not overcome the Yankees. Captain Patterson was placed under arrest by the court sitting at Easton as the result of a complaint filed against him by one of his victims, Abigail Jameson. On November 27th, Armstrong with most of the men moved out of Fort Dickinson and adjacent buildings, marching over the Sullivan road to Easton. "Thus the Pennamite horde vamoosed from Wyoming, never again to return with force of arms!"[311] Three days later the Yankees totally destroyed Fort Dickinson. This marked the end of the Second Yankee-Pennamite War.

CHAPTER 19
Right of Soil Still at Stake

The Susquehanna Company Revitalized

The end of the Second Yankee-Pennamite War left all of the burning issues unresolved. The question of the right of soil remained unanswered and there was still no effective representative government operating in the several townships.

In this vacuum, the Susquehanna Company became revitalized, no doubt sensing the opportunity to reinforce its claim over the lands it had purchased. At its meeting of July 1785 a committee was appointed to go to Bennington, Vermont to seek the assistance of General Ethan Allen, who had just completed the organization of the State of Vermont. Allen agreed with the committee to go to Wyoming with a small detachment of his Green Mountain Boys to assist the settlers in their claims to the right of soil. In developing this agreement, the Susquehanna Company allotted certain shares to Allen, as compensation for his support.

Allen was unable to go to Wyoming at this time. However, news of his intent spread among the Yankee settlers and encouraged them to become "more strenuous and in some instances more violent." [312] The same news cast consternation and alarm among the Pennsylvania Assembly. Consequently, the Supreme Executive Council of Pennsylvania petitioned the General Assembly to take some action in the matter. As a result the Honorable John Bayard wrote to Colonel Zebulon Butler pleading with him to maintain peace and to continue to seek resolution of the conflict by legal means. The latter pled for more time to permit the state assembly to act.

The matter had already been placed before this body several months previously and had been tabled. Under the date of February 26, 1785, Councillor James Wilson had written

President Dickinson in part as follows: "The controversy respecting the settlements at Wyoming depends before Congress in a very disadvantageous state of suspense. I think that both the interest and the honor of Pennsylvania require that a speedy and explicit decision should be had upon the complaints, and representations which have been made against her."[313]

Yankee Settlers United Under Franklin

The Wyoming settlers now found unity and a new determination, sparked by their powerful leader, Colonel John Franklin. It was he who travelled to and from Connecticut to spread news of the situation in Wyoming, forming sympathy throughout New England and kindling enthusiasm among the members of the Susquehanna Company. Franklin realized that many of the settlers were lukewarm toward taking any action and consequently he called a series of town meetings at which he addressed the people, encouraging them to persist in defense of their rights.

At the July meeting of the Susquehanna Company a remarkable paper was issued. Miner [314] calls it "a state paper of altogether too much consequence to be omitted or passed lightly over; nor can it be regarded as much less than a manifest of war." It set forth the policy and intent of the Susquehanna Company to be followed for the next several years. After some paragraphs reciting the history of the Connecticut claim and the Susquehanna purchase, it stated that "our right to those lands in possession, as found in law and justice, is clear and unquestionable; and we cannot and will not give it up." The Company vowed to support the proprietors and owners in their application to Congress for a trial of the right of soil. Every able bodied man who would go to Wyoming would become a half share proprietor. He must agree to remain there for three years and must be approved by the Company's Committee. The total of these new half share proprietors must not exceed four hundred. A half share owner received a quantity of land not exceeding two thousand acres, three hundred of which would be located in a township. In addition, the standing committee was further authorized "to dispose of six hundred rights in the general tract of country for the use of the said Company, using their discretion therein."

The intent of the Company was clearly stated: To move as many new proprietors to Wyoming as was possible and thus to flood the area with New England Yankees. The overwhelming numbers would establish the flavor and the political philosophy of New England throughout this vast area of northeastern Pennsylvania.

Colonel Franklin had attended this Company meeting and shortly thereafter departed for Wyoming. Immediately after his arrival there he called a town meeting in Kingston and carefully explained the salient points of the state paper cited above. He then visited each of the towns on both sides of the river, addressing the gathered settlers so that everyone was informed as to the measures to be taken. Franklin invited many "adventurers" to purchase half share rights during this visit, and he was busy for several days issuing certificates from the Susquehanna Company.

In May of 1786, the Company appointed a committee with full power and authority to locate townships within the territory. Members of this committee were Colonel John Franklin, General Ethan Allen, Major John Jenkins, and Colonel Zebulon Butler. The Company voted to "support and maintain their claims to the land aforesaid, and effectually justify and support their settlers therein."[315]

This fresh resolve of the Susquehanna Company caused a flow of new settlers to go to the lands claimed by it, now opening up that part of the original Susquehanna purchase upstream as far as Athens. Many of these people were investing as land speculators and most of them were newcomers to the scene.

The Wyoming settlement was peaceful and quiet at this time. The nucleus of old settlers—those who had arrived prior to the Trenton Decree—formed a stable, rather conservative group. Not resentful of the new immigrants, they nevertheless looked upon them as something different. This difference created two action parties, one conservative, and the other liberal and even radical; during the forthcoming struggle for right of soil and for integration into the state government these two bodies became increasingly recognizable.

The 14th Commonwealth Versus a New County

General Ethan Allen did visit Wyoming in April of 1786 as promised. He indicated a willingness to settle in Wyoming and proposed to bring a number of Green Mountain Boys with him. There was a secret plan to create a new state from the lands of the purchase and from some lands in New York State. News of this daring plan leaked out and spread rapidly among the settlers. The long established conservatives were vehemently opposed to the plan, whereas the radicals were all for it. The conservative objection was based upon a concern that creating a new state would dash their hopes for an early settlement of their land claims. All they had fought and struggled for would be lost forever.

When the news of this daring plan reached the state government, a general alarm developed. Should the state send troops back to Wyoming to try once again to settle the dispute by military means? This was suggested but rejected. Colonel Montgomery, in a letter to the Supreme Executive Council suggested that "If our General Assembly...go on to set that district off as a separate county, I believe it would tend to the same happy purpose, as it will open the way to some of the honors and emoluments of a county which will act as a counterpoise to (those) of a new state." [316]Montgomery goes on to condemn any use of the militia. On Saturday, September 23, 1786, the Pennsylvania Assembly called up the Bill for making the seventeen townships into a separate county. The Honorable Thomas Mifflin, as speaker of the Assembly, signed the Bill into law on September 25th. The new county, subsequently named Luzerne, was huge, extending from Nescopeck Creek on the south, to the New York State line on the north.

The Pennsylvania Assembly then passed a supplement to this Act, designating Colonel Timothy Pickering, Colonel Zebulon Butler and Colonel John Franklin as commissioners, notifying the settlers in the new county that election of county officers would take place on February 1, 1787. Meanwhile, Colonel Pickering was called upon to proceed to Wyoming to begin the task of persuading the settlers to approve the Act.

"The Pumpkin Fresh"

This grand strategy was interrupted in October by a flood. Miner states:[317] "The waters of the Susquehanna rose to a height never known except at the ice flood....This was termed the 'pumpkin fresh,' from the immense number that floated downstream, to the astonishment of the people below. Great and irreparable losses were sustained in hay, grain and cattle, causing much suffering during the ensuing winter. Several houses and barns were swept away, and one or two lives lost.

As soon as the water receded, Pickering arrived. Colonel Pickering, born in Massachusetts, had been the Quartermaster General of the Armies in the Revolution and held the respect of Congress. He was dispatched to Wyoming to perform a difficult task. The population in the settlement was now much more complex due to the influx of many people of diverse background. It was no longer a closely knit homogeneous group. Nevertheless Colonel Pickering began his assigned task with vigor and enthusiasm. During this period he moved up and down both sides of the river, meeting groups wherever and whenever possible, explaining patiently the details of the new county government.

He found the older settlers to be friendly and willing to support the creation of a new county. The more recent arrivals and some of the radicals were opposed, wanting to make a new state, independent of Pennsylvania. On a few occasions, he met with Bennet, either alone or as a member of a group.

Thomas Bennet maintained an active interest in the politics of the settlement long after the close of the Second Yankee-Pennamite War. His opinion was sought from time to time by community leaders. Pickering states: [318] "Thursday, June 11th (1787) This morning I dispatched James Whitney with copies of the Act, and notifications signed by Colonel Butler and me...to deliver the post up through the whole settlement from Lackawanna to Tioga, on both sides of the river. In the afternoon Major (John) Jenkins from Exeter, old Mr. Thomas Bennet from Abraham's Plains, Major McCormick from Kingston, Captain John Swift from Shawnee, and diverse others, came to my lodgings to speak and hear in relation to the proposed election."

Bennet Tenacity

It is remarkable that the Bennets had managed to avoid confiscation and dispossession during the vicious Yankee-Pennamite conflict of June-December 1784, particularly when many properties changed hands three or four times in those few months. One reason for this stability might be that the Bennet farm was located not far from Fort Defence, the Yankee stronghold on Abraham's Creek and was less vulnerable to attack than those dwellings closer to the Pennamites at Fort Dickinson.

In addition, there is evidence to indicate that the female Bennets maintained an active production of marketable clothing and various garments which could have been sold or bartered to the Pennamites. The production of cloth and of twine was a "cash crop" of the Bennet family. During those troubled days there was very little wool available, because the sheep were driven away or slaughtered by the Pennamites; and there was no locally produced cotton. Much needed clothing had to be made from flax; this grew well in Wyoming Valley and the plants were not likely to be plundered by wandering soldiers or civilians.

Flax was a tough and durable plant. To harvest it, a powerful tug pulled it out of the ground. Whereupon it was dried in the field, then "rippled" by dragging the stalks through a course wooden comb to strip off the seed pods. These pods were gathered together and pressed to deliver linseed oil. After rippling, the stalks were soaked under water for at least five days. This made the central core of the plant brittle, so that it could be broken into smaller pieces in a flax "brake." In order to get at the broken bits of core, both sides of it were then attacked by swinging a long wooden knife, using downward, scraping strokes against a vertical stalk.

Harvesting the flax and bringing the process up to this point was clearly the work of men—it was heavy and hard labor. The few fibers were then combed out straight and cleaned of the broken pieces. Then the women would spin the fibers into thread on a flax wheel. Cloth required quantities of spun yarn, so that the women spun at every opportunity. Linen fabric was made into clothing, napkins, sheets and bedding. Coarser fibers were made into much needed twine, or into canvas for sacking and bags.[319]

The Bennets created what must have been a thriving industry for that time. Colonel Timothy Pickering has this entry in his journal: "Tuesday, January 16th [1787]. With Colonel Butler and Captain Schott went to old Thomas Bennet's on Abrahams' Plains...I have seen more industry at Mr. Bennet's than at all other places in the County. The old man was near his house, with another hand, breaking flax, and when we entered the house we found his wife and two daughters spinning. The room, too, was hung round with clothing, chiefly of their own spinning, and hanks of linen yarn like in the Dutch houses in Jersey. The old man put on a brown linen coat, waist-coat, and breeches of their own fabric. ...His wife said since their sheep had been destroyed, they were obliged to content themselves with linen garments. ...They dined us well and hospitably."[320]

Pickering usually rode from town to town accompanied by a small staff. On Monday, January 15, he "crossed the river to Kingston with Colonel Butler and Captain Schott, and went to Mr. Lawrence Myers. He and his brother and another young man (all from Maryland) keep a small store of goods, wet and dry. Lawrence Myers was formerly a Lieutenant in Schott's Company."

The leader of the radical opposition, Colonel John Franklin, also canvased the settlements for support, having the determined goal of creating the new state. Franklin was a match for Pickering, being equally persuasive and possessing a powerful personality. Franklin would prove to be relentless in his pursuit of this goal, an effort which in time would lead to disaster.

CHAPTER 20

Luzerne County Established

Luzerne County Elections

The General Assembly in Harrisburg named the new county "Luzerne" in honor of Le Chevalier de la Luzerne, who was France's Minister to the United States from 1779-1784. The Act creating the County called for the election of officers. To become qualified, it was necessary to give an oath of allegiance to the Commonwealth of Pennsylvania. A number of inhabitants had already done this, but Colonels Pickering and Butler signed up several more, the final list showing names of 146 men eligible to vote.[321] The election on February 1, 1787, took place in the home of Colonel Zebulon Butler at the corner of River and Northampton Streets in Wilkes-Barre. Additional voters arrived from settlements some distance from Wilkes-Barre. The first elected officers of Luzerne County were: Colonel John Franklin, Representative to the General Assembly; Colonel Nathan Denison, Councillor; Lord Butler and Mason F. Allen, Sheriffs; Nathan Carey and John Dorrance, Coroners; Jonah Rogers and Nathan Kingsley, Commissioners. Franklin refused to serve, remaining true to his vow to establish the new state.

Franklin Pushes for 14th Commonwealth

Colonel Franklin now increased his efforts to gain support for his venture, moving his headquarters to Athens, close to the Pennsylvania-New York border. From this point he conducted his land office, issuing a large number of Susquehanna grants and actually populating the northern tier. People from New England poured in to develop new towns and settlements throughout the upper reaches of the new County of Luzerne.

The Confirming Act

Alarmed by these developments, the General Assembly meeting in Philadelphia voted to approve a bill which had been presented by Colonel Pickering. This bill stated that "All the said rights or lots now laying within the County of Luzerne, which were occupied or acquired by Connecticut claimants who were actual settlers there at or before the termination of the claim of the State of Connecticut, by the (Trenton) Decree, agreeably to the regulations then in force among them, be and they are hereby confirmed to them and their heirs and assigns."[322] This bill was enacted on March 28th, 1787, and became popularly known as the "Confirming Act."

There arose a strong difference among settlers whether to accept and support this Act or to ignore it. Some cast their fortunes with Pickering while others vehemently wanted to follow the lead of John Franklin towards separation. The Pickering allies were Colonel Denison, Matthias Hollenback, James Sutton and Dr. William Smith. Most of the people living up the river were followers of Colonel Franklin, as were the Slocums, Jenkins, Spauldings and Satterlees.

Open Town Meeting at Forty Fort

So intense were the two sides that it was decided to hold an open meeting, inviting all interested parties to attend. On April 19th the meeting was held in Forty Fort. Brewster called it the "greatest gathering ever held in the Wyoming settlements. The prosperous established farmers living in the old settling towns of Kingston, Plymouth, Hanover, Wilkes-Barre, Pittston and Exeter were all there."[323] In addition, representatives came from remote areas such as Ulster, Claverack and Salem.

A platform had been built for the moderator and clerks of the meeting, and there was a stand for the speakers; James Sutton presided. Sutton's daughter attended and described what took place: "When the people were called together to vote upon the question of submitting to the Laws of Pennsylvania, my father was appointed moderator, and it devolved upon him to receive the votes and report the result. The Franklin men, beginning to doubt their strength, took father away, and carried him into the woods. A general melee followed. The men rushed into the thicket and cut clubs; it was an awful scene. ...Heavy green clubs were lifted and brandished in all directions. Father was found and brought back...no one was killed or very seriously injured."[324]

The Bennets also attended, and Miss Martha gives a more colorful description of the event. "Colonel Pickering made an eloquent speech in favor of submission to the jurisdiction of Pennsylvania, giving the most ample assurances that the government would protect the settlers in all their rights as citizens, and that there should be no more harassing procedures instituted against them. Colonel Franklin then arose and rehearsed the grievances of the settlers, and denounced the 'pretended compromise' and all its supporters in the most unmeasured terms. The blood of the old Yankees was stirred. Some were on one side, and others on the other, but all were excited and determined on victory. The old argument of physical force was not yet quite out of date, and, in the absence of firearms, each man ran to the grove hard by and cut a club. Many blows were dealt on both sides. ...There was a general melee. Esquire Sutton was driven from the stage and disappeared. Supposing that he was spirited away, and was about to be victimized by the hare-brained partisans of Franklin, a party scoured the woods and by-places, and found him. ...Colonel Hollenback cracked Colonel Franklin about the ears with his riding-whip, loading him with a volley of epithets. A rather informal vote to sustain the Laws of Pennsylvania and accept the proposed compromise was passed and the gathering dispersed." [325]

Martha Bennet Marries Philip Myers

The Bennets now became occupied with the impending marriage of Miss Martha to Philip Myers. At the urging of his brother, Lawrence, Philip had come to Wyoming from the family home in Frederick, Maryland. Arriving there in 1785, he assisted his older brother in maintaining a general store and tavern at Kingston Corners. For several months he sought the hand of Martha Bennet, and they were married on July 15, 1787. He was age twenty-seven and she was twenty-five.

"Thomas Bennet gave his new son-in-law a town lot on the north line of old Forty-Fort. On this he (Philip) erected a comfortable house constructed of yellow pine logs, hewed and pointed with lime mortar and lined on the inside."[326]

Thomas and Martha Bennet now had to adjust to the departure of Miss Martha from their family home. In addition to the loss of their oldest daughter, they experienced the departure of Solomon. He had purchased from the Susquehanna Company at least one-half share in the new development up river at Athens, and moved there to establish his own home. This left young Andrew and Miss Polly to help with the farm and the spinning and weaving. One or more hired hands were employed as the domestic situation required.

County Officially Organized

The structure of the county was now established, with elected officials in place. The first court met on May 29, 1787, at the home of Colonel Butler. On advice of Colonel Pickering, the state authorized the establishment of a county militia. Officers of the 7th Company, representing volunteers from the upper district of Kingston, were: Major Lawrence Myers, commanding; Benjamin Smith, captain; Philip Myers, lieutenant; and Andrew Bennet, ensign. The Wilkes-Barre Company was under the command of Captain William Ross. The Hanover boys were under Captain Rosewell Franklin, and a troop of horses was commanded by Captain John Paul Schott. All companies were under the direction of Lord Butler, Esquire, who had been elected high sheriff of the county.

Franklin had been empowered by the Susquehanna Company to sell whole or half shares, and soon spirited speculation in their lands developed in Pennsylvania, New York, New Jersey and Connecticut. He sent members of his party to survey lost titles. Some, long forgotten, were revived and activated. In all of this, Franklin was the prime mover. Contact with newcomers gave him an increasingly wide basis of support, especially among those settling upriver from Wyoming.

Franklin Arrested

Franklin's activities were closely followed by those governing Pennsylvania and a warrant for his arrest was soon issued by Chief Justice McKean of the Supreme Court of Pennsylvania. This action was taken when, on September 23rd, Franklin wrote the following note: "Sir, you are requested to give notice to the half share men and settlers at Wysox and Towanda who expect to support their lands under the

Susquehanna Company that they will appear to Abel Yarrington's in Wilkes-Barre on Tuesday the 9th of October at 9 o'clock in the morning complete in arms and equipped."[327] He signed his name as John Franklin, Commandant, in several of these communications. These notes were widely distributed by Franklin and his supporters.

In order to activate the warrant, the Supreme Executive Committee directed Colonel Craig, commanding lieutenant of the Northampton County Militia, to proceed to Wyoming to take Franklin into custody. Craig chose to take just a few older experienced continental officers with him rather than a company of militia. Miner states [328] that four men surprised Franklin, tricking him by informing him that his presence was requested in the red house near the ferry. Franklin was standing in front of Yarrington's home, close by. The four men identified themselves as interested in purchasing some land from the Susquehanna Company. Franklin was enticed to walk to the nearby red house when he was suddenly seized from behind. Franklin was big and strong and shook off his would-be captors repeatedly.

The fight that transpired grew increasingly violent, and Franklin received a powerful blow to the head which for the moment made him almost senseless. Blood streamed down his face. Miner quotes Colonel Pickering: "The four gentlemen seized him, two of their horses were in my stable, which were sent to them; but soon my servant returned on one of them with a message ... that the people were assembling in numbers, and requested me to come with what men were near me, to prevent a rescue. I took two loaded pistols in my hands, and went with another servant to their aid. Just as I met them, Franklin threw himself off his horse, and renewed his struggle with them. His hair was disheveled and face bloody with the preceding efforts. I told the gentlemen they would never carry him off unless his feet were tied under his horse's belly. I sent for a cord. The gentlemen remounted him, and my servant tied his feet. Then one taking his bridle, another following behind, and the others riding one on each side, they whipped up his horse, and were soon beyond the reach of his friends." With considerable haste, he was thus carried off to the jail in Philadelphia.

CHAPTER 21
Pennsylvania and the New Constitution

The Constitutional Convention of 1787

1787 was the year during which was created the great new nation, the United States of America. The Constitutional Convention had been called for May 14, 1787, but because of late arrivals, it did not convene until May 25th. The remarkable document was completed fourteen weeks later. Page Smith termed it the most serviceable written constitution. "It rose out of a strange conjunction of political and theological ideas several thousand years fermenting."[329]

A condensed version of how this was accomplished is justified in view of its supreme effect upon the affairs of the world during the ensuing years. Since it passed by the narrowest of margins, it had to be the result of remarkably clever political maneuvering. Its progress was guided largely by men who had experienced the struggle leading up to the Declaration of Independence, and who had suffered through the Revolution. They had also lived under the inadequate government of the Articles of Confederation and realized something better was badly needed. People living in the several states as well as their elected delegates shared these experiences in common.

Delegates to the convention from Pennsylvania were Gouverneur Morris, James Wilson, Robert Morris, Thomas Fitzsimmons and Benjamin Franklin. As soon as the delegates were seated Robert Morris rose to inform the assembly that his state had instructed him to nominate General George Washington, Esquire, to preside over the convention. Washington promptly took the chair and graciously thanked the delegates for this honor, taking the responsibility most seriously. He was the most widely respected leader of the land, and his presence proved to be of enormous importance in maintaining an orderly and dignified ambience despite the intensity of the debates.

On Tuesday, May 29th, Edmond Randolph of Virginia presented a plan for a new constitution. In it he listed those issues which he thought ought to be matters for consideration. Known then as the Virginia Plan, it is remarkable that the final draft of the Constitution for the most part resembled this plan. Much thought had gone into the preparation of the Virginia Plan; it shortened the work of the convention by giving it a template for organized and structured debate.

Among the most contested issues, a few stand out as remaining unsettled even today: How to limit the power of the executive to prevent the arrogant seizure of that power by an ambitious president? How long the term of office and should he be eligible for re-election? How to create a federal judiciary and make the Supreme Court the watchdog or guardian of the constitution? How to elect the president, and make him truly the choice of the people? How to remove him (and others) from office should the need arise? What should be the terms of office for members of the Congress?

The Preamble Completed

On Saturday, September 8th, a committee was created to edit all material to date and to put it in the best literary style. On Wednesday, September 12th, the committee reported printed copies of a digest of the plan. The report began:

"We the people of the United States, in order to form a more perfect union, to establish justice, insure domestic tranquility, provide for the common defense, promote the general welfare, and secure the blessings of liberty to ourselves and our posterity, do ordain and establish this constitution for the United States of America."[330]

Franklin Addresses the Convention

This preamble was followed by several pages on which the body of the constitution was printed. By Monday, September 17th, the reading was completed, whereupon Benjamin Franklin rose to deliver some words of wisdom: "...when you assemble a number of men to have the advantage of their joint wisdom, you inevitably assemble with those men, all their prejudices, their passions, their errors of opinion, their local interests, and their selfish views. From such an assembly can a perfect production be expected? It therefore astonishes me...

to find this system approaching so near to perfection as it does, and I think it will astonish our enemies...I hope therefore that for our own sakes as *a part of the people,* we shall act heartily and unanimously in recommending this constitution ... and turn our future thoughts and endeavors to the means of having it well administered."[331]

The Federalist Papers

The constitution was then printed and copies distributed throughout the states, for it was now necessary to pilot the ship through the murky waters of state politics. Hamilton, Madison and John Jay hastened to write a series of papers in which were detailed an explanation and defense of the major principles of the constitution. The series was printed in a number of newspapers in all states. Known as the Federalist papers, they became the recognized statement of the constitution.

Hamilton, writing the first of these papers, set their purpose as intending to discuss "the utility of the Union to your political prosperity. The insufficiency of the present Confederation to preserve that union—the necessity of a government at least equally energetic with the one proposed, to the attainment of their object—the conformity of the proposed Constitution to the true principles of republican government—its analogy to your own state constitution—and lastly, additional security which its adoption will afford to the preservation of that species of government, to liberty, and to property."[332]

Anti-constitutionalists were widespread and threatening, particularly in Massachusetts, New Hampshire and Virginia. Final ratification did occur in all three states, but only by a narrow majority—in Massachusetts, only by ten votes.

A copy of the Constitution appears to have reached the Pennsylvania House of Assembly promptly. In a letter to Colonel Pickering dated September 17th, Samuel Hogdon (his business partner) wrote:[333] "This a.m. the new constitution was read in our House of Assembly to a crowded audience and seems to be generally approved. Indeed, we have been in high glee ever since, bells ringing and congratulations in every street."

Pickering Participates in Convention

Pickering had been elected by a large majority from Luzerne County to be delegate to the Pennsylvania Convention for state ratification of the proposed Constitution. He was known to be a supporter of the new Constitution and thus reflected the attitude of the majority of voters in the County. Thomas Bennet and his family were strong Federalists. Lawrence Myers, a close friend of the Bennets, was described by Miner as follows: "Myers was a zealous Federalist, but too liberal and kind to cherish a particle of ill will against his opponents...for several years (he) gave that party great influence, aiding to preserve it in the ascendancy."[334] In general, the Bennet and Myers families shared the same political philosophy.

On December 12, 1787, the Pennsylvania delegates ratified the Constitution, being the second state of the new union to subscribe to the document. Concerning this process, Colonel Pickering noted:[335] "After a great deal of discussion, the Convention assembled and ratified the Constitution. It was engrossed on parchment, and received the signatures of nearly all the Delegates, including the opposers while under discussion, with the exception of three of four obstinate men, and, to the best of my recollection of their characters, as ignorant as obstinate. Opposers of its adoption were the extra republicans or democrats—the same sort of men who afterwards were called anti-federalists and who uniformly oppose all leading measures of the federal administration of the general government."

Joseph Wilson was the strong leader in the Pennsylvania Assembly. Although the Assembly very likely would have voted for the Constitution much earlier, Wilson insisted the entire document be studied, item by item, before submitting it to a vote.

Ratification

As can be seen by the table from Cooke,[336]ratification proceeded rapidly in some states such as Delaware and Pennsylvania, but was delayed almost two years by Rhode Island, carrying by a vote of 34-32 on May 29, 1790.

Cooke states that celebrations to honor the final ratification were held everywhere. "Stone masons, bricklayers, carpenters, wire merchants, brewers and apprentices of every trade marched with tailors, hatters, wigmakers and other craftsmen behind banners and floats proclaiming support for the new government." [337]

RATIFICATION of the CONSTITUTION

State	Date	Vote
Delaware	Dec. 7, 1787	Unanimous
Pennsylvania	Dec. 12, 1787	46-23
New Jersey	Dec. 18, 1787	Unanimous
Georgia	Jan. 2, 1788	Unanimous
Connecticut	Jan. 9, 1788	128-40
Massachusetts	Feb. 6, 1788	187-168
Maryland	Apr. 26, 1788	63-11
South Carolina	May 23, 1788	149-73
New Hampshire	June 21, 1788	57-47
Virginia	June 25, 1788	89-79
New York	July 26, 1788	30-27
North Carolina	Nov. 21, 1788	195-77
Rhode Island	May 29, 1790	34-32

Washington Becomes President

In April 1789, the electors met to select the first president. George Washington received a unanimous vote and was inaugurated in New York City on April 30, 1789. With Washington at its helm, the new government began to function. Again, Washington proved to be a wise and fortunate choice, carrying with him the respect and admiration of the people. This was crucial in the early, uncertain days of his administration.

Page Smith [338] states "The most crucial element in the success of the new government was undoubtedly the fact that Washington had accepted the presidency. He gave the entire government the sanction and authority that no one else could have. By being president he authenticated the Constitution."

Subsequent generations of citizens in the United States and elsewhere in the world have drawn benefit and inspiration from the Constitution. They all owe a debt of gratitude to the framers of the instrument and to the people who had the courage and wisdom to carry it into practice and to support it.

CHAPTER 22

An Era Draws to an End

Colonel Pickering Taken Captive in June 1788

Colonel Pickering returned to Wyoming in January 1788, and in June he was seized at about 11 p.m. when he was in bed, sleeping. He was taken up river by his captors. The kidnapping was planned and carried out by followers of Colonel Franklin, and had the motive of forcing Franklin's release from the Philadelphia jail. At one point, Pickering was kept in chains. "Colonel Franklin... had been put in irons in the Philadelphia jail, and they must put irons on me, although it was not agreeable to them to do it." [339]

Following the abduction of Colonel Pickering, the Luzerne County Sheriff immediately called out the four companies of militia. Near Meshoppen, Captain Ross and his company encountered "a party of the wild Yankees under the lead of Gideon Dudley. An action ensued in which Captain Ross received a severe wound,...the ball passing through him, lodged in the skin of the opposite side, from which it was some time after extracted. He was removed with all possible care to Wilkes-Barre where he slowly recovered. A ball struck Dudley in the wrist, when his party retreated"[340]No other injuries appear to have occurred during this pursuit by the militia.

Release of Pickering

After nineteen days of captivity, Colonel Pickering was voluntarily released by his captors and returned to his home in Wilkes-Barre, there joining his wife and children. Several fleeing captors were captured and placed under arrest. Of the twenty-seven indicted either for direct participation or for being accessories, nine had pleaded guilty in preliminary hearings and were brought up from Easton jail for sentencing.

In September 1788, the Court of Quarter Sessions was held at Wilkes-Barre to hear the testimonies of those involved with the abduction of Pickering. A special Grand Jury was selected and impaneled, consisting of Lawrence Myers, foreman, Benjamin Bailey, Jabez Fitch, Solomon Avery, Elisha Blackman, Daniel Dawling, Jacob Patrick, Thomas Bennet, John Dorrance, Philip Myers, Samuel Dailey, Stephen Harting, Isaac Allen, Elijah Sillsby, Samuel Miller, John Scott, Benjamin Jones, Joseph Wheeler, Leonard Westbrook, Justus Gaylord, and Joseph Elliott.[341]

Colonel Franklin Indicted

A Supreme Court was opened at Wilkes-Barre in early November 1788. Colonel Franklin was finally indicted on a charge of high treason, "In endeavoring to subvert the government and to erect a new and independent state in the room and stead thereof."[342] His attorney moved for a postponement of the trial on the grounds that important defense witnesses were absent. The motion was granted. Franklin was released on temporary bail, and seems to have spent the next two weeks in the Wilkes-Barre area, visiting his many friends.

He was then transferred to the Easton jail, and later returned to Philadelphia accompanied by Captain William Ross. He spent an additional year there before being released. He was thus detained for a total of about one and a half years, much of that time without an indictment and all of it without actual trial. Franklin was given his liberty in September 1789, making his way back to Wilkes-Barre "on a canoe, carrying five passengers, that he sold on his arrival for three dollars to pay a debt."[343] He left Wyoming for Athens on April 26, 1790, and walked the entire way, arriving in Athens five days later.

Franklin Pardoned

Franklin was finally pardoned by Governor Mifflin on January 9, 1792. After an arduous and lengthy incarceration in the Philadelphia jail, he had lost much weight and was in general depleted. He quickly regained his strength and became a vigorous farmer. His popularity among the settlers of the Susquehanna basin never diminished. In 1793 he was named a Lieutenant Colonel of Militia and he served intermittently over several years as an elected member of the state legislature.

Meanwhile Pickering's career in Wyoming came to its close. He was elected a delegate to the Pennsylvania Constitutional Convention in the fall elections of 1789 and served in this capacity until the new state constitution was completed and passed on September 2, 1790 . On the 4th of September he was appointed to be head of the Indian Commission by George Washington. He seems to have won the approval and support of the Six Nations, holding conferences over a long period at Tioga Point. Late in June 1791, he had a second conference with the Indians, this time at Newtown, New York.

Pickering Becomes U. S. Postmaster General

In the fall of 1791, Pickering left Wyoming to serve as the U.S. Postmaster General, and finally moved his family to their new home in Philadelphia. His illustrious and honest administration of affairs at Wyoming came to an end. He was widely admired and respected by the settlers, and had repeatedly shown his leadership on their behalf.

Pennsylvania Constitution Revised

Ratification of the U.S. Constitution forced the several member states to construct new constitutions to bring state governments into agreement with the federal document. In the 1780s the government of Pennsylvania had foundered. Neither the U. S. Articles of Confederation nor the State Constitution of 1776 provided for adequate governing authority. The citizens of the state were restless and wanted a convention to write the new constitution. This was finally called at Philadelphia in November 1789.

Tinkcom states that "the electorate showed wisdom in its selection of some of the best political and legal talent from both factions for and against a new constitution."[344] Thomas Mifflin was elected to preside. Debate was on a high plane and many compromises were made quite smoothly. The new Pennsylvania Constitution owed much to the federal plan of government. Full legislative power was vested in a Senate and a House of Representatives. Senators were to serve four years, while the representatives were to be elected annually from the counties and the city of Philadelphia.

A popularly elected Governor was the supreme executive authority, given veto power, large appointive privileges, and was commander-in-chief of the armed forces of the state when they were not in the service of the United States. He held a three year term and could not serve more than nine of any twelve years. A judiciary system was established which permitted judges of the Supreme and Common Pleas Courts to hold office during good behavior. Article IX, consisting of twenty-six sections, carefully outlined a Bill of Rights. [345]

This new state constitution gave stability to its people and served to put a stamp of finality on a phase of potential ferment that was peculiar to American History. Nowhere was this appreciated more than among the settlers at Wyoming. Traditionally obsessed with the law and its careful administration, they now at last had a structure through which their many conflicting land titles could be quieted. Particularly they considered that their "right of soil" might be honored.

Thomas Bennet was among those early Connecticut settlers who held title to his extensive lands from the Susquehanna Company. He had established his right in 1770, and had, more than most, occupied his land continuously since then. Forcibly required to leave on occasion, he would return just as soon as possible, usually after an absence of a few weeks.

The romance and excitement of his life gradually faded in the closing years of the decade 1780-1790, even though he was involved in his farming and watching his family grow. That he was considered a symbol of his time was shown by his jury selection in the never completed trial of Colonel Franklin.

Bennets Buried at Forty Fort Cemetery

Thomas Bennet died in 1796 at age seventy-five, quietly and at his home in Forty Fort. His wife Martha died in May, 1811, at age eighty. During her widowhood she lived among her four children and twenty-four grandchildren. She slowly lost her sight and became increasingly dependent on her family. Nevertheless she was recognized by Miner as one of the clearest chroniclers of early scenes.

Both Mr. and Mrs. Bennet were buried in a plot at Forty Fort Cemetery. In 1770 the proprietors of Kingston Township had set apart as a burying ground a square acre of land in the town plot, lying north and east of the present meeting house. In November 1779, the proprietors noted that the burial ground was overgrown with briar and bush and they resolved to grub it out. They then enclosed the grounds with a fence, so as to keep out prowling cattle. It has become the oldest burial ground still in use in Northern Pennsylvania.[346]

In June 1972 a severe hurricane struck the basin of the north branch of the Susquehanna River. The raging waters of the river washed out part of the cemetery, carrying coffins and cadavers downstream. The extent of the damage was considerable, but it stopped just short of the grave of Thomas Bennet. He may be said to have once again clung to his beloved land, demonstrating symbolically for perhaps the last time the tenacious spirit of the old settlers from Connecticut.

Settlement of the Land Titles

Land and its possession was the fuel feeding the continued struggle in Wyoming. As stated earlier, the Confirming Act was passed by the State Legislature on March 28, 1787. All Connecticut claimants who were there prior to the Trenton Decree of 1782 had their property rights confirmed by this Act. It was repealed on April 1, 1788, after little more than one year.

The disputed titles remained unsettled until the State legislature passed the Compromising Act on April 4, 1799. By this Act three Commissioners "were appointed to examine and to ascertain the quantity, quality and situation of all lands in the seventeen townships held or claimed under Pennsylvania title and to divide the same according to the value into four classes."[347] The Act required that all those claiming under Pennsylvania to the extent of 40,000 acres must file deeds of release in the land office, and that all Connecticut settlers file their submission to the Commissioners determination. No lands could be examined except those released as described above.

The Act was amended repeatedly over the next decade, allowing extensions of the time limit for filing, altering and updating land values, liberalizing methods of payment, allowing civil suit against the State of Pennsylvania, authorizing the Land Office to issue patents for lands certified by the Commissioners, etc. The general philosophy pursued by the State of Pennsylvania was liberal, a radical change from previous years.

Thomas Cooper, Chairman of the Commission, was its soul, acting with firmness and impartiality, "rendering a just compensation to Pennsylvania claimants and confirming to the actual settlers, the Connecticut people, the fruits of their toil."[348]

Regardless of the statutes of the State of Pennsylvania, the Connecticut settlers were quite active in the sale and transfer of their lands from 1772 onward. Brewster describes in detail this activity in Kingston Township (p. 505-525). Some lots showed many transfers of title, for example Lot #1, Third Division, initially drawn by Ezra Belding, was deeded to a new owner nine times between 1772 and 1811!

Several instances show an attempt to consolidate ever larger estates, as, for example, by the Shoemakers, the Dorrances, the Myers family, and others. Thomas Bennet is listed as sometime owner of Lots #8 and 19, 1st Division; #13, 2nd Division; #8, 24, 28, 33,3rd Division; and #34,4th Division. During the final decade of his life he deeded parcels to Andrew, his son, and to John Tuttle and Philip Myers, both sons-in-law. His eldest son, Solomon, who moved to Athens, does not appear as an inheritor of Wyoming lands.

All of the lots of the original Kingston Township were certified titles under the Act of 1799, and all were ultimately issued Patents by the Pennsylvania Land Office. Each one had to be examined by the Land Commission and certified by it. Nevertheless, a number of title lawsuits are on record during this period. The final one, Bird vs. Snyder (8 Watts) was decided by Chief Justice Gibson in 1839.

It is worth noting that the ultimate secure title was from the State of Pennsylvania, through its Special Commission and the Land Office. The bulk of legal opinion agreed with Chief Justice Tilghman in Satterlee vs. Mathewson (13 5. & R.133). He said, in 1825 "It is very clear that one who entered on land in Pennsylvania, under a title derived from the State of Connecticut, acquired no right in law or equity. What is called an improvement or settlement right arises from an implied contract between the settler and the Commonwealth, that the settler should have the right of preemption, in consideration of the benefit rendered to the public by his improvement.... From the time of the Decree of Trenton, the Courts of Pennsylvania must consider the title of Connecticut as of no validity either in law or in equity, except as it may have been confirmed by an Act of Assembly."[349] That so many of the Connecticut settlers ultimately received certification and patent for their titles is a measure of the final wisdom and bounty of the Commonwealth.

CHAPTER 23

Reflections

Although the written record of the life of Thomas Bennet presents some gaps which interrupted the continuity of our narrative, there is a surprising body of reference scattered in several books. Indeed, there is enough to create a fairly accurate picture of the man and his family as their lives wind through this exciting and challenging period.

Once he had decided to migrate to Wyoming he never deviated from accomplishing this difficult task. He returned again and again to occupy the lands on the west side of the Susquehanna River for which he had drawn possession in 1772.

He was a tall, strong, quiet man, enjoying his own counsel. His steadfast devotion to his Wyoming lands was exceeded only by devotion to his family, without whose strength he could not have accomplished his goal. Not at all militant he nevertheless could fight effectively when challenged—witness his leadership and fighting skill when he and his party were kidnapped by the Indians in 1782. It was he who plotted and carried out the escape and who led his small party back to Forty Fort.

The period during which he lived witnessed momentous changes in the thirteen colonies. Citizens of his time grew through the Declaration of Independence, the War of the Revolution, the Articles of Confederation, and the development and ratification of the United States Constitution. Although communications were primitive, there was a sense of immediacy, of being a part of what was created.

Many nations of today owe a debt of gratitude to those men for their courage, wisdom, and political maturity. They fashioned a document which any society might follow, using it as a template for constructing democracy.

Many years have passed since the last voices of these brave men and women have been stilled. The stamp of New

England was made upon a large area of Northeastern Pennsylvania and some of it remains. This is more noticeable as one travels up river through Tunkhannock, Laceyville, Wyalusing, and Towanda to Athens. Many of their towns could just as well be in Connecticut. The physical planning and the architecture, the conservation of land, the quiet sense of order—all are reminders of New England. In many instances, the people are fifth or sixth generation descendents of the Yankee settlers. They remain fiercely independent, suspicious of "government," protective of their lands, intensely loyal to one another. But when fully informed they are able to generate surprising enthusiasm for or against a project.

It is their stewardship of land and river that has kept both remarkably beautiful. Indeed the river remains Northeastern Pennsylvania's greatest natural resource, largely as a result of care given by the people upriver.

In the twenty mile traverse of the river through Wyoming Valley there are also lingering marks of the first settlers. Take a walk north along Susquehanna Avenue in West Pittston and follow the river along its bend towards the gap at Coxton. Several homes look down upon you in quiet and dignified repose, creating an ambiance augmented by the gentle mantle of evening. Some of this experience may also occur on River Street, Forty Fort, beginning where the old church and meeting house still stand.

During the 19th century, the burgeoning anthracite industry drew large numbers of immigrants from central and southern Europe as well as from Wales, Ireland, Scotland and Britain. Even so, the descendants of the Yankee settlers have continued in the forefront of leadership throughout the community. In Wilkes-Barre, the orderly city plan, with its central square, was laid out in 1772. From Plymouth to Exeter, the "great road" – Wyoming Avenue–was also drawn in 1772.

There remains a remarkable social stability despite the extensive mixture of ethnic cultures. The several towns jealously guard their independence of governing, holding open council meetings in which all citizens may participate. Freedom to worship as one desires is a community blessing. The area has a remarkably varied church architecture, mirroring the spread of ethnicity here; it may be that the early lessons of tolerance have filtered down through subsequent generations.

It is fair to say the Connecticut settlement of Wyoming was driven primarily by economics. Tillable and productive lands of Connecticut had been fully occupied and used by 1760, and it was logical to develop new settlements to the west—a beckoning, fertile, undeveloped land whose westward limitations were yet unknown.

It is not surprising that this movement would be resisted by those already possessing the land or planning to do so. Confusion over boundaries was common because maps of the time were inaccurate. Most land had not been surveyed and there was widespread speculation on the part of ambitious men desiring to profit from land ownership, if not from settlement.

In Northeast Pennsylvania, the confrontation resulted in a civil war lasting from 1770 to 1784, interrupted temporarily by the War for Independence. This struggle was fanned by land speculators who had no real desire to settle the land themselves. Influential land lobbies prevented resolution of the dispute over titles through negotiation, and determination of the "right of soil" was never resolved in court. Not until 1799 did the Pennsylvania legislature attack the problem of land titles with maturity and compassion.

It might be that this punishing conflict could have been avoided. But men's feelings ride high in these circumstances and the student has the feeling that relentless forces are at work. There seems to be a requirement that the play must find its own finale, with participants tossed along impersonally to the end.

Charles E. Myers
Larksville, Pennsylvania
1993

Footnotes

1. Oscar Jewell Harvey and Ernest G. Smith, *A History of Wilkes-Barre and Wyoming Valley,* 6 vols. (Wilkes-Barre, PA: The Raeder Co., 1909, 1927, 1929), 3: 1240. Following the death of Oscar Harvey in 1922, the final four volumes were completed by Ernest G. Smith.
2. Harvey, *History of Wilkes-Barre* (Wilkes-Barre, PA: Raeder Press, 1909), 1: 240-243.
3. Isaac A. Chapman, *The History of Wyoming* (1830; reprinted., Danbury, CT: Pantens, Inc., 1971) p. 40.
4. Ibid., p. 43,
5. Harvey, *History of Wilkes-Barre,* 1: 250.
6. Ibid., p. 253.
7. Ibid., pp. 254-255.
8. Julian Boyd, ed., *Minutes of the Susquehanna Company* (Ithaca, NY: Cornell University Press, 1930), p. 193.
9. Harvey, *History of Wilkes-Barre,* 1: 263-284.
10. Ibid., p. 293.
11. Charles Miner, *History of Wyoming* (Philadelphia: J. Crissy, 1845), p. 464.
12. Rev. George Peck, *Story of Wyoming* (New York: Harper and Brothers, 1858), p. 14.
13. Chapman, *History of Wyoming, p.* 6.
14. Francis Beck Brandt, *The Majestic Delaware* (Union City, NJ: William Wise and Co., 1981), p. 17.
15. Richard Smith, *A Tour of Four Great Rivers in 1769,* ed. Francis W. Halsey (Long Island City, NY: Ira I. Friedman, Inc., 1964), p. 70-80.
16. Harvey & Smith, *History of Wilkes-Barre,* 3:1210.
17. Peck, *Story of Wyoming,* p. 172.
18. William Brewster, *The Pennsylvania and New York Frontier* (Philadelphia: George McManus Co., 1954), p. 113.
19. Harvey, *History of Wilkes-Barre,* 1:401.
20. Ibid., p. 402.
21. *Minutes of the Susquehanna Company,* p. 400.
22. Harvey, *History of Wilkes-Barre,* 1: 403.
23. Peck, *Story of Wyoming, p.* 134.
24. P. H. Smith, *The History of Dutchess County, New York* (Pawling, NY: Published by the author, 1877), pp. 174-214
25. Rittenburg & Clark, *History of Orange County, New York* (Philadelphia: Evarts & Peck, 1881), p. 295.
26. Smith, *A Tour of Four Great Rivers,* p. 8.
27. Peck, *Story of Wyoming, p.* 135.
28. Rittenburg & Clark, *History of Orange County,* p. 699.
29. Smith, A *Tour of Four Great Rivers,* p. 76.
30. Rittenburg & Clark, *History of Orange County,* p. 699.
31. Harvey, *History of Wilkes-Barre,* 1: 441.
32. Ibid., pp. 430-431.
33. William F. Henn, *The Story of the River Road: Life Along the Delaware from Bushkill to Milford, Pike County, Pa.* (Published by the author, 1975), p. 89.

34. Peck, *Story of Wyoming*, p. 135.
35. Harvey, *History of Wilkes-Barre*, 1:430, 448.
36. Ibid., p. 465.
37. Ibid., p. 418.
38. Ibid., p. 444.
39. Ibid., pp. 452-453.
40. Ibid., p. 460.
41. Paul A. Wallace, (n. p.: Pennsylvania Historical Museum Collection, 1965), p. 2.
42. H. Holister, *The History of Lackawanna Valley* (New York: W. H. Tinson, 1857), p. 28.
43. Harvey, *History of Wilkes-Barre*, 1: 465.
44. Wm. Brewster, *History of Certified Township of Kingston, Pennsylvania* (Kingston, PA: School District of the Borough of Kingston, 1930), p. 31.
45. Henn, *Story of the River Road*, p. 4.
46. Harvey, *History of Wilkes-Barre*, 1: 477.
47. *Pennsylvania Archives*, 1771, p. 391.
48. Harvey, *History of Wilkes-Barre*, 1: 487, 481.
49. Peck, *Story of Wyoming*, 1: 134.
50. Harvey, *History of Wilkes-Barre*, 1: 488.
51. Ibid., 1: 493.
52. Ibid., 1: 507.
53. Ibid., 2: 626-627.
54. Ibid., 2: 633.
55. Ibid., 2: 643, 644.
56. Ibid., 2: 652.
57. Ibid., 2: 658, 659.
58. Ibid., 2: 661.
59. Brewster, *History of Certified Township of Kingston*, p. 80.
60. Ibid., p. 61 .
61. Ibid., p. 80.
62. Harvey, *History of Wilkes-Barre*, 2: 672.
63. Peck, *Story of Wyoming*, p. 366.
64. Harvey, *History of Wilkes-Barre*, 2: 669-671.
65. Ibid., p. 672.
66. Miner, *History of Wyoming*, p. 121.
67. Peck, *Story of Wyoming*, p. 366-370.
68. Harvey, *History of Wilkes-Barre*, 2: 672.
69. Ibid., 2: 676.
70. Ibid., 2: 678.
71. Ibid., 2: 681.
72. Peck,. *Story of Wyoming*, p. 143.
73. Harvey, 2: 740, 741.
74. Peck, *Story of Wyoming*, p. 143.
75. Ibid., p. 143-145.
76. Harvey, *History of Wilkes-Barre*, 2: 691.
77. Ibid., p. 694.
78. Ibid, p. 698.
79. Peck, *Story of Wyoming*. p. 147.
80. Peck, *Story of Wyoming*, p. 149.
81. Harvey, *History of Wilkes-Barre*, p. 756.
82. Sheldon Reynolds, "The Frontier Forts Within the Wyoming Valley, Pennsylvania," Read before the Wyoming Historical and Geological Society December 1894. Published in the State Report 1896, p. 20.

83. Peck, *Story of Wyoming*, p. 170.
84. Chapman, *History of Wyoming*, p. 99.
85. F. C. Johnson, Collection of Wyoming Valley Pamphlets. See address of Hon. John N. Conyngham delivered in 1856.
86. Julian Boyd, ed., *The Susquehanna Papers,* Published for Wyoming Historical and Geological Society, Wilkes-Barre, Pennsylvania (Ithaca, N. Y.: Cornell University Press, 1930. Reissued 1962),1: xxx-xxxi.
87. Brewster, *History of Certified Township of Kingston,* p. 109.
88. Ibid., p. 87.
89. Miner, *History of Wyoming*, p. 141.
90. Brewster, *History of Certified Township of Kingston,* p. 88.
91. Harvey, *History of Wilkes-Barre,* 2: 758.
92. Ibid., 2: 636.
93. Ibid., 2: 755.
94. Miner, *History of Wyoming*, p. 136.
95. Harvey, *History of Wilkes-Barre,* 2: 750.
96. Ibid., p. 760.
97. Chapman, *History of Wyoming*, p. 111.
98. Ibid., p. 111.
99. Harvey, *History of Wilkes-Barre,* 2: 793.
100. Chapman, *History of Wyoming*, p. 112.
101. Harvey, *History of Wilkes-Barre,* 2: 826.
102. W. W. Greener, *The Gun and Its Development,* 9th ed. (New York: Bonanza Books, 1967), pp. 119-120.
103. Edward Tunis, *Colonial Living,* 1st ed. (Cleveland, World Publishing Co., 1957.), p. 104.
104. Wm. S. Dutton, *One Thousand Years of Explosives* (New York: Rinehart and Winston, 1960), p. 12.
105. Tunis, *Colonial Living*, p. 123.
106. Harvey, *History of Wilkes-Barre,* 2: 858.
107. Ibid., p. 635.
108. Ibid., p. 787.
109. Ibid., p. 850.
110. Miner, *History of Wyoming*, p. 171.
111. Ibid., p. 171.
112. Peck, *Story of Wyoming*, p. 149.
113. Harvey, *History of Wilkes-Barre,* 2: 862.
114. This account of the Battle of Rampart Rocks is a synthesis of the stories told in Miner, Harvey, Brewster, and Plum.
115. Peck, *Story of Wyoming*, p. 149.
116. Adrienne Koch, ed., *The American Enlightenment* (New York: George Braziller, Inc., 1965), p. 287-290. Quoting Thomas Jefferson's essay *Intellectual Leadership for Independence.*
117. Ibid., p. 80.
118. Barbara W. Tuchman, *The March of Folly* (New York: Alfred A. Knopf, 1984), p. 130.
119. Ibid., p. 229.
120. George Otto Trevelyan, *The American Revolution,* ed. Richard B. Morris (New York: David McKay Company, Inc.,1969), p. 10.
121. Koch, *American Enlightenment*, p. 169.
122. Trevelyan, *American Revolution*, p. 2.
123. Thomas Paine, *Common Sense and Other Political Writings,* ed. Nelson F. Adkins (Indianapolis: Bobbs-Merrill Co., Inc., n. d.), p. 34.

124. Bernard A. Weisberger, *The American Heritage History of the American People* (New York: American Heritage Publishing Co., 1971), p. 97.
125. Bruce Catlin, *American Heritage Book of the Revolution* (New York: American Heritage Publishing Co., 1958), introduction.
126. Henry Steele Commager and Richard B. Morris, eds., *The Spirit of Seventy-Six* (New York: Harper and Row, 1975): p. 325.
127. Koch. *American Enlightenment*, pp. 181-182. Letters of John Adams attachment to England, and for An American Republic.
128. Joseph J. Kelley, Jr., *Pennsylvania. The Colonial Years* (New York: Doubleday & Co., Inc., 1980), p. 752.
129. Ibid.
130. Catherine Drinker Bowen, *John Adams and the American Revolution* (Boston: Little Brown & Co., 1949), p. 472.
131. Page Smith, *A New Age Begins* (New York: McGraw-Hill Book Co., 1976), 1: 656.
132. Commager and Morris, *Spirit of Seventy-Six, p.* 1062-1063.
133. Koch, *American Enlightenment*, pp. 290-292. From the Papers of Thomas Jefferson, The Debate on Independence.
134. Ibid., pp. 290-292.
135. Harvey, *History of Wilkes-Barre,* 2: 874-875.
136. Koch, *American Enlightenment*, p. 293.
137. Kelley, *Pennsylvania: The Colonial Years*, p. 764.
138. Peck, *Story of Wyoming*, p. 153.
139. Harvey, *History of Wilkes-Barre,* 2: 871.
140. Miner, *History of Wyoming*, p. 189.
141. Commager and Morris, *Spirit of Seventy-Six*, p. 327.
142. Harvey, *History of Wilkes-Barre,* 2: 878 .
143. Miner, *History of Wyoming*, p. 190
144. Harvey, *History of Wilkes-Barre*, 2: 870.
145. Ibid., 2: 883.
146. Reynolds, *Frontier Forts*, p. 20.
147. Harvey, *History of Wilkes-Barre,* 2: 884.
148 . Reynolds, *Frontier Forts*, p. 20.
149. Commager and Morris, *Spirit of Seventy-Six, p.* 495. "Bagging the Fox."
150. Harvey, *History of Wilkes-Barre,* 2: 900.
151. Commager and Morris, *Spirit of Seventy-Six*, p. 504.
152. Ibid., p. 505.
153. Miner, *History of Wyoming*, p. 207.
154. Commager and Morris, *Spirit of Seventy-Six*, pp. 538-539.
155. Ibid., p. 131-132.
156. Miner, *History of Wyoming*, p. 207.
157. Commager and Morris, *Spirit of Seventy-Six*, p. 642.
158. Ibid., p. 637.
159. Ibid., pp. 637-644.
160. Ibid., p. 644
161. Ibid., p. 656.
162. Ibid., p. 656-660.
163. Harvey, *History of Wilkes-Barre,* 2: 976.
164. Commager and Morris, *Spirit of Seventy-Six*, p. 999.
165. Ibid., p. 998.
166. Ernest Cruikshank, *The Story of Butler's Rangers and the Settlement of Niagara* (n.p.: Tribune Printing House, 1895),p.41.

167. Harvey, *History of Wilkes-Barre,* 2: 938.
168. Cruikshank, *Butler's Rangers, p.* 34.
169. Harvey, *History of Wilkes-Barre,* 2: 940.
170. William Stone, *The Life of Joseph Brant.* 2 vol. (New York: Alexander V. Blake, 1838).
171. William Halsey, *The Old New York Frontier* (New York: Charles Scribner & Sons, 1901), p. 207.
172. Harvey, *History of Wilkes-Barre,* 2: 984 footnote.
173. Peck, *Story of Wyoming,* p. 154.
174. Harvey, *History of Wilkes-Barre,* 2: 956.
175. Ibid., 2: 977.
176. Ibid., 2: 978.
177. Peck, *Story of Wyoming,* p. 155.
178. Harvey, *History of Wilkes-Barre,* 2: 985.
179. Ibid., pp. 986-987.
180. Miner, *History of Wyoming,* p. 219.
181. Harvey, *History of Wilkes-Barre,* 2: 1005.
182. Ibid., 2: 811 .
183. Ibid., 2: 826-829.
184. Ibid., 2: 995-996.
185. Ibid., 2: 992.
186. Ibid., 2: 993.
187. Ibid., 2: 994-995.
188. Ibid., 2: 1005.
189. Miner, *History of Wyoming,* p. 219.
190. Chapman, *History of Wyoming,* p. 122-123.
191. Harvey, *History of Wilkes-Barre,* 2: 1007.
192. Ibid., 2: 1010.
193. Stewart Pearce, *Annals of Luzerne County* (Philadelphia: B. Lippincott & Co., 1866), p. 100.
194. Brewster, *The Pennsylvania-New York Frontier, p.* 66.
195. Chapman, *History of Wyoming,* p. 143.
196. Harvey, *History of Wilkes-Barre,* 2: 1006-1011.
197. Chapman, *History of Wyoming,* p. 126.
198. Cruikshank, *Butler's Rangers,* p. 45-46.
199. Harvey, *History of Wilkes-Barre,* 2: 1040.
200. Alfonso Stanley Zawadski, "The British Vewpoint of The Battle of Wyoming" (M. A. thesis, University of Scranton, 1968).
201. *The Annual Register,* vol. 21 (Pall Mall: J. Dodsley printer, London, 1779), quoted in Zawadski, "British Viewpoint."
202. Harvey, *History of Wilkes-Barre,* 2: 1056.
203. Ibid., 2: 1065.
204. Ibid., 2: 1065.
205. William L. Stone, *Life of Brant* (New York: Alexander V. Blake, 1838), p. xiv.
206. Peck, *Story of Wyoming,* p. 160.
207. Harvey, *History of Wilkes-Barre,* 2: 994, 1028.
208. Peck, *Story of Wyoming,* p. 159.
209. Ibid., p. 161 .
210. Miner, *History of Wyoming,* p. 229.
211. Peck, *Story of Wyoming,* p. 162.
212. Ibid., pp. 162-165.
213. Ibid., p. 168.
214. Ibid., p. 169.

215. Brewster, *History of Certified Township of Kingston,* p. 166
216. Peck, *Story of Wyoming,* p. 170.
217. Miner, *History of Wyoming,* p. 230.
218. Harvey, *History of Wilkes-Barre,* 2: 1054-1055.
219. Ibid., 2: 1047.
220. Rolf Ridgway Hillman, *Old Dansbury and the Moravian Mission* (Buffalo, NY: Kenworthy Printing Co., 1934), p. 8
221. William A. Hunter, *Forts on the Pennsylvania Frontier, 1753-1758* (Harrisburg, PA: Pennsylvania Historical and Museum Commission, 1960), p. 215.
222. Margaret Smith and Nedra Patrick, eds., *History of Monroe County, Pennsylvania, 1725-1976,* (East Stroudsburg, PA: Pocono Hospital Auxiliary, 1976), pp. 10-12.
223. Miner, *History of Wyoming,* p. 239.
224. Harvey, *History of Wilkes-Barre,* 2: 1058.
225. Ibid., 2: 1059.
226. Peck, *Story of Wyoming,* p. 171.
227. Harvey, *History of Wilkes-Barre,* 2: 1081.
228. Ibid., 2: 1086.
229. *Proceedings and Collections of the Wyoming Historical and Geological Society,* 7: 132.
230. Peck, *Story of Wyoming,* p. 171.
231. Brewster, *History of Certified Township of Kingston,* p. 170.
232. Harvey, *History of Wilkes-Barre,* 2: 1081.
233. *Proceedings,* 7: 135.
234. Harvey, *History of Wilkes-Barre,* 2: 1090.
235. Ibid., 2: 1095.
236. *Proceedings,* 7: 142-144.
237. Commager and Morris, *The Spirit of Seventy-Six,* p. 836.
238. Harvey, *History of Wilkes-Barre,* 2: 1098.
239. Miner, *History of Wyoming,* pp. 239-248.
240. Ibid., p. 261.
241. Harvey, *History of Wilkes-Barre,* 2: 1158.
242. Charles P. Whittemore, *A General of the Revolution—John Sullivan of New Hampshire* (New York and London: Columbia University Press, 1961), p. 151 .
243. Harvey, *History of Wilkes-Barre,* 2: 1161.
244. Ibid., 2: 1171-1176.
245. Thomas C. Amory, *Military Services and Public Life of Major-General John Sullivan* (Port Washington, NY: Kennikat Press, Inc., 1868), pp. 104-105.
246. Harvey, *History of Wilkes-Barre,* 2: 1166.
247. Ibid., 2: 1180.
248. Ibid., 2: 1189.
249. Order Book of General Sullivan p. 39. As reproduced in "Notes from Craft Collection in Tioga Point Museum on the Sullivan Expedition of 1779." Ed. and copyright by Louise Welles Murray, Director of Tioga Point Museum, 1930.
250. Harvey, *History of Wilkes-Barre,* 2: 1225.
251. Ibid., 2: 1225 .
252. Ibid., 2: 1225-1227.
253. Peck, *Story of Wyoming,* p. 172.
254. Ibid., p. 173.
255. Miner, *History of Wyoming,* p. 278.

256. Peck, *Story of Wyoming*, pp. 175-176.
257. Brewster, *History of Certified Township of Kingston*, p. 178.
258. Harvey and Smith, *A History of Wilkes-Barre*, 3: 1241-1242.
259. Brewster, *History of Certified Township of Kingston*, p. 178.
260. Harvey and Smith, *History of Wilkes-Barre*, 3: 1243.
261. Brewster, *History of Certified Township of Kingston*, p. 182-184.
262. Peck, *Story of Wyoming*, p. 176.
263. Miner, *History of Wyoming*, pp. 278-308.
264. Harvey and Smith, *History of Wilkes-Barre*, 3: 1311.
265. Miner, *History of Wyoming*, p. 287.
266. Ibid., p. 288.
267. Ibid., pp. 305-307.
268. Harvey and Smith, *History of Wilkes-Barre*, 3: 1292.
269 . Ibid., 3: 1293 .
270. Page Smith, *The Constitution. A Documentary and Narrative History* (New York: William Morris and Company, Inc., 1978), p. 76.
271. Miner, *History of Wyoming*, p. 308.
272. Robert J. Taylor, "Trial at Trenton." Offprint from the *William and Mary Quarterly*, Third Series, 26 (1969).
273. Chapman, *History of Wyoming*, p. 135.
274. Harvey and Smith, *History of Wilkes-Barre*, 3: 1309.
275. Ibid., 3: 1315.
276. Harvey and Smith, *History of Wilkes-Barre*, 3: 1333.
277. Chapman, *History of Wyoming*, p. 138.
278. Brewster, *History of Certified Township of Kingston*, p. 194.
279. Chapman, *History of Wyoming*, p. 139.
280. Peck, *Story of Wyoming*, p. 178-179.
281. Harvey and Smith, *History of Wilkes-Barre*, 3: 1370.
282. Miner, *History of Wyoming*, p. 344.
283. Harvey and Smith, *History of Wilkes-Barre*, 3: 1379.
284. Brewster, *History of Certified Township of Kingston*, p. 195.
285. Ibid., p. 199.
286. Miner, *History of Wyoming*, p. 345.
287. Peck, *Story of Wyoming*, pp. 181-182
288. Chapman, *History of Wyoming*, p. 142.
289. Harvey and Smith, *History of Wilkes-Barre*, 3: 1387-1388.
290. Ibid., 3: 1385.
291. Miner, *History of Wyoming*, p. 346.
292. Page Smith, *The Constitution*, p. 69.
293. Ibid., p. 82.
294. Page Smith, *The Shaping of America* (New York: McGraw Hill Book Co., 1980), 3: i.
295. Miner, *History of Wyoming*, p. 347.
296. Ibid., p. 348.
297. Peck, *Story of Wyoming*, p. 189.
298. Chapman, *History of Wyoming*, p. 147.
299. Harvey and Smith, *History of Wilkes-Barre*, 3: 1406.
300. Miner, *History of Wyoming*, p. 352-353.
301. Ibid., p. 354.
302. Harvey and Smith, *History of Wilkes-Barre*, 3: 1422.
303. Chapman, *History of Wyoming*, p. 152.
304. Harvey and Smith, *History of Wilkes-Barre*, 3: 1431.

305. Miner, *History of Wyoming*, p. 361.
306. Harvey and Smith, *History of Wilkes-Barre*, 3: 1444.
307. Ibid., p. 1445.
308. Peck. *Story of Wyoming*, p. 183.
309. Miner, *History of Wyoming*, p. 366.
310. Harvey and Smith, *History of Wilkes-Barre*, 3: 1450.
311. Ibid., 3: 1454-1455.
312. Ibid., 3: 1487.
313. Ibid., 3: 1461.
314. Miner, *History of Wyoming*, p. 383.
315. Harvey and Smith, *History of Wilkes-Barre*, 3: 1508.
316. Ibid., 3: 1507 .
317. Miner, *History of Wyoming*, pp. 399-400.
318. Harvey and Smith, *History of Wilkes-Barre*, 3:1545
319. Tunis, *Colonial Living*, pp. 48-50.
320. Harvey and Smith, *History of Wilkes-Barre*, 3: 1546.
321. Ibid., 3: 1553.
322. Miner, *History of Wyoming*, p. 407.
323. Brewster, *History of Certified Township of Kingston*, p. 221.
324. Peck, *History of Wyoming*, p. 218.
325. Ibid., pp. 192-193.
326. Ibid., pp. 193.
327. Harvey and Smith, *History of Wilkes-Barre*, 3: 1583.
328. Miner, *History of Wyoming*, p. 413-414.
329. Page Smith, *The Constitution*, p. 527.
330. Ibid., p. 215.
331. Ibid., p. 230.
332. Alexander Hamilton, James Madison, and John Jay. "The Federalist" in William Benton, ed., *Great Books of the Western World* (Chicago: Encyclopedia Britannica., 19th printing, 1971), p. 30.
333. Harvey and Smith, *History of Wilkes-Barre*, 3: 1591.
334. Miner, *History of Wyoming*, p. 304.
335. Harvey and Smith, *History of Wilkes-Barre*, 3: 1592.
336. Donald E. Cooke, *Our Nations' Great Heritage* (Maplewood,NJ: Hammond, Inc., 1972), p. 189.
337. Ibid., p. 195.
338. Page Smith, *The Constitution*, p. 290.
339. Miner, *History of Wyoming*, p. 425.
340. Ibid., p. 431.
341. Harvey and Smith, *History of Wilkes-Barre*, 3: 1613.
342. Miner, *History of Wyoming*, p. 437.
343. Harvey and Smith, *History of Wilkes-Barre*, 3: 1647.
344. Harry Marlin Tinkcom, *The Republicans and Federalists in Pennsylvania 1790-1801* (Harrisburg: Pennsylvania Historical and Museum Commission, 1950), pp. 7-8.
345. Ibid., p. 16.
346. Brewster, *History of Certified Township of Kingston*, p. 256.
347. Ibid., p. 233.
348. Ibid., p. 236.
349. Ibid., p. 240.

Index